Leonidas LaFayette Polk
AGRARIAN CRUSADER

L. L. Polk at Fifty

Leonidas LaFayette Polk

AGRARIAN CRUSADER

by

STUART NOBLIN

Chapel Hill
THE UNIVERSITY OF NORTH CAROLINA PRESS
1949

Copyright, 1949, by
THE UNIVERSITY OF NORTH CAROLINA PRESS

TO
MY MOTHER
AND TO THE MEMORY OF
MY FATHER

PREFACE

The two words that best capture the personality of L. L. Polk are, I think, "ardent" and "sanguine." An ardent man is warm-hearted, energetic, zealous, and devoted; but he may also be impetuous and erratic. A sanguine man is cheerful, hopeful, enthusiastic, and ever-confident; but he may also be naïve and unrealistic.

The ardent, sanguine man who is the subject of this biography became nationally famous in the early 1890's as a farmers' champion. He headed the National Farmers' Alliance and Industrial Union, the largest agricultural organization in American history, and, had he lived four weeks longer, would surely have won the nomination of the People's Party for President of the United States in 1892. In his native North Carolina, he fathered the state Department of Agriculture and was appointed the first Commissioner of Agriculture; he founded and edited the weekly *Progressive Farmer,* which soon reached the greatest circulation of any newspaper in the state's history and exerted a nation-wide influence; he was the most important single factor in the establishment of North Carolina's land-grant agricultural and mechanical college, now the North Carolina State College of Agriculture and Engineering; and he provided the impetus that the leaders of his denomination needed for the creation of the Baptist school for girls that is now Meredith College.

Such a man deserves study. The living, flourishing, enduring monuments he left behind him in his home state may well rank him as its most significant citizen between 1865 and 1900, while his leadership of the powerful farmers' movement during the early 'nineties makes him, without doubt, an individual of national significance.

Yet L. L. Polk is not a familiar figure to the present generation, even in North Carolina. Unlike his closest counterparts in the South, he never enjoyed the advertising that long and sometimes spectacular tenure of high public office afforded. When he came within reach of his showiest prize, death cut him down. Although he passed from the scene two years before the Populists and the Republicans joined forces in North Carolina—and would have repudiated that move—his name for many years unfortunately shared the special odium reserved for Fusionists by the dominant Democrats. His most devoted followers were not the scholars, editors, and political officials who record the history and mythology of the state, but simple farmers.

Sources of information about Polk and the forces that produced him are numerous, though a number of the best have not become available until recent years. They cover well most periods of his life. There exists, however, a dearth of material on his personal and family life that I cannot help but regret; and some Polk material, notably much of his correspondence as president of the Alliance, is known to have been destroyed.

Many good people have assisted me. At the head of the list stand Polk's three grandchildren who live in Raleigh. Miss Leonita Denmark allowed me complete freedom in using the fine L. L. Polk Collection in her possession, supplied important information that documents sometimes failed to convey, and provided work facilities in the old Polk home that any investigator would have pronounced ideal. Mr. L. Polk Denmark contributed much time and energy to my problems, and shared with me frankly his intimate knowledge of all phases of his grandfather's career. Mr. James W. Denmark, a professional photographer, expertly prepared the book's illustrations. The encouragement of Dr. Clarence Poe, of Raleigh, was a constant inspiration; and through him the board of directors of the *Progressive Farmer,* which he has guided with distinction for the past fifty years, granted me generous financial aid in meeting the costs of publication.

I owe much to four members of the University of North Carolina history department: Dean W. W. Pierson, Jr., for friendly interest and wise guidance; Professor A. R. Newsome, for excellent advice and suggestions and for clarifying several problems of North Carolina history; Professor Hugh T. Lefler, for introducing me to Polk's descendants and for carefully reading the book in manuscript; and especially Professor Howard K. Beale, now of the University of Wisconsin, for giving the whole manuscript the benefit of his exceptionally thorough criticism. I am also grateful to President R. B. Purdum and the board of trustees of Davis and Elkins College for granting me a year's leave of absence in 1945-46 for work on the project.

In footnotes and bibliography appear the names of several persons who kindly wrote letters, gave interviews, or donated material, and of libraries whose staff members were uniformly efficient and helpful in making their resources available. My wife, Evelyn Blanchard Noblin, deserves thanks for helping me check proof and compile the index, and for enduring the project's many vicissitudes from beginning to end.

STUART NOBLIN

North Carolina State College
Raleigh, N. C.

CONTENTS

CHAPTER		PAGE
	Preface	vii
I.	A Speech in Kansas	3
II.	Up to Manhood	22
III.	The Conscience of a Whig	40
IV.	The Soul of a Soldier	50
V.	A Chapter in Reconstruction	73
VI.	Genesis of a Department of Agriculture	87
VII.	Mr. Commissioner	109
VIII.	The Early 'Eighties	134
IX.	"The Progressive Farmer"	147
X.	The Farmer Builds a College	163
XI.	On the Education of Women	183
XII.	The Wrong	190
XIII.	The Remedy	201
XIV.	The National Scene	215
XV.	The Alliance in North Carolina	229
XVI.	Mr. President	254
XVII.	The People's Party	268
XVIII.	"I Am Standing Now . . ."	282
	Bibliography	299
	Index	311

ILLUSTRATIONS

Frontispiece
L. L. POLK AT FIFTY

Between pages 194 and 195
WEDDING PICTURES OF SARAH PAMELA GADDY AND L. L. POLK

POLK AS A MEMBER OF THE NORTH CAROLINA HOUSE OF COMMONS, 1861

POLK FAMILY GROUP

MASTHEADS AND SALUTATORIES OF POLKTON "ANSONIAN" AND "PROGRESSIVE FARMER"

FIRST PAGE OF NEW YORK "REVIEW OF REVIEWS," MAY, 1892, FEATURING PHOTOGRAPH OF POLK

Leonidas LaFayette Polk
AGRARIAN CRUSADER

Chapter I

A SPEECH IN KANSAS

On the Fourth of July in the year 1890 the town of Winfield, Kansas, overflowed with a great crowd of six thousand people. They were farmers, most of them, and since dawn, with their wives, children, horses, wagons, buggies, and lunch baskets, they had poured into this seat of Cowley County from all over the southern part of the state. It was not only Independence Day, but "Alliance Day" as well—the biggest day of the year.

Kansas seethed with revolt. In protest against economic forces and conditions that oppressed and impoverished them more and more each season, the individualistic, hard-headed farmers had finally organized in self-protection. A large number of the sun-browned people who now congregated on the Chautauqua Assembly grounds belonged to the Farmers' Alliance. Over the whole country their organization and its affiliates embraced more than two million voters, chiefly in the Northwest and the South. As neither Republicans nor Democrats seemed disposed to legislate for their relief, many of these Kansas farmers had already joined a new third party—the People's Party. On this day they had come to Winfield largely to see and hear a man whose fame had preceded him, the national president of the Alliance, Colonel L. L. Polk of North Carolina.

A little past ten o'clock, officers of the Chautauqua met the Southern Kansas train that brought President Polk and his party. Paced by a brass band, the group marched to the Assembly grounds, where Polk and Ralph Beaumont, the labor leader who accompanied him on this trip, shook hands with many of the people. After the band played again, Beaumont made a long speech. When he had finished, the crowd moved to "the grove" to enjoy a basket dinner.

At two-thirty the farmers and their friends filled the large Tabernacle to hear Colonel Polk.[1] Benjamin H. Clover, the Cowley County farmer who was national vice-president of the Alliance, introduced him, and he came forward amid applause.

The audience focused its attention upon a rather handsome man of medium height and build who appeared to be about fifty years of age. As he smiled in response to the greeting of the crowd his face was decidedly pleasant. His hair and skin were dark, and, in the hirsute mode of the time, he wore a heavy mustache and long beard, which were well streaked with gray. His body gave the impression of leanness and solidness. His height must have reached five feet eight inches, and his weight 160 pounds. He carried himself as erect as a soldier. The farmers noticed that his square head was set compactly on broad shoulders, that his hips were narrow, and that his hands were large and capable-looking. L. L. Polk made a favorable first impression.

Those who had eaten and talked with him an hour earlier had observed more closely the thick black hair, only slightly grayed, which he parted neatly on the left side; the medium forehead; the dark brows; the large and remarkably luminous and expressive brown eyes, the most striking of all his features; the prominent nose; the large ears, with their unusually long lobes; the clean-shaven cheeks and jaws; the dark but clear complexion; and the long whiskers, which partly hid a determined mouth, completely covered a sharp chin, and extended some six inches below. He wore a low and comfortable white starched collar and a suit and shoes of excellent quality. The president of the Alliance

---

[1] Winfield, Kansas, *Courier*, July 10, 1890, is the source both for the foregoing description of events and for the text of the speech that makes up the bulk of this chapter.

struck this Kansas crowd as a most friendly, courteous, and affable Southerner.

True, President Polk could hardly be at his best on this occasion. For ten days he had been riding trains and speaking to vast assemblies in the open air, while the temperature ranged from 95 to 104 degrees. Now he was suffering the miseries of a bad cold. Nevertheless, he made ready to speak, and the audience adjusted itself to listen. Clover, Beaumont, and the others near him on the platform may have noticed that his knees shook—a violent muscular tremor that never failed to pass over him as he began a public speech. Yet the throng facing him saw only a poised, experienced, smiling orator.

"Ladies and gentlemen, and Brothers of the Alliance of Kansas:
"I desire first to express my profound appreciation of the distinguished honor conferred upon me through the kindness of the secretary and managers of this Assembly, who have afforded me the opportunity which I have so long sought,—an opportunity to visit the great and enterprising state of Kansas, and meet and mingle with its intelligent, industrious, and plucky people. As has been intimated by Brother Clover, I am physically unfit to do the cause which I represent or myself justice on this occasion. I am here, however, in obedience to that call to which I have never yet turned a deaf ear. I beg your indulgence in view of the laborious task imposed upon me by my cold, and ask that you be patient and give your best attention to the few rambling remarks which I propose to submit to you."

Here the speaker paused. He had spoken slowly and deliberately, enunciating his words carefully and distinctly. Though affected somewhat by his cold at the moment, his voice was soft, smooth, and low-pitched, with good carrying power.

"I hear, in all my travels from one end of the country to the other, expressions of appreciation of the future of this country.

I confess to you that when I look on one side of the picture, apprehensions all disappear. When I go from one of the great cities to another in this country and see the mammoth enterprises, I see evidences of growth and financial prosperity. When I witness the rapid strides we are making, and the material advancement; when I go to our capital city at Washington and look at those grand Government buildings with their magnificent and perfect architecture, and look at that massive building the Capitol, and look at the machinery of the Government, I feel that we are a great people, and, perchance, a great destiny awaits us.

"But when I leave the scenes of opulence and wealth and go into the country and visit that Christian family—the patriotic father, the godly mother, surrounded by their helpful, bright, and happy boys and girls—and listen to their words of wisdom gained by their conservative course in life, and look at that type of Christian manhood and womanhood illustrated in that home, it is then that I forget for the time being all this magnificence of wealth and show of power. I say in my heart, after all, the great power and strength of this country rests upon the perpetuity of this humble Christian home of its farmers." (Great Applause.)

This opening, with its popular sentiment, gave Polk's hearers the first indication of the eloquence that they had been led to expect. Clover, Beaumont, and a few others present had heard him before. They knew how he could electrify an audience, and for two or two and a half hours hold its attention so closely that scarcely anyone would stir. Others had heard how the oratorical magic of this North Carolinian sometimes moved men to tears. The crowd under the big Chautauqua tent looked and listened carefully as Polk proceeded.

"I congratulate the management of this Association in providing this means of education, and I bid it, in the name of the coming men and women, Godspeed in its noble work.

"For after all, brother farmers, thank God we have at last

reached the point where we recognize the great truth that it is brain-power that moves the world. When I was a boy I well remember that my father carted his produce to the distant market through rain and snow, water and slush, ten or fifteen miles per day. I tell you, my friends, that was the day of muscle! Today I stand anywhere in this beautiful country of ours and see your engines spinning around your hills and skimming over your plains and carrying one million pounds of freight in a single train, and running at the rate of thirty miles per hour. And I would be a blind man if I did not see that this is the age of brains.

"I remember I took my scythe and cradle and worked from early morning till dewy eve to harvest three acres of grain—and it was a good day's work. That was muscle! Today I see you farmers riding around on your harvesters—with your umbrellas over you, if you please—whistling 'Yankee Doodle,' and at night you have lying at your feet twelve to fourteen acres ready for shock. This is the age of brain.

"I remember that when we gave one of our ladies enough goods for a dress, she stitched away for six days to make it. That was the age of muscle. Today they do the same work on an improved sewing machine run by an electric motor in less than that number of hours. This is the age of brain.

"Your woodman, when he enters the forest to clear away the brush and establish his home, hears the screaming of the locomotive as it throbs up behind him. Steel rails, steam power, printing presses, steam ships, and electricity have revolutionized the world. Electricity and steam, the twin giants of power, are harnessed to the blazing chariot of human progress, and have startled the human mind with their achievements. Young men of Kansas who are on the farm, let me tell you if you have not already learned it, that the God of mercies has endowed you with brains. He has something more for you to do than to run a straight furrow across a field.

"National prosperity, national happiness, and national independence must be based upon the virtue, and the virtue upon the intelligence, of the people. A nation can no more live without it than your body can live without blood and brain. That nation which neglects to educate its masses of people to higher ability and to a higher plane of thought and action is on a sure road to inevitable decay and death. Therefore I bid Godspeed to this Association. With such charming surroundings and the opportunity of hearing such men of letters, you should come here prepared to enjoy this festival of soul. But especially the boys and girls of the farms of your state should come here that they may learn to become virtuous and intelligent people.

"It has been my good fortune within the past few years to travel over a large extent of territory in this country. I have traveled from Maine to the Rio Grande. I have traveled much in the central states of this Union. I have looked into the manufactories of these and the New England states, and I want to say to you that on my first trip to the great West I see many evidences of skill, industry, and enterprise. You have one of the most beautiful countries the sun shines upon. Any man who witnesses the evidences of your enterprise, skill, industry, and hard, plucky work would conclude that under favorable conditions you should be among the thriftiest, the most prosperous, the most contented and happy people the world has ever seen.

"But ladies and gentlemen, candor and truth compel us to say there is something wrong in this country. Never in our history—"

Suddenly the Colonel's voice became quite weak. His afflicted vocal cords almost failed him. He rallied, however, made a few apologetic remarks, and after a brief autobiographical digression returned to his theme.

"I said there was something wrong with this country. Never in the history of the United States have we seen such an era of prosperity among the railroads as we see today. Never have we seen money capital seek investment in railroad enterprises as today. Never have we seen manufacturing in all departments so active and flourishing as we do today. Never have we seen speculation so rife, and men grasp fortunes so easily as today. Never have we seen cities grow up and flourish as we do today. But you must excuse your American friend when he tells you he has never seen agriculture languish as it does today.

"I remember that, when a boy, I read in my school textbook that there were two men who were millionaires in the United States—Stephen Girard and John Jacob Astor. How difficult it was to grasp the idea of that vast sum! Now you can count the millionaires by the thousands; and only the other day I stood in the Capitol at Washington and looked down upon eighty-two representatives, forty-two of whom, it is said, are millionaires. Today 6,600 men control two-thirds of the wealth of the United States, and the other one-third belongs to over sixty millions of people.

"In 1850 the farmers owned seventy per cent of the wealth of the country, and paid eighty-five per cent of the taxes; in 1880 they owned one-half the wealth, and paid eighty-seven per cent of the taxes; today they own less than twenty-three per cent, and still pay over eighty per cent of the taxes. And when I say that, I do not mean the indirect tax, but the tax that is collected from the people on what they own. From 1850 to 1860 the actual valuation of farms had increased 101 per cent; from 1860 to 1870, they had increased forty-three per cent; from 1870 to 1880 they had increased only nine per cent. And notwithstanding the total wealth of the country had increased forty-five per cent, and the population twenty-nine per cent.

"Suppose an intelligent man from some far-off country, who had heard of this Government, suppose he had heard this statement; suppose that he had traveled over Kansas, had visited your farms, had witnessed your industry, and had seen these honest men who have cultivated these rich lands since 1865—men who had worked hard and lived hard and had cultivated these lands for twenty years and are poorer today than they were twenty years ago. Suppose he had heard this statement which I have just made. He would say: 'Sir, I have heard you had the greatest government on earth. I have been taught that prosperity has thrown its arm around, and over, and about the citizens to protect and shield them from all harm. But if your statement be true, I am forced to believe there is something wrong—something radically and ruinously wrong.' Suppose I had made this statement to this foreigner: that a man had recently died in this country and left his son a fortune which was so great that if he did not but draw the interest at four per cent (he need not speculate or invest his money in any way, and I would allow him $5,000,000 a year for pocket change, and he need do nothing but collect his interest and his rents), if he should live as long as his father, drawing the interest all that time, he could buy the whole of this country and put it into his vest pocket; what would he say? And yet that statement is true.

"I know nothing of the extent of your mortgaged indebtedness in Kansas, but we hear much about it. This I know: that the product of your labor costs you more than you receive for it. I do know that the farmers of Kansas have made no money in the last five years, and they are poorer today than they were five years ago. You are going down the scale of our prosperity; you feel it and you know it.

"Here are eight or ten millions of farmers in this country, who by nature of their vocation live isolated lives. Their employment removes them from the sharp contact of shrewd money men, and from the workings of political machinery of today, and tends to make them quiet, dignified and law-abiding and contented citizens. It is so from one end of the country to the other. But I tell you this afternoon that, from New York to the Golden Gate, the farmers have risen up and have inaugurated a movement such as the world has never seen. It is a revolution of thought.

A revolution which I pray God may be peaceful and bloodless. A revolution which shall roll on and on and on till some of the great wrongs of the world shall be righted. A revolution that cannot be stayed. A revolution of honest, earnest thought. And it will go forward until it shall accomplish the glorious mission for which it was inaugurated.

"Men wonder why the farmers are so agitated. If you want to know, go to the register of deeds office, or the office of the recorder of your state, and you will see the cause. If you go to the homes, you will find the children working in the corn fields who ought to be in the school rooms. Go to that old man; see him denying himself and family the comforts of life because of the short reward of his labors. Then turn your eyes and see the princely fortunes that are being accumulated all over the land, and tell me why the farmers are separated on this question, when we have reached the great bed rock.

"We know that it is to our interests to stand together and not to go down at their bidding. The American has inherited the strength of his father and the faith of his mother, and it is a heritage he should prize—yes, a fortune. He has a fruitful soil. He has health, muscle, will, industry, and desires to build himself up, and he sees that everything else is prosperous while he alone is at a standstill. And he would not be worthy his heritage if he did not seek to know the reason for this great discrimination. Illinois last year produced 64,000,000 more bushels of corn than it consumed, and 20,000,000 bushels of wheat. And yet I tell you farmers of Kansas, if every bushel of wheat and corn had been applied to paying the interest on the indebtedness, it would have fallen short $3,840,000. The corn cost $9,885,000 more than it was worth when raised.

"But lay aside all of these facts; shut our eyes to all these truths; and stand here and ask why it is in this great country of ours, the best on the globe, with all our rich soil, improved as it has been, admirably adapted to cultivation, with great lines of transportation, and equal productive power and protected as it is, and then ask in the name of justice why it is that a man in this country should work hard, live hard, and die poor. These are the questions that are moving the masses of people as they were never moved before. They are talked by the firesides all over the land. They see that one of the means used to bring about this vast state of affairs is organized, cooperative effort. It is a mighty power that is moving the world today. They see that organization is the watchword everywhere. There is not the class of people today that is not sustained by an organization—none but the farmer. He was an open prey to every other interest. He is beginning to recognize the law of common safety, the law of God and nature. And he is beginning to make demands from this rapidly progressing age.

"But I hear farmers constantly say, 'Oh, I have been brought up under that law of God which says I must earn my bread by the sweat of my face.' That man stands aloof from all organizations. I want to say to that man I have read another law somewhere—perhaps you can find it—and that is this: No man liveth to himself alone. I said it was a law of God. Brothers of Kansas, sisters of Kansas, whether you believe it or not, whether you will aid each other or not, whether you join in this fraternal spirit in which God intended you should join, whether you believe it or not, I want to tell you people of Kansas here today that the farmer of North Carolina, Georgia, Texas, South Carolina is your brother, whether you want it so or not!" (Applause.)

"Thank God that I can stand on this platform this afternoon without being interfered with any sectional feeling, and tell you that your destiny is my destiny!" (Applause.) "Tell you that you are my brother! Tell you that there is a common interest between us! Tell you that we are bound by common peril! Tell you that we have a common interest, and must make common cause in spite of all that sectional feeling! Tell you we must acknowledge but one name and one flag!" (Applause.) "And one common country. The struggle is *not* between the North and the South—thank God, no!" (Applause.) "And so long as we live there will *never* be a North and South!" (Applause.)

The last several sentences, delivered rapidly and vehemently, struck like the blows of a sledge hammer, firing the enthusiasm of the audience. Polk's plain-spoken, graphic English and the directness, vigor, and power of his speech appealed vastly to the farmers.

"Some people have stirred up sectional feeling and have kept us apart for twenty-five years. I tell you that I believe in my heart of hearts that the man, North or South, who urged on the war—I care not what his name may be, or what position he may hold—that man helped to light the flame of war, and when it was ablaze all around the horizon fired your minds and sent you to the front and then skulked out of it himself. And who in 1865 found out that we had a war, got mad, and has been mad ever since. That man who was 'invisible in war and invincible in peace.' The man who never smelt gun powder or heard a minnie ball. The man who has to use the sacred dust of the grave and has scattered it to the winds, and tried to work upon our passions. The man who has waved the bloody shirt. The man who has taught his children the poisonous doctrine of hate. I say, and I have declared it before, I believe him to be the worst of our enemies on the face of the earth!" (Applause.)

"No, sir! The politicians would keep you and me apart, and by so doing they have chained us hand and foot. They have placed upon us manacles that are worse than those that have fallen from the African slaves. They know that if we get together and shake hands and look each other in the face and feel the touch of kinship, their doom is sealed." (Applause.)

"I stand here today, commissioned by hundreds of thousands of Southern farmers, to beg the farmers of Kansas to stand by them. And they assure you that they will never, no never, never, no never give prominence to any man who stirs up this question which was settled by Lee and Grant at Appomattox. I point these men to a man who did not fear to fight. I point these men to a man whose name will last when theirs' have been forgotten. None other in this country was braver than Ulysses S. Grant. He was a great general, and as true to his flag as ever a man was. I want to take these men, when they are flaunting the bloody shirt, to the bedside at Mt. McGregor and let them hear his last parting word.

"When I returned from the St. Louis convention, I told my family how our Northern brethren had received us, and they rejoiced. Afterward I spoke in Metropolitan Hall in Raleigh, to a large gathering of people, the most of whom were ex-Rebel soldiers. I told how the six Alliances, or the Alliances from six Northern states had received us, and there was not a dry eye in the house when I got through. They received it with tears of joy and shouts of exultation. I told the same thing at a strong Democratic gathering in Kentucky last week, and it would have done your hearts good to have heard the shouts of applause. I have told it among Union soldiers, and it is the same. The spirit of love and fraternity is growing. Thank God, Brother Clover, the day has come when a man from the South and a man from Kansas, Kentucky, or the Eastern states are permitted to stand on the same platform!" (Applause.) "So long as they can contrive to keep us apart, they will succeed in keeping us down.

"Some fellow says, 'I told you he is going into politics.' I know, but in my country a man who says that is nothing but a small political fry." (Laughter.) "Getting into politics! Over half of them don't know the difference between partisanism and politics. I say—and I say it privately for L. L. Polk, and I think I can say it officially—that if the Alliance is not as full of politics as an egg is full of meat, I would not give a snap of my finger for it!" (Laughter and applause.)

"Let me ask you a question or two about the Alliance going into politics. Let us be honest today. I have no sugar-coated pills in my pocket for anyone. I have come to tell the truth, the whole truth, and nothing but the truth, so help me God." (Applause.) "I believe that any man who has the confidence and respect of a large number like this, when he speaks on questions relating to the public weal, if he suppress the truth or fear to express it, he is unworthy of your confidence. Now, my little political friend, you who are so afraid of running into politics, will you please tell me who has a better right in America to go into politics, than the farmers? Who does your party belong to anyhow? If I had met any of you farmers on the road twelve months ago, and had asked you what party you belonged to, you would have said at once: I belong to the Democratic or the Republican party as the case might be. Now, you would have put the cart before the horse; you don't belong to any party, the *party* belongs to *you!*" (Applause.) "I know how the parties are run in my section of the country. They are run by bosses who sprang up while we were trying to get something to eat after the war, and they have managed things so long that they have come to the conclusion that all the farmers ought to do is to vote as they tell them and pay taxes.

"I want to tell you an Alliance secret. I don't believe Brother Clover has told it to you men who are outside of the Alliance, and I suppose there are two or three hundred Alliance men here today, and they will bear testimony that what I say is true. When a man joins the Alliance, before he takes the obligation he enters the hall and is taken before the proper officer, who says to him, 'There is nothing in this obligation which will interfere with your freedom of political or religious views.' " (Cries of "That's true.") "This is one of our secrets. We don't tell him we are going to control the caucus and he must obey the caucus. That would be an oligarchy which all would resent. We do not say that you must go by certain rules. No, sir! We take him by the hand and say, 'You are a free man.' I would like to know what right we have to control the great principles of religion and political freedom. We leave it to his judgment. We have no more right to tell a man he should belong to the Democratic party, or to the Baptist church, than we have to tell him he should belong to the Republican party or Methodist church. If a man comes up and says, 'I believe I can do a better work by remaining in the Republican party,' the Alliance has nothing to say, and assumes that he is going to act as an honest man. If he says, 'I am a Democrat, and believe that I can further the interest of the Alliance by remaining with my party,' the Alliance has not one word to say. If a man says, 'I do not see a chance to get anything through these parties, and I am going to join a new one,' the Alliance is absolutely still. It has not one word to say.

"It reminds me of an old fellow who was a great horse-swapper; you don't know what that means until you go to North Carolina. His name was Roark. He was a Union man, but he stayed home from the war and sent a substitute. He did not make much at his trade during the war. In 1864 some cavalry went into his county, and he swapped the boys out of a good horse. The horse was poor, but his practiced eye discovered his fine qualities, so he made the trade. He took him home and fatted and fixed him up, and he had a fine horse. In 1865 General Kilpatrick was coming through that section of the country with his cavalry, on a raid. Roark wanted to see a live Yankee and also wanted to see if he could be of some service to him, so he put on his best clothes and mounted this horse and started to meet him. As he came up, the captain who was in advance said, 'Halt!' Roark halted. He put on his blandest and said, 'Good morning.' He noticed the captain looking at his horse. 'Dismount!' said the captain. He looked at the captain, and he seemed to mean it, so he dismounted. 'Take the saddle off that horse and strap it onto this one!' he said, motioning to a horse which was so poor that it could scarcely stand. Roark did as he was bid. 'Mount!' said the captain. Roark mounted. 'Now take yourself home!' Roark stopped. 'I want to say just one word. I have been swapping horses for years, but this is the first time I ever swapped horses that I did not have one word to say.'" (Laughter and applause.)

"How many of you have been making such swaps during the last twenty-five years, and did not have one word to say? I want to say one word to you men who cling to party. I voted with a party, and I stand in this presence to tell you now, I have done some things that I am ashamed of—I suppose the most of you have done the same." (Laughter.) "I have voted for men, and if God will forgive me I will never do it again." (Applause.) "I have done some things of a mere partisan character, and I have determined hereafter never to vote for any man, be he high or low, or of whatever party, so long as I live, neither for the legislature nor for Congress, whom I have any reason to believe is not a true and loyal friend of my people." (Applause.) "And if that be political treason, make the most of it, and turn up your noses. George Washington never gave better advice than when he told us to beware of the baneful party spirit, and he never gave us advice which has been so little heeded, for the last twenty-five years.

"Some will ask, 'How are you going to remedy it?' By observing closely we have found out that some of the leading politicians of both North and South have not been telling us the truth. I propose to be plain and honest. In the last campaign they told us the great question was the tariff—that if we had protective tariff the farmers would have a remedy for their ills. But just the other day I saw where 442 farmers had left their homes in New Hampshire, right under the shadow and within the sound of the whistles of the workshops and factories, because they could not make a living. In free trade England they are as bad off as they are in this country. Why should this conflict come between theory and practice? I think it was a sham battle gotten up to fool us. Now I am not trying to get any man to leave his party, but I do say it is a sham battle. It is a party bone put out for the people to scramble over while *they* get the money and offices." (Applause.)

"I will tell you what you are going to see. You are going to see a party that will be mindful of the interests of the people. It may be called Republican and it may be called Democratic, but I believe you will live to see this. You will see the great issues of state, and they will be laid down as they ought to be. You will see arrayed on the one side the great magnates of the country, and Wall Street brokers, and the plutocratic power; and on the other you will see the people.

"How are we to get relief? We have a bill which we have been trying to get passed, and Congress could give us relief in twenty-four hours if it had a mind to. I do not say it is the best bill that can be devised, but if anyone can show us a better one we will abandon this one immediately. When we sent it in, the answer we received was 'old hayseed socialists—demagogues.' For 108 years we farmers have not asked for anything from this Government. We went to Congress for the first time. We were in a deplorable condition. And we showed them our condition and they acknowledged that it was true. We went before the House Committee and stated our case. But what have they done? They have done nothing, and they are going to do nothing. They are in a quandary. If they don't pass the bill, the people are going to sit down on them; and if they do pass the bill, Wall Street is going to sit down upon them. I believe that both of the parties are afraid of Wall Street. They are not afraid of the people.

"They say to me, 'Don't you know that you can buy more with a dollar now than you ever could in the history of our country?' That may be true. But suppose you owed a thousand dollars. Ten years ago six hundred bushels of wheat would have paid the debt; now it requires fourteen hundred bushels to pay it. Suppose you had five dollars. How much more taxes will it pay? how much more interest on your debt? how many more physician's bills? How many more lawyer's fees will a dollar pay? Will it pay four times as much as it did? And how much will the dollar cost to get it?

"A tramp ran up to a gentleman one day and asked him if he could tell him where he could get a good square meal. The gentleman pointed out a place where he could get a meal for a quarter. The tramp thanked him and started off, but had not gone far before he came running back. 'You were so kind to tell me where I could get a nice meal for a quarter. Will you now tell me where I can get the quarter?'" (Laughter.) "And that is the way with the politicians. They keep telling us what we can buy with a dollar, but they do not tell us where we can get the dollar.

"When I went up to Washington City and showed them statistics from all over the country, they said it was overproduction that had caused our trouble. Mr. Morrill declared from his seat that it was overproduction and Mr. Dodge says it is overproduction—that is what troubles you farmers. If Mr. Morrill had come out onto the streets of Washington on a cold November morning, he would have seen the children picking bits of coal out of the ash piles to warm themselves by, and morsels of food out of the heaps of garbage to satisfy their hunger. As long as those things exist there is no overproduction. As long as a single cry for bread is heard it is underproduction and underconsumption. And in that great and final Day, when all the crime and misery shall be revealed, some one will have to answer for this lack of food. There is something besides overproduction that has caused it. I believe that it is not God's fault that we are in this bad condition. Congress could give us a bill in forty-eight hours that would relieve us, but Wall Street says nay.

"I will tell you where the revolution must commence. It must come through Congress, and you must make your representatives stand or fall by their own records. When they return from Congress ask your representatives whether or not they have done anything to pass these bills; and if they have not, ask them if they have tried to pass any substitute for them. If they have done nothing, do not send them back. If we cannot get Congress to pass these bills for us we will have to change the men in Congress." (Applause.) "If they believe our bill is impracticable, let them provide one that shall be practicable. But we must have relief of some kind. Now I reach a point where I intend to call upon my people—you may call it politics if you like—I tell them that if they want relief, they will have to send different men to Congress than those who are there now."

At this point the speaker prepared to close. First, however, he exhorted the boys in the audience to be morally strong, called upon Alliance men to do their duty in the present crisis, and paid a compliment or two to Kansas and its people. Then in conclusion he said:

"I believe there is fast coming a further revolution when there will be but two classes—the extreme rich and the extreme poor. The middle class has been the great source of strength; they have been the bulwark of this country. They have fought the battles, and have preserved our free institutions. I want to see the middle class rise up. Let the Alliance take them by the hand and speak to them words of encouragement, and tell them that when God made them he never made larger men. Let us lift them up and make them feel that the country belongs to them and is depending upon them. Let us encourage them to go forward and remain as they have been, the great source of strength of this country.

"Now I want to tell you that the people all over the country are watching what the Farmers' Alliance is doing in Kansas today. They are looking to see what attitude you will take. Let us go forward, therefore, and do the right, and the right will triumph.

"When I go back to my home, I will tell with pleasure what I have been made to feel in the great state of Kansas. I assure you that I shall be pleased to meet you on my own soil, and should any of you ever come down that way you will receive a hearty welcome. There shall be no Mason and Dixon line on the Alliance maps of the future. It shall be one nation and one flag!" (Applause.)

"And now I am like the fellow who asked his girl to marry him. She said she would, and he leaned back against the wall and said never a word for a half hour. Finally the girl could endure it no longer, and said, 'Willie, why don't you say something?' 'Well,' he replied, 'I feel as if there has been enough said.'" (Laughter.) "And so I will say, God bless you till we meet again. Good-bye!" (Applause.)

Polk had captivated his hearers, as he usually did. His temporarily poor physical condition prevented this speech from being one of his best, yet in style and content it was quite typical. Like any gifted orator, he had to be both seen and heard to be fully appreciated. Obviously he delighted in crowds and they delighted in him. His fine presence, ready smile, soft accent, fluent delivery, superb voice, and graceful gestures made a lasting impression. Even an implacable enemy could call him "a man of fine address and great plausibility."[2] Polk also left this impression: "a strong impression of defiance—a man of wrath who stood up and hurled his curses at the world that was."[3]

What forces fashioned this North Carolinian, and brought him, talking of a farmers' revolution, to Winfield, Kansas, on the Fourth of July, 1890? And what happened to him and his cause afterward? That is the story to follow.

[2] Samuel A. Ashe, *History of North Carolina*, II, 1195.
[3] William Allen White, Emporia, Kansas, to the author, June 24, 1937.

CHAPTER II

UP TO MANHOOD

"I WAS BORN and raised on the farm," L. L. Polk also told his Winfield audience. "I was raised by one of those plain old farmers; he was an old fogy in some respects. He believed a man ought to make his money honestly, no matter how slowly it came in. He believed that if he was worth a million of dollars, his sons ought to be taught to work just the same. He had another old fogy idea. He believed that it took twenty-one years to make a man out of his son, and he had no fourteen year old young gentleman about his premises."[1]

The "old fogy" was made of sturdy stuff. He was a small planter, a middle-class farmer, who toiled long and hard on the rolling acres he owned in Anson County, North Carolina. He was never worth a million dollars and never dreamed he would be. But Andrew Polk's lifetime of labor—with cotton and timber and produce—won for him and his family a living that was comfortable and secure. When he died, at harvest-time in 1850, an official inventory of his personal property revealed his status clearly.[2]

Thirty-two Negro slaves, two gins, and twenty-one bales told of hours in the service of King Cotton. Seven hundred bushels of corn, thirty stacks of fodder, six stacks of oats, a thresher, sixteen head of cattle, forty head of hogs, and ten head of geese spoke eloquently of a wise diversification that provided food sup-

[1] Winfield *Courier*, July 10, 1890.
[2] "Record of Inventories, 1849-1856," p. 64, Anson County courthouse, Wadesboro.

plies for both farm and market. The eight mules, yoke of oxen and ox cart, four-horse wagon and barouche indicated heavy work in the fields and woods, trips to church and town, and visits to relatives and neighbors. There were the usual farm tools and equipment, as well as "10 Fine Chairs," "2 Folding tables," and other household items of a well-furnished plantation. For the enlightenment of mind and spirit, one "bible & hymn Book," two treatises on law and one on medicine, three volumes of "Buchanan works" (probably George Buchanan's *History of Scotland*), a map, and "3 small Books" stood ready to serve. There was $656.15 in cash. In addition to the personal property, some 1,848 acres of land remained to be divided among the widow and four sons.

Andrew Polk was probably a typical representative of his class, in ante-bellum times the backbone of North Carolina and the South. The middle-class farmer, descended from Scotch Presbyterians, English Baptists, German Protestants, or French Huguenots, believed in industry and frugality, boldness and independence. He treated his slaves kindly and supervised their work in the fields himself rather than employ an overseer. His home often stood as the hospitable social center of the neighborhood, where one could find good things to eat and hear local gossip, the state of the weather, the progress of crops, and politics exhaustively discussed. Pure in morals and strict in religious principles, he followed in the tradition of evangelical forbears. A contemporary observer remarked:

> The middle-class farmer of the South (when religious) is practically pious and God-fearing. . . . He keeps away from race-courses, cockpits, groggeries, brothels, and the like; makes no bets; plays no cards; shuns profane company as much as possible; attends to his own business diligently . . . endeavors to raise up his children "in the nurture and admonition of the Lord."[3]

[3] Daniel R. Hundley, *Social Relations in Our Southern States*, pp. 82-94 *passim*.

Anson is one of the southern border counties of the state, midway between the mountains and the sea. Here the Piedmont Plateau shades into the Coastal Plain. The sandy and red clay soil, nourished by tributaries of the Pee Dee River, has always been productive. In 1840 the county led all others in the number of pounds of cotton produced; and ten years later, even after being partially dismembered by the creation of Union County to the west, Anson ranked second. In a total population of 13,489 the blacks outnumbered the whites by a few hundred.[4]

Born in Mecklenburg County in 1792, Andrew came with his father to Anson in early life. At twenty-five he announced his intention of marrying Miss Colin Caraway. Thomas Polk thereupon deeded to him, for a very reasonable consideration, 740 acres of fine land along Little Creek, signing the document by mark. Both father and son bought and sold much land and apparently prospered. Andrew and Colin eventually became the parents of three sons. Living in a dramatic era of lusty American nationalism, they gave their boys patriotic, inspiring names—Thomas Jefferson, James, and Marshall. As Polks, too, they were expected to live up to the worthy standards of an honorable ancestry.

The Polks of the United States trace their lineage back to medieval Scotland. Originally the name was Pollok. During the seventeenth and eighteenth centuries the family became part and parcel of the great "Scotch-Irish migration." Responding to the inducements of James I of England, who needed an Irish population upon which he could rely for support, the Polloks and thousands of their Lowland brethren migrated to Ulster. As they would surely retain their uncompromising Protestantism and would never intermarry with the native Irish, the Stuarts regarded them as invaluable allies. Industrious and thrifty, the Scots developed North Ireland wonderfully. Later, however, their position came to be so formidable that severe religious and econo-

[4] *United States Census of 1850*, pp. 309, 321.

mic restrictions were imposed upon them. Their churches were threatened and their property rights jeopardized. This state of affairs inspired large numbers to set sail for America in search of religious freedom and economic opportunity.

The immigrant head of the Polk clan, Robert Bruce Pollok, settled in Somerset County, on Maryland's eastern shore, some time before 1687. About sixty years later his grandson, William Polk, of Carlisle, Pennsylvania, found himself in the path of a flood sweeping southward. The Scots were on the move again. A great new wave of immigrants passed through Philadelphia to seek farms in the interior. But they found the most desirable lands either occupied already or priced too high; and they were keenly aware of the presence of hampering religious restrictions in Virginia. So, hearing of a vast unoccupied tract of fertile territory between the Yadkin and Catawba rivers, they began their four-hundred-mile trek into North Carolina.

Here they would have rich fields to till. And here, in company with kindred spirits, they would build churches of their own. William Polk saw the vision with the rest and set out with his family for the promised land. From Pennsylvania through the Shenandoah Valley and across the Dan River to western Anson they poured by thousands. The county from 1749 to 1762 extended "to the mountains and beyond"; but the Rocky River region, center of the settlements, filled up so rapidly that a new county—Mecklenburg—had to be carved from Anson in the latter year. The "many hundreds" of land grants issued during those years denoted a vigorous young rural community. The pioneer generation was a hardy one whose virtues have been the theme of many a panegyric. Brave and independent, deeply religious, loyal and home-loving the Scots undoubtedly were; yet the very intensity of their natures often made them austere, opinionated, narrow, and clannish.

Of such most probably were the Polks. Most of them lived in Mecklenburg and Anson, though some had settled in South

Carolina. William, according to the published genealogy of the family, stands as the common ancestor of all the North Carolina Polks. One of his grandsons was Thomas, the father of Andrew.[5] Unpretentious and unassuming small farmers these people were, microcosms of their rural commonwealth.

Three members of the family, however, in successive generations of a collateral line, towered well above the others.

First came Colonel Thomas Polk, a son of William, who, like his father, emigrated from Pennsylvania. An able and trusted leader of good education, he figured prominently in the establishment of Mecklenburg County and the town of Charlotte. In the military and political affairs of North Carolina before, during, and after the American Revolution he attained considerable distinction. In the 1760's he was a prime factor in the "War of Sugar Creek," a fierce struggle between land-hungry settlers and the local land agent. He served as representative in the House of Commons, captain of militia, and surveyor of the North Carolina-South Carolina boundary line. As revolutionary sentiment in the colony grew, he proved to be a zealous patriot who fired the public mind. As a colonel during the conflict with Great Britain, his most notable achievement was the procuring of supplies for the army under most difficult and discouraging circumstances.

His son, Colonel William Polk, shared his father's glory as a hero of the Revolution. Widely known as a brave and competent young officer, he fought at Brandywine and Germantown and spent the winter with Washington at Valley Forge. After the war he too became a member of the North Carolina House of Commons. In later years he was one of the state's most prominent citizens, influential particularly in business, politics, and social affairs. He became Supervisor of Internal Revenue and president of the State Bank, and for forty-four years he was an active and devoted trustee of the University of North Carolina. A Federalist,

---

[5] William H. Polk, *Polk Family and Kinsmen*, pp. 95, 132.

he opposed the War of 1812 so stoutly that he refused a major-generalship, even though President Madison himself urged it upon him. When General Lafayette returned to America in 1824 and made his triumphal tour of the various states, Colonel Polk was commissioned to welcome him officially to North Carolina.

Third in the line to attain distinction was Leonidas Polk, gifted churchman, educator, and soldier. As a young man he attended the University of North Carolina. But soon he decided, in keeping with the military tradition of his father and grandfather, to enter West Point. During his final year there, however, he was converted to the church. He then studied in the Virginia Theological Seminary and embarked upon a career of great usefulness in the Protestant Episcopal denomination. As "missionary bishop of the Southwest" and founder of the University of the South at Sewanee his influence upon the religious and educational life of his section was powerfully felt. Believing in the "sacredness" of the Southern cause in the Civil War, he accepted a commission as lieutenant-general and was killed in action in 1864.

To say that one was connected with the "Mecklenburg Polks" carried weight in North Carolina.

In the course of a trip between his old home in Raleigh and his parish in Tennessee, not long after his father's death in 1834, Leonidas Polk stopped in Anson County to enjoy the hospitality of his cousin Andrew. The two men talked of many things. They spoke of the passing of old Colonel William and remarked upon his long and useful life, filled with adventure and honor. His experiences in the Revolution, his friendship with Lafayette, and his royal reception of the gallant old Frenchman just ten years before made a deep impression upon Andrew Polk. Now Lafayette too was dead. The old order was indeed changing. The country was growing up—just as fast as Andrew's boys! The farmer talked about his sons and his farm, while the fine-looking young churchman recalled his Chapel Hill and West Point days and spoke of his conversion, the work of his parish, and of his high hopes for the future. Everyone agreed that it was a "nice family visit."[6]

About this time, in the middle 1830's, Colin Polk died. A little later Andrew Polk married Serena Autry, and in the spring of 1837, on April 24, their only child was born. It was Andrew's fourth son. True to his old predilection, he gave the boy a name inspiring and patriotic—Leonidas LaFayette Polk. With such a name and such a heritage his proud parents doubtless expected great things of him.

The childhood of L. L. Polk has long been a secret. No youthful scribblings, autobiographical reminiscences of later years, or recollections of doting friends can be found to aid in the sketching of an early portrait. Only occasional references to boyhood in the speeches and writings of maturity, a few family traditions, and various inferences drawn from the character and attitudes he revealed during manhood remain to form the faint outlines of what must have been an interesting picture. He grew up on the farm—"away out in the country in a sparsely settled neighborhood." There he spent the "sweetest" hours of his life with his "old black mammy" and "little colored playmates." They were his constant companions, since his three half-brothers, all much older than he, had already left home. Most important of all during childhood, he was blessed, as he put it, with the "society of the best mother" a boy could have asked for, as well as that of a father who commanded respect and admiration.[7]

The great turning point of the boy's life came in his early teens, when he lost both his parents. His father died in 1850 at the age of fifty-eight, thus leaving to others unfinished the twenty-one-year task of making a man of his son. Two years later, when Leonidas was fifteen, his mother died. Bereaved so early of both

[6] Conversations with Miss Leonita Denmark and Mr. L. Polk Denmark, of Raleigh; William M. Polk, *Leonidas Polk: Bishop and General*, I, 151.
[7] L. L. Polk to Mrs. Polk, Dec. 25, 1863; Winfield *Courier*, July 10, 1890.

father and mother, the orphaned youth faced a number of new and difficult adjustments.

In spite of the successive blows that shattered his childhood world and indeed hastened the transformation from boy to man, Leonidas still enjoyed certain advantages. He was placed under the legal guardianship of John Broadaway, who took good care of him and administered the boy's share in his father's estate. Leonidas, moreover, had many friends, and these were ever eager with their sympathy and advice. One was John Edwards, whom Serena Polk was planning to marry at the time of her death. Another was Thomas S. Ashe, a man prominent in the legal and political life of the state, who remained a life-long mentor. So close to him seemed the members of the W. H. Benton family that he spent about half his time with them and claimed them as his "kinfolks." After the death of his parents he made it a habit to turn to experienced men like these for counsel, a practice that stimulated his mind and nourished his ambitions.[8] From a material standpoint also he fared well. After his mother had been specially provided for, he and his half-brothers shared equally in the estate of their father. Each received a parcel of land valued at $1,600 and a number of slaves valued at $3,100. His portion amounted to 353 acres and seven slaves.[9]

This division of property accentuated one of the young man's most serious personal problems: his relations with his half-brothers. Because they were considerably older than he, they were never his natural comrades, and more than a suggestion of ill feeling flared up between them. Relations with "Brother Jeff" were particularly strained. Leonidas carried with him far into manhood the conviction that Jeff, administrator of their father's

---

[8] "Record of Inventories, 1849-1856," pp. 219, 268; "John Edwards to Cyrena [sic] C Polk," Aug. 12, 1852, MS. marriage contract, Wadesboro; *Progressive Farmer*, Feb. 9, 1887; James W. Denmark, undated MS.; interview with Mrs. Bettie Beachum, Polkton, N. C., Feb. 24, 1938.

[9] "Record of Deeds, Anson County," XIII, 391, 566; "Record of Inventories," p. 84.

estate, had appropriated to himself money that had rightfully belonged to Leonidas. The coolness between them existed for many years. James, the second brother, sold his land in the early 'fifties and emigrated to Texas. Of his three "buddies," as he called his brothers, Leonidas apparently stayed on best terms with Marshall, who for the next twenty years seems to have been as close to him as Jeff was distant. The real and fancied wrongs they committed against him assumed great proportions in his vivid imagination and helped to fix upon him a "persecution complex" that clung to him for the rest of his life.[10]

Young Polk inherited far more than land and slaves. The sound body, alert mind, ardent nature, strenuous temperament, and friendly disposition that were his found their roots in his father and mother and in the generations that had gone before. The Polk in him intimated pride and moral tone and qualities of leadership; while an inner part of him, expressing itself in characteristic charity and affection, suggested his mother's very name, Serena.

He attended the schools of the neighborhood as a matter of course. This formal education, whatever may have been its limitations, he generously supplemented. His diligent reading ranged all the way from Major Walter Campbell's *The Old Forest Ranger; or, Wild Sports of India* to a brightly illustrated compendium of "modern events" called *The Historical Cabinet*. In view of his lifetime success as an orator, it is safe to conjecture that he frequently drove to Wadesboro, the county seat, for the "speaking" that was the essential feature of patriotic celebrations, political campaigns, and court week. At many of the "house-raisings," "corn-shuckings," and "singing schools" held in the county he was present also, lively and popular, as the chosen leader of the young people.[11]

---

[10] Confidential information; L. L. Polk to T. J. Polk, [May 30, 1871]; L. L. Polk to Mrs. Polk, May 2, Nov. 17, Dec. 6, 1864.

[11] Wadesboro *North Carolina Argus,* May 21, 1863; J. W. Denmark, undated MS.

Leonidas experienced little difficulty in choosing his career. In a sense his decision was inevitable. The blood of farmers ran in his veins, and his mind and body were attuned to rural life. He knew both the delights and hardships of the farm. His father had been a competent and successful tiller of land and master of slaves, and shortly he himself would come into full possession of land and slaves of his own. At the precise time of his decision to become a farmer—in the middle 'fifties—the doctrines of scientific agriculture were being felt in North Carolina. Stimulated by the organization of the State Agricultural Society and the first annual State Fair, and by the appearance of several able periodicals devoted to agriculture, the movement for improved farming was making noticeable headway. The state's crying need was a sizable group of farmers trained in the science of seeds and soils and up-to-date methods.

Partly to prepare himself for his chosen profession, then, and partly to receive the liberal education that a young man of his station should have, L. L. Polk at eighteen decided to go to college. He was financially able, and he was eager to learn. With his friends Risden Bennett Gaddy and Robert A. Little, he entered Davidson College in the autumn of 1855.

This institution, which first opened its doors to students the year of Polk's birth (1837), was founded by descendants of those Scotch Presbyterians who had settled in Piedmont North Carolina the century before. They were people deeply interested in education and were particularly concerned about the training of young ministers for Presbyterian churches in the South. Hence the atmosphere of Davidson was highly religious, and the spirit powerfully evangelical. That the students were required to profess belief in God, the Christian religion, and the "inspiration and divine authority of the Holy Scriptures" went without question. The president and professors, moreover, were obliged to express their "sincere adoption of the Confession of Faith and Form of Government of the Presbyterian Church" and were pledged to teach nothing "subversive of the fundamental principles of Presbyterianism." During its brief existence the school had become well-anchored, in spite of the storms, financial and otherwise, it had sometimes been forced to weather.

The moral life of the students was an object of great solicitude. First of all, the school was located, not in Charlotte or some other town, but "on the Plank Road" twenty miles north of Charlotte, and thereby "as removed from temptations to vice and dissipation as any other locality in the State." The original charter strictly prohibited any gaming or billiard tables, games of chance or gambling devices, "sl[e]ight of hand, theatrical or equestrian performances, dramatic recitations, rope or wire dancing," and the like. The matter of morals appeared succinctly in the college rules: "No student shall play at cards, dice, or any other immoral game; or buy, keep, or use in his room or elsewhere, any intoxicating liquors; or keep a dirk, pistol, or any deadly weapon; or visit tip[p]ling houses, or other places of ill-fame; or use profane language; or be guilty of any grossly immoral conduct whatever, under severe punishment." [12]

As for the physical aspect of the institution in 1855:

> It was exceedingly plain and primitive and small. There was not one imposing or impressive feature. The Chapel was a rather insignificant-looking building—the Chapel upstairs and four lecture rooms downstairs. The dormitories consisted of a row of low brick buildings, one story each, one room deep, each room opening out doors. There were two or three residences of Professors and two Society Halls. These latter were by far the most attractive buildings in sight. There was a straggling village—a few houses—a Postoffice and two stores. . . .
>
> Student life was primitive, as viewed from the comforts of a later time. We chopped most of the wood we used. We drew water from a well and brought it to our rooms. . . . If we felt the need of exercise, there were the axe and the

[12] Davidson College, *Catalogue for 1855*, pp. 9, 15-16, 30; *1858*, p. 25.

wood pile; there were the bucket and the well, there were roads where we could walk without fee or hindrance. The morning bell rang at 15 minutes before sunrise. Then five minutes before sunrise it rang again, sounding its last stroke at the rising of the sun. When it ceased to ring every student was expected to be in his place in the chapel. . . . [13]

In such a simple, isolated community expenses were naturally moderate. Tuition amounted to $30 for the full school year, while one could get board for $70, room for $4, servant hire for $2, and "washing, wood and lights" for $12—a total of $118 for the ten-month session.

When Polk attended Davidson there were eighty-eight students and five professors, including the president of the college. Clement Daniel Fishburne taught "Greek and Ancient History," the Reverend Elijah Frink Rockwell "Latin and Modern History," and John Adams Leland "Natural Philosophy and Astronomy." They were "scholarly Christian gentlemen" who were also able teachers. The president, the Reverend Drury Lacy, was the "heart" of the institution. He managed the affairs of the college, served as professor of "Moral Philosophy, Sacred Literature and Evidences of Christianity," and, as pastor of the college community, "preached to large assemblies, rarely without tears." Earnest and sincere, kind and courteous, he was devoted to his students. His attractive home, always open to the young men, imparted a "healthy influence which went with them into future years." If President Lacy was Davidson's heart, then Major Daniel Harvey Hill, professor of "Mathematics and Civil Engineering," was its strong right arm. A graduate of West Point who had distinguished himself in the Mexican War, he brought to Davidson something of the discipline he had learned in the army. Grades, demerits, and thorough drill were in his opinion essential elements of a sound system of pedagogy. The military ideas of the provocative Major combined readily enough with the stern

---

[13] George L. Petrie, in Cornelia R. Shaw, *Davidson College*, pp. 82, 83.

Calvinism of the community to set firmly the style of instruction. The excessive demands and rigorous drilling caused many students to leave college in disgust and deterred many boys from entering.[14]

In comparison with other colleges of the period, the standards of Davidson were high. Of course the curriculum emphasized the classics. Thorough preparation in Greek, Latin, and mathematics was required for entrance, and the work of the freshman year was devoted chiefly to Greek, Latin, and mathematics. Probably because he lacked the necessary classical foundation, and because he had an eye for utilitarian subjects, young L. L. Polk enrolled as an "irregular" student. An "irregular" could plan his own schedule, subject to the approval of the faculty. Thus Polk was able to concentrate almost entirely upon the courses that specially interested him, even though they were junior or senior studies. That he was a very good student is shown by the marks he made, figured down to Major Hill's smallest fraction:

First Semester		Second Semester	
Agricultural chemistry	89.9	"Dr. Lacy's Dept."	92.66
Logic and rhetoric	91	Mathematics	90.33
Mathematics	95.32	Declamation	95.5
Declamation	97	Composition	100 [15]
Composition	95		

Outside classes and religious exercises, student activity at Davidson centered in the two literary societies, Eumenean and Philanthropic. They sprang up soon after the college first opened and became an integral part of student life. The small but substantial red-brick structures that housed them were of simple and beautiful Greek-Colonial design, and with their white columns and air of quiet dignity were the most pleasing architectural features

---

[14] Robert Z. Johnston, "The Administration of Rev. Drury Lacy," Davidson College *Semi-Centenary Addresses*, pp. 123-25, 129-30.

[15] *Catalogue for 1855*, pp. 12-13; *1856*, pp. 8, 10; [Charles Robson], *Representative Men of the South*, p. 354; Faculty Minutes, Feb., June, 1856, Davidson College Library.

of the campus. Fortnightly the organizations provided experience in the parliamentary procedure, committee work, discussions, declamations, and debates that were commonly associated with the small college literary society.

At "Regular Meeting No 191," on October 13, 1855, L. L. Polk appeared as one of fifteen to join the Eumenean Society. Almost immediately his active participation began. He "was fined 6¼ cts for not handing in a Question [for debate] at the proper time" and was appointed member of a committee "to examine the Chandelier, and procure some burning fluid for the lamps." During the year he also served on committees "to examine the Library," "to examine Books worthy of rebinding," to consider "exchanging our book cases for shelves," "to sweep out the Hall," "to procure a veil for the bust of J C Calhoun," and "to extend politeness to the Annual Orator." Once he was fined 6¼ cents for "speaking more than twice without leave" on the same subject; another time 75 cents (which he did not pay) for being absent from a meeting without satisfactory excuse. Evidently he was a facile writer, for almost invariably he was a member of the committees chosen to notify prominent men of their election as honorary members of the Society.

Young Polk took part in five regular debates. His side lost four of them. In the two debates he helped to judge, however, he and his colleagues were more fortunate: their decision was "sustained by the house" each time. The questions that year ran the traditional gamut, from the perennial "Was the execution of Mary, Queen of Scots, justifiable?" to the timely "Would the annexation of Cuba to the United States be beneficial to the latter?" The Society held two general debates on topics of current interest: "Is the American party beneficial to the Union?" and "Has the downfall of Poland strengthened the cause of despotism in Europe?" In these the whole membership participated. In the preparation of their speeches the members had recourse, not only to the College Library, but to the Society Library of over a thousand volumes. *"Pulchrum est colere mentem"*—"It is a fine thing to cultivate the mind"—was the Eumenean motto.[16]

Soon Leonidas had made his mark as a forceful and fluent speaker. When in February the time came for the Society to choose its three commencement orators, the members elected him their "Third Representative," despite the fact that he was only a "freshman irregular." The "Exhibition" of the two societies took place on the evening of June 27. "Speech is the golden harvest that followeth the flowering thought," declared the printed program. "Speech is Reason's brother, and a kingly prerogative of Man."[17] The Philanthropic speakers discoursed on "Cromwell," "Spain," and "Literature—Its Toils and Rewards"; the first two Eumenean representatives, on "The Triumphs of Intellect in the Physical World" and "Intelligence Essential to Liberty." Polk spoke on "The Glory of America," a subject doubtless based upon a book of that title in his possession, a book which recounted the heroism of American military leaders in the Revolution and the War of 1812.

With "The Glory of America" Polk said farewell to Davidson; his college education ended with his return to Anson in the summer of 1856. Like Davidson's most famous "alumnus," Woodrow Wilson, he attended the college but a year. He had absorbed already, he believed, the chemistry and mathematics that would make him a good planter, the logic and rhetoric that would make him an effective speaker and writer, and the inspiration that would make him a better Christian. He did not go to college again, for he had come to feel the stronger pull of the farm, home, and love.

Fifteen months later he married. His bride was Sarah Pamela Gaddy, sister of his friend "Rit" Gaddy, and daughter of Joel T. Gaddy and Mary A. Bennett Gaddy. "Sallie," as they called her,

[16] "Record of Minutes of the Eumenean Society [1852-1859]," Oct. 13, 1855—June 21, 1856, "Eumenean Society Treasurer's Book," Oct. 27, Nov. 8, 1855, Feb. 18, April 18, 1856, Davidson Library.
[17] Leaflet, Davidson Library.

was petite and pretty—barely five feet tall, and slender, with brown hair and blue eyes. She had attended Salem Academy, North Carolina's best-known school for girls, to which her father, a prosperous Anson planter, had proudly sent her. Leonidas and Sallie were married on September 23, 1857, when he was twenty and she seventeen.[18]

The following January, three months before his twenty-first birthday, Leonidas secured from John Broadaway, his guardian, three hundred acres of land along Brown Creek. This tract, valued at $2,400, included his father's old homestead, on which the young couple now began their married life. With plenty of land, a good number of slaves, and abundant energy and ambition, he seemed well on the way toward becoming a "gentleman farmer." He read the *North-Carolina Planter* and other new agricultural periodicals, which condemned the common methods of cultivation and advocated deep plowing, terracing of rolling lands, and use of commercial fertilizers. Willingly he allied himself with them, and practiced what they preached.[19]

There was time and inclination for other reading, too, especially during the long winter evenings. That part of Polk's library which has been preserved suggests a variety of rather substantial fare.[20] For example, history and biography are represented by David Hume's *History of England,* William Grimshaw's *History of the Wars of the French Revolution,* the *Life and Public Services of Henry Clay* by Epes Sargent and Horace Greeley, and *Washington and the Generals of the American Revolution;* poetry by late editions of the *Poetical Works* of Milton, Pope, and Martin Tupper, a popular poet-philosopher of the day; philosophy by George Combe's *Constitution of Man, Considered in Relation to External Objects,* which Polk warmly recommended to Rit Gaddy; religion by *A Guide for Young Disciples, Spurgeon's Gems, The Sacred*

---

[18] Conversations with Miss Leonita Denmark; Polk and Gaddy "family Bibles."
[19] "Record of Deeds, Anson County," XV, 679; Raleigh *News,* June 23, 1880.
[20] A part of the L. L. Polk material in the possession of Miss Leonita Denmark.

Mountains, and George W. Purefoy's *History of the Sandy Creek Baptist Association.*

The Bible occupied a prominent place in that library, for the young man was religiously inclined. Leonidas was a Baptist and one of the superintendents of the "Piney Grove Sabbath School," though the earlier Polks had been Presbyterians, and he himself had attended Davidson College. His church belonged to the Sandy Creek Association, which was steeped in the spirit of the camp-meeting revival and was noted for its vigorous campaigns against liquor.[21]

Marriage, the advent of a daughter, and the wholesome life of the farm apparently broadened and deepened his spiritual life. His preoccupation with moral subjects and homely virtues is revealed in a fragment of the commonplace book he kept at this time. "It is not by great deeds, like those of the martyrs, that good is to be done," he wrote, "but by the daily and quiet virtues of the life, the Christian temper, and good qualities of relatives and friends. . . ." Such silent moral influence is not like a flood or a torrent but rather like the small, never-ending stream that waters the farm. "It is a rill—a rivulet—a river—an ocean, boundless and fathomless as eternity. . . . Straws swim on the surface, but pearls lie at the bottom." Neither wealth nor power makes a good man, but a character of moral worth that fears only God. To enrich a man's life his spiritual instinct should be carefully developed. "The richest genius like the most fertile soil, when uncultivated shoots often in the rankest weeds; and instead of vines and olives for the pleasure and use of man, produces to its slothful owner the most abundant crop of poisons." A word to the wise is sufficient: "What a fool does in the end, a wise man does in the beginning. . . . The wise man is happy, when he gains his own approbation,—the fool, when he gains the applause of those about him." Pay no heed to the ill-considered opinions of others, but always strive to bring out the best that is in you on

[21] Wadesboro *North Carolina Argus,* Sept. 29, 1859.

every occasion. Above all, in this business of living, "We should exercise charity toward those who differ with us in opinion. To err is human, and it is best to defer final judgment, until it is clearly ascertained who is in error, lest the just be condemned and the wrong approved. . . . In taking revenge a man is but equal with his enemy, but in passing it over he is his superior."

Polk penned these thoughts in December, 1858.

Chapter III

THE CONSCIENCE OF A WHIG

The late 'fifties excited North Carolina as well as the rest of the country. As the breach between North and South gradually widened, men apprehensively wondered what the final outcome would be. Some said that war was inevitable, that the "irrepressible conflict" was at hand. One heard impassioned pleas for secession, for union, for compromise. Momentous issues were under serious discussion by people, press, and politicians.

L. L. Polk, young as he was, found it impossible to ignore the passing parade of state and national events. Politics had become an essential part of his experience. At Davidson he had participated earnestly in the many informal arguments over slavery, sovereignty, and state rights. Those closest to him at home had always been keenly interested in the political news from Wadesboro, Raleigh, and Washington. He was ambitious, and in the South bright and personable young men of ambition were generally expected to take an active part in politics. Aware of his own talents, encouraged by his many friends, and prompted by some categorical imperative, he soon plunged in.

Leonidas was a zealous Union Whig, a disciple of Henry Clay. The Whig Party as such had pretty well passed from the national scene. Its elements had been absorbed by the Southern Democracy as well as by Northern Republicanism. None the less, it was still a potent force in North Carolina. In no other Southern state had the old-line Whigs left so fine a record of constructive statesmanship. When the moribund party was revived in the late 'fifties and took its stand upon a platform exalting nationalism and decrying sectionalism, it was soon able to challenge the Democracy, which had dominated the state for ten years. The Democrats saw their supremacy threatened by the rise of new issues and by faction and dissension within the party; the presidential campaign of 1860 revealed clearly the sharp cleavage into radical state rights men and conservative union men. In this situation the Whigs' patriotic appeal to stand by the Union and the Constitution attracted wide support and made them strong contenders in the elections. One of the first local rallies young Polk attended passed resolutions that declared:

> We are tired and sick of the useless agitation of the slavery question . . . the defeat of the Democratic party is, in our opinion, indispensable to the welfare and continuance of the Union . . . as Whigs of North Carolina, we are determined to know no geographical parties, no sectional distinctions, no North, no South, no East, no West—but our country—our whole country.[1]

In contrast to their position in other Southern states, the Whigs of North Carolina were strongest in the regions where the slave system did not predominate—the western mountains, a large part of the Piedmont and center, and the eastern coast. In great need of better transportation facilities and the development of their natural resources, these regions favored the Whig program of internal improvements by state aid.

The Whigs effectively made use of another issue—"equal taxation." When the Constitution of 1835 was formed, the "Slaveocracy" inserted provisions that, along with later legislative enactments, placed a heavier tax burden upon non-slaveholders and mechanics than upon slaveholders. Slave property was exempt from all taxes except the poll tax, and slaves under twelve and over fifty were exempt from that. Proportionately, land was taxed much more heavily than slaves. For instance, the owner

[1] Wadesboro *North Carolina Argus,* April 14, 1859.

of a tract of land worth $1,000 paid a land tax of $1.50, while the owner of a slave worth $1,000 paid a poll tax of only fifty cents. A white mechanic who earned at least $500 a year had to pay, in addition to his poll tax of fifty cents, a license tax of $5; but the owner of a slave mechanic, who might compete with the free white mechanic, paid only the fifty-cent poll tax.

Such discrimination bore especially hard upon landless laborers and upon non-slaveholding tenants and small farmers. These classes, largely under the influence of the new common schools, were developing class consciousness and becoming articulate. Workingmen's associations and other groups, demanding the "*ad valorem* taxation of slave property," looked to the revived Whig Party as the palladium of their rights. And the Whigs, having forsaken their "Know-nothingism" and "Americanism," now appeared, in one of those reversals characteristic of American politics, as liberals fighting for democracy against the vested interests of the conservative Democracy.

Polk's home county was stalwartly Whig, though the Seventh Congressional District, of which it was a part, was represented by a Democrat. Anson ranked decidedly Unionist and "*ad valorem.*" The proposed construction of a railroad through the county, extending from Wilmington on the coast to Charlotte and the mountains beyond, had excited the active interest of many citizens. In this traditionally nationalistic, conservative spot even the slaveholders—and Anson was a large slaveholding county— were inclined to accept "equal taxation" if they could also have the railroad that would carry their cotton to the sea. But with the crisis of 1860 all such local issues were held in abeyance, overshadowed by the greater issue of Union versus Secession.

As a delegate from Diamond Hill Precinct, Polk in 1859 faithfully attended county meetings in Wadesboro, often serving as secretary. He was present at the Seventh District gathering in Charlotte and was later appointed a member of the "District Committee" from Anson County. Early in 1860 he journeyed to

Raleigh for the state convention of the "Opposition Party," as the Whigs sometimes preferred to call themselves.[2] Political activity of this kind continually widened his circle of friends and acquaintances as his remarkable ability as an orator became known and his personal charm was felt. Both he and his friends believed that the time had come for him to take that familiar first step of the aspiring young statesman: to run for the House of Commons. Accordingly, the formal announcement of his candidacy for one of the county's two seats in that body was published in the Wadesboro *Argus* in April, when he was twenty-three years old. The first of such notices to appear, it bore the signature "MANY CITIZENS." Two more candidates eventually announced.[3]

Young Polk strongly favored both "equal taxation" and internal improvements, but he campaigned almost exclusively on the "simple issue of Union or Disunion."[4] The result of the August election was proof of his popularity. With his strength well distributed throughout the county, he led this three-man all-Whig ticket by polling 791 votes. In second place with 733 votes came Edward R. Liles (almost as young as Polk), who thus won Anson's other seat in the House. The third man received 521.[5] In the race for governor, incidentally, Anson County gave 890 votes to John Pool, Whig, and only 290 to John W. Ellis, Democrat; but Ellis won the state as a whole.

Abraham Lincoln's election to the Presidency in 1860 naturally intensified the widespread discussion of North Carolina's federal relations. Before deciding upon any definite line of action, however, most of the state's political leaders were content to wait for the opening of the General Assembly and the Governor's message. The important session began on November 19. The

[2] *Argus*, April 14, June 2, Oct. 13, 1859, Jan. 12, March 1, 1860.
[3] *Argus*, April 12 *et seq.*, 1860.
[4] [Charles Robson], *Representative Men of the South*, p. 355.
[5] *Argus*, Aug. 9, 1860.

Senate contained thirty-two Democrats and eighteen Whigs, and the House sixty-five Democrats and fifty-five Whigs. Governor Ellis, a member of the radical state rights school, recommended in his message a conference of Southern states, a convention of the people of North Carolina, and the organization of the state on a military basis so as to resist possible federal coercion. Obviously in the direction of secession, these proposals caused legislative battle lines to be swiftly drawn.

The Whig minority of course opposed the Governor's program. The radical Democrats, taking the offensive, supported it completely. The conservative Democrats, while believing in the right of secession, did not favor its application; they preferred for the present to "watch and wait." Together with the Whigs, these conservative Democrats formed a pacific group that effectively prevented the radicals from taking any precipitate action. This alignment in the legislature accurately reflected the sentiments of the people back home. Resolutions embodying the dominant ideas of each group were presented in the House early in the session, and the political battle was on.

Much vehement debate and no conclusive legislation marked the month preceding the Christmas recess. The recommendations of Governor Ellis could not win the necessary support. "The general feeling of North Carolina is conservative," one writer observed. "She would respond to any fair proposition for an equitable adjustment of present national difficulties, but will insist on her rights at all hazards." [6] These things the legislators learned in the two weeks with their constituents.

After the General Assembly reconvened in January the picture gradually changed. South Carolina had seceded, and the states of the lower South followed one by one. Secession meetings in North Carolina took place in ever-increasing numbers. As the national situation became more critical, sentiment for a state convention grew rapidly. The aggressive radical Democrats, with

[6] *American Annual Cyclopaedia, 1861*, pp. 537-40.

their well-knit organization and coherent program, persuaded their conservative colleagues to stand with them, thus leaving the Whigs in a clear minority. Yet even many Whigs favored the convention as the best method of checking the secessionists— as "the conducting steel to the lightning-freighted cloud." The convention bill, major issue of the regular session, passed both houses late in January. It authorized the people of the state to choose 120 delegates and vote for or against a convention.

On February 28, following a month of thorough discussion, the people voted. In view of external events, particularly of the fact that most of the Southern states had already seceded, the results were indeed surprising: two-thirds of the elected delegates were Unionists, and the convention was defeated by a narrow margin. Conservative North Carolina was not yet ready for secession; the policy of "watch and wait" won a temporary victory. The chagrined secessionists nevertheless redoubled their efforts, aided now by the failure of the Peace Conference at Washington and the general distrust of the new Lincoln administration. They began the systematic organization of the state, holding a series of mass meetings that culminated in a great "Southern Rights" convention at Goldsboro in March. But the events of "fateful April," 1861, made further agitation unnecessary.

The firing on Fort Sumter, President Lincoln's call for troops, and the secession of Virginia combined to render North Carolina's decision inevitable. The state readied itself for war. Governor Ellis ordered the seizure of the Federal forts and called for a special session of the legislature. Meeting on May 1, that body quickly passed a bill authorizing the Governor to call a convention, commended him for his prompt action in the crisis, proffered military assistance to Virginia, and took steps to prepare the state for combat. Composed of the ablest of the Whigs and Democrats, the Convention that assembled on May 20 forthwith cut the bonds that had bound North Carolina to the Union for seventy years. Without regard to former political differences, the representatives of the people were now united in resistance.

What a time for a young man to begin his public life! Polk could never forget, as he wrote in later years, "the flourish with which Holden unfurled the Southern Cross, over the office of the Standard—the air of conscious superiority, which bore conspicuously, the blue cockade on the beaver of Judge Cantwell—the constant and fiery appeals of Erwin, for war—the impatient and furious ravings of V. C. Barringer, for blood . . . the pledge made in the House on the 10th Jan., 1861, by the lamented and noble-hearted Crumpler, in reply to taunts and derisions from these same men. . . ." [7]

During the regular session Polk joined his fellow Whigs in their steadfast opposition to the radical program of the secessionists, especially on the question of arming the state. It was a losing fight, however, for the two Democratic factions eventually demonstrated that they could and would vote together. In view of this fact, Polk was one of those Whigs who felt it wise to support the movement for a state convention.[8] He, Liles, and S. H. Walkup, state senator from Anson, addressed a circular letter to their constituents urging them to remain true to the Union, whether a convention were called or not. If it should be called, they wrote, send good Union men to it.[9] The people of the county were predisposed to do just that, but the convention was defeated.

Immediately after the adjournment of the legislature on February 25, Polk returned home to watch closely the trend of state and national affairs—and to be on hand for the birth of his second daughter. The events of April stirred him profoundly. Upon receiving the proclamation of Governor Ellis requesting the legislators to reassemble on May 1, he was moved to state,

---

[7] Polkton *Ansonian*, April 23, 1874.

[8] *North Carolina House Journal, 1860-'61*, pp. 196-391 *passim* (Dec. 18–Jan. 25).

[9] *Argus*, Feb. 14, 1861.

as he put it, "the sentiments by which I shall be governed during the extra session." In a letter to the *Argus* he told how he had pointed out during the winter that "Lincoln's fanatical horde" would meet "fierce and bitter resistance" in North Carolina. "I was then a Union man, exerting all my power to aid in averting civil war, and continued to labor untiringly until the last hope was extinguished." But since Lincoln's threatening call for troops, "*I am now for resistance to the bitter end.*" The youthful Representative invited the citizens to express their views, declaring that if they should differ with his own he would "cheerfully resign." Finally, he warned, "We are not battling for any minor consideration but for our lives, our property, our honor, in short, *our all.*" [10]

In the extra session Polk belonged to the overwhelming majority that prepared the state for war. Still, he did not vote on some questions that implied approval of secession and the Southern Confederacy. During the brief two-week sitting most of the measures offered went through practically without opposition. A large number of men in the House—Polk among them—insisted upon referring to the people for ratification any act connecting North Carolina with "any other Government." They were quickly compelled, however, to surrender to the forces of hard circumstance and public opinion.[11] After this Polk doubtless echoed the words of the eminent Union Whig, Jonathan Worth: "With sorrow I now co-operate and unite with a majority of my State."[12]

As a representative Polk in these sessions was said to have been "quite attentive." He introduced minor bills relating to free Negroes, county revenue, internal police, and individual relief, and was assigned to the joint committee on public buildings and grounds. While in Raleigh he boarded at the Yarborough,

---

[10] *Argus*, April 25, 1861.
[11] *House Journal, 1861*, first extra session, pp. 15-17 (May 1), and *passim*.
[12] Jonathan Worth, *Correspondence* (J. G. deRoulhac Hamilton, ed.), I, 140.

the leading hotel and political headquarters of the capital. A novice in legislative politics and debate, he wisely followed the lead of the more experienced men in his party.

A second extra session of the General Assembly convened, and in it Polk played an active role. The State Convention had ordered the legislature to meet on August 15 for the purpose of furthering the preparations for war. Toward this end strenuous efforts were made to raise and equip troops; a new stay law, a revenue bill, and a militia bill were passed; and two Confederate senators were elected.

Polk's work came in connection with the militia bill. On the second day of the session he introduced a resolution "That a message be sent to the Senate proposing to raise a joint select committee of five on the part of the House and three on the part of the Senate, to be styled 'The Committee on the Militia.'" The resolution was adopted, and the Senate concurred. Polk, Stephen W. Davis, Dennis D. Ferebee, Henry G. Woodfin, and Charles C. Clark were appointed from the House, and Alfred Dockery, H. H. Street, and F. L. Simpson from the Senate. After two weeks of investigation, deliberation, and preparation, Polk, chairman of the committee, reported a bill. It easily passed its first reading in the House, but on second and third readings it had to run the gantlet of amendments. Yet under Polk's guidance the bill was approved and sent to the Senate within four days. Two more weeks, and the finished product emerged from the upper house.[18]

Ratified on September 20, 1861, the bill provided that the State Militia be organized into twenty-eight brigades composed of 116 regiments. There was one regiment to each county except in the larger ones, and they were numbered from east to west. All free white males between the ages of eighteen and fifty, with certain obvious exemptions, were subject to service. The bill specially exempted persons "having scruples of conscience against

[18] *House Journal, 1861*, 2nd ex. sess., pp. 16 (Aug. 16), 20 (Aug. 17), 26 (Aug. 20), 43 (Aug. 23), 49 (Aug. 26), 90-125 *passim* (Sept. 2-6), 189-90 (Sept. 13).

bearing arms," but only after Polk and his friends had beaten down, by a vote of 53 to 38, a motion to strike out the clause. Appointments and elections of officers, arms and requisitions, drills and musters, flags, districts and taxes, drafts and terms of service, courts-martial, fines and arrests, duties of surgeons, use of the militia by the governor in defense of the state, pay, and similar subjects were carefully detailed. The ninety-four sections of the long bill appeared to be ably drawn and amended.[14]

Ten days before the legislature adjourned, when it was evident that the militia bill would pass, Polk obtained leave of absence and went home to do the work he had more or less cut out for himself. He received the commission of colonel and soon began to organize the militia in Anson County in accordance with the law he had helped to make. Since the law was rigid, that was not an easy task. This "delicate and difficult service" required men of "unusual energy and determination, as well as of stern impartiality." Young Polk found the undertaking peculiarly trying because of the fact that he was placed in his own county, where he "personally knew almost every citizen." Nevertheless, he performed the duties of his position from September, 1861, to May, 1862.[15] "General Orders" concerning drill and parade and equipment appeared intermittently in the *Argus* during that time, signed by "L. L. POLK, Col. Commanding, 81st Reg. N. C. Militia" through "R. B. Gaddy, Adjutant." One item alone indicates how completely the pleasant paths of peace were necessarily abandoned for the perilous roads of war: "Col. L. L. Polk requests the officers, commissioned and non-commissioned, of the 81st regiment, to meet at Piney Grove Church, on Friday, the 7th of February, at 9½ o'clock, for the purpose of drill."[16]

With North Carolina he had cast his lot.

[14] *North Carolina Public Laws, 1861,* 2nd ex. sess., pp. 18-46 (ch. 17).
[15] [Robson], *Representative Men of the South,* p. 355.
[16] *Argus,* Jan. 30, 1862, and *passim.*

Chapter IV

THE SOUL OF A SOLDIER

By the spring of 1862, war had been grimly brought home to the people of the South—the importance of it by the military preparations of the national administration and the presence of Yankees on Southern soil, the pinch of it by booming prices and dwindling supplies, the horror of it by bloody battles and casualty lists. As the great war entered its second year, there seemed to be small hope that the issue could be settled in the near future. The conviction grew that the struggle would be long and drawn out.

In May, Polk gave up organizing the militia and turned to a wider field. He attempted to raise a company, which he called the "Anson Plough Boys," to serve with the Twenty-sixth Regiment of North Carolina volunteers commanded by Colonel Zeb Vance. He was offered a captaincy by Vance, but declined it. Young Polk chose rather to serve as a private in the ranks than to lead in the fight for Southern independence. He belonged to Company K, the "Pee Dee Wildcats." Soon, however, he accepted appointment to his colonel's staff as sergeant-major.[1]

The Twenty-sixth was well known. Composed of companies from the central and western counties of the state, it had mobilized the previous summer and had distinguished itself in the New Bern campaign against General Burnside. Yet to Polk the greatest attraction of the regiment was its colonel. Zebulon Baird Vance was a picturesque product of the North Carolina

---

[1] Wadesboro *North Carolina Argus*, May 1, June 26, 1862.

mountains, a stout Union Whig who had fought against secession until April, 1861. At thirty-two he had already served one term in the legislature and two terms in Congress, and his "ready wit, broad humor, quick repartee, and boisterous eloquence" had marked him as one of the most powerful advocates and stump speakers in the state. As colonel of the Twenty-sixth he was no military genius, but his personality and his gallantry endeared him to his men. Under Vance the regiment operated near Kinston, North Carolina, in May and June, 1862. Then it was ordered to Virginia, where it participated with credit in the Seven Days' fight around Richmond, ending with the battle of Malvern Hill. In August, Vance was elected governor of North Carolina and soon took leave of his men. When on his departure the officers presented a sword to him, Sergeant-Major Polk made the speech. During the fall and winter the Twenty-sixth maneuvered in eastern Virginia and eastern North Carolina as a part of Pettigrew's brigade.[2]

Polk became dissatisfied with his position after Vance had gone, and in February, 1863, transferred to the Forty-third Regiment as a second lieutenant. Under the leadership of Colonel Thomas S. Kenan this body campaigned in the Kinston region during the spring. It was attached to the command of General D. H. Hill, the old Davidson disciplinarian. One of its duties was to distract the enemy while foraging trains penetrated Hyde and Tyrrell counties for corn. In one skirmish Polk and another lieutenant, in charge of a detail of eighteen men, conducted themselves with considerable skill and success against a Yankee picket force.

That spring there was no serious or prolonged engagement, but life was miserable and dangerous just the same. "The Spring," wrote Polk, "was unusually cold, rainy and disagreeable, camp

[2] George C. Underwood, "Twenty-Sixth Regiment," *Histories of the Several Regiments and Battalions from North Carolina in the Great War, 1861-'65* (Walter Clark, ed.), II, 303-39.

duties close and constant, drilling heavy, sick list unusually lengthy, and furloughs sought by nearly all the boys." [3]

Soon the Forty-third packed off to Virginia to fight at Fredericksburg. Polk was left behind, sick with liver trouble. When, however, the regiment moved north to take part in Lee's invasion of Pennsylvania, he set out to overtake it. After some of the hardest marching he ever did, once "having walked *74 miles in 2 1/2 days*," he caught up with it at Chambersburg. He had retraced the Shenandoah Valley route by which his ancestors had come to North Carolina. From Carlisle, home of his great-great-grandfather, he wrote that the Confederates had made good their threat to "carry the war into Africa." [4]

Then came Gettysburg. Polk's next letter to his wife was written in Petersburg, Virginia, two weeks later:

> I was in the terrible ordeal of the 1st 2nd & 3rd insts. at Gettysburg Pa. I am wounded, though happy to inform you that *it is not serious*. I was wounded on the 1st just before dark in our last charge upon the enemy's lines. I was in the act of catching James Brily who was shot dead & fell back, when a shell burst immediately in my front, a piece striking me on the right foot & another on the right hip. The concussion shocked me so dreadfully that I have not yet recovered from it & fear it will be some time before I do. I was struck to the ground, but recovered & went through the charge & was not sensible of the character of the wound until we all stopped. I stayed near the battlefield until the 3^{d} when all who could travel had to leave. . . . I am stopping with Mrs. [C. M.] Page who is as attentive & kind as a mother. I applied for a furlough this morning but was flatly refused.

[3] Polkton *Ansonian,* April 12–May 3, 1876. The best printed account of the Forty-third Regiment is Polk's "The 43rd N. C. Regiment during the War: Whiffs from My Old Camp Pipe," which ran serially in the *Ansonian* from April 12, 1876, to April 25, 1877. It was based upon letters to his wife during the war, a small line-a-day diary he kept from April 14 to Dec. 4, 1864, his own memory, and correspondence later with officers of the regiment (Thomas S. Kenan to Polk, April 21, 1876, W. G. Lewis to Polk, May 8, July 27, 1876). Thomas S. Kenan's "Forty-Third Regiment," *Histories of the Several Regiments* (Walter Clark, ed.), III, 4-15, is very brief.

[4] Polk to Mrs. Polk, May 16–June 28, 1863.

> ...*One thing is certain,* if I can't get one I *will remain here as long as I please.* I have some money, but no clothes, the Yankees having captured all my clothing, except what I have on.... I was struck by three spent balls & two pieces of shell, none of which entered the skin, though they pierced my clothes....

More than his stiff leg and the Gettysburg defeat troubled him: "Vicksburg is gone! ! ... Lee is yet beyond the Potomac. ... My liver is in a torpid condition...."[5]

After a convalescence of six weeks in Petersburg, part of the time on crutches, Polk prepared to rejoin his group. "I know I shall miss my comfortable lounge, nice table & kind attentions, when I get back, & I am loth to exchange them for the very rough fare which our boys are getting but *duty* impels me," he declared.

The Forty-third found itself in the thick of the fight at Gettysburg. Its casualties amounted to twenty-one killed and 129 wounded. Of these, Polk's company suffered one killed and eleven wounded. On the retreat south the Forty-third acted as rear guard of the entire army and at length encamped at Orange Courthouse.

The regiment spent the rest of 1863 along the Rapidan River, skirmishing and constructing fortifications, until cold weather made it necessary to go into winter quarters. Ingeniously the men used their fortifications to protect themselves from the bitter cold. "As a means of comfort, which aided us to take any sleep, we were compelled to build fires in the ditches, and after warming the ground would remove the fire, and 'pack' as many together as the capacity of the ditch could allow." They also built shanties, vying with each other for originality; but, as luck would have it, just as they were finished the regiment was ordered back to North Carolina.[6]

A season of maneuvers in the eastern part of the state was

---

[5] Polk to Mrs. Polk, July 12, 14, 1863.
[6] Polk to Mrs. Polk, July 16–Dec. 28 *passim*, 1863; *Ansonian,* May 17–June 28, 1876; *Argus,* July 23, 30, Aug. 6, 1863.

climaxed by the successful siege of the fort at Plymouth, a most satisfying victory for the Confederate forces in North Carolina. Not long afterward Polk's regiment journeyed again to Virginia —this time to assist Lee in his great duel with Grant. Traveling on flatcars of the Wilmington and Weldon Railroad, the men suffered "only what soldiers can feel on crowded trains." At Drewry's Bluff and other points near Richmond and Petersburg in May, 1864, the Forty-third faced some of the heaviest fire of its career. Against Grant and Butler, Polk wrote, "we are *continually* on the tramp, or throwing up breastworks, or fighting." [7]

But the worst was yet to come. In the torrid months of June and July the regiment undertook its most grueling campaign. Indeed it ranked as one of the notable campaigns of the war. Leaving Lee's army on June 13, it advanced first to Charlottesville and then Lynchburg, where the order was given to pursue Hunter, who had moved farther west. At "quick and double quick" the men pressed on "in hot pursuit, with empty haversacks, and on a terrible rough road." "We had no bread," Polk wrote, "and the raw bacon was greatly relished without it . . . a terrible day's march. . . . Nothing to eat; heat and dust almost beyond endurance . . . so great was the heat and exhaustion that men actually dropped dead in ranks. . . . Still pursuing Hunter. The hardest days march I have ever done. Am almost perished. . . ." They marched as far west as Salem, where at last they found plenty of food to eat, and "cool sparkling waters to drink from the rock base of the Alleghany" mountains. No respite was ever more welcomed or enjoyed.

Learning that its quarry had proceeded down the Valley of Virginia, the Forty-third turned toward the northeast and again gave chase. By way of Buchanan, Lexington, where respect was paid the remains of "Stonewall" Jackson, Staunton, and New Market, through heat and dust and over rough roads, the men

---

[7] Polk to Mrs. Polk, April 20, 23, 24, May 17, 20, 25, June 7, 1864; Diary, April 14–June 3, 1864; *Argus*, May 5, 1864; *Ansonian*, July 5–Aug. 30, 1876.

pushed on, averaging twenty-two miles a day. Though their hardships were many, the magnificent Valley charmed them. "Many were the exclamations of admiration," said Polk, "even from the ragged, foot-sore soldiers. . . . Scenery beautiful! Sublime!"

On July 4 the regiment reached Harper's Ferry, rudely interrupting a Yankee Independence Day celebration. Two days later the troops gratefully greeted the first rain that had fallen since the campaign began. They continued into Maryland, however, under the "most oppressively hot sun" they remembered ever having endured, and "men fainted and fell all along the march."

General Early, commander of the division to which the Forty-third Regiment belonged, now boldly determined to march on Washington. The Confederates invaded the District of Columbia, coming within sight of the Capitol, and the fall of the city seemed imminent. Yet Early decided not to attack. His decision was wise, in Polk's opinion, because of the exhaustion of the men, their exposed position, and the approach of Hunter. Retreat became necessary. After more severe marching, the ragged, dirty, and worn-out troops recrossed the Potomac and finally established their base of operations in the lower Valley of Virginia. The great campaign was over. In a month the Forty-third had traveled six hundred miles and had met the enemy nine times. Since leaving Kinston in April, the regiment had marched over a thousand miles in three months with only eight days of rest.[8]

During the latter half of 1864 the Forty-third fought in the Valley. Fortifying its positions, destroying railroads and bridges, battling and skirmishing against the crack United States Sixth Army Corps, marching and maneuvering among the mountains and along the streams, it was very busily employed as Early sought to keep Sheridan occupied and thus prevent him from

---

[8] *Ansonian,* Sept. 6–Nov. 8, 1876; Diary, June 17–July 10, 1864; Polk to Mrs. Polk, June 16, [22], 24, 27, 30, July 17, 1864; Bryan Grimes, *Extracts of Letters . . . to His Wife . . .* (Pulaski Cowper, comp.), pp. 56-57.

reinforcing Grant near Richmond. Polk left the regiment in December, as he had been elected again to the North Carolina House of Commons.[9]

The discomfort, frustration, and danger Leonidas experienced as a soldier was matched by the burden of responsibility, loneliness, and anxiety that Sallie Polk had to bear at home. They corresponded constantly, and his letters have been preserved. Far more than a mere source for his military movements, they are striking documents revealing candidly the thoughts and feelings that fashioned his character and motivated his actions. Amid the perils of war, when each letter might well be the last, there was little reason to hold anything back. "Is there a man in the Confederate States who writes as many letters to his wife as I do? I doubt it. . . . You say you receive so many letters from me that you cannot keep up with them. I write so often that I do not know what I write or what I omit. I guess however that I write 'it all.'. . . I have no confidents, when away from you, & like some old woman, there are many things I want to talk about which no one can hear but you. I am altogether out of my sphere when away from home. . . ." Their correspondence was, inevitably, an admixture of the spiritual and the material. "I received on Friday," Leonidas would write, "your kind & I might say *noble* letter, together with the tobacco, drawers, & suspenders."[10]

Strong and tender were the ties that bound these two together. Their marriage, animated by a love still young, was strengthened by the presence of their two small daughters. In the course of his hurried march down the Valley of Virginia, Polk could find time to write:

> I think of them when bowed before
> The God who rules & reigns above
> His richest blessings to implore
> Upon the heads of *those I love.*

[9] *Ansonian*, Nov. 15, 1876—April 25, 1877; Polk to Mrs. Polk, July–Dec. *passim*, 1864; Diary, Sept.–Oct., 1864; Grimes, *Letters*, pp. 58-65.
[10] Polk to Mrs. Polk, May 12, Aug. 9, 1863, March 11, 26, June 30, 1864.

The inspiration of this love was his successful defense against the soldier's special temptations. When he saw certain officers come from roadside women and then write their wives, he could sign his own letters "your *true & devoted husband*" and mean it. When he was "pressed by a 'parlour warrior' to drink" he had the strength of habit and conviction to decline. So much was it all a part of his religion that he wrote, entirely without sanctimony: "The boys & girls of Kinston have balls & parties nearly every night. I stay in my tent & read my Bible—pays better." [11]

"Back home" during the war, leadership passed to the women. Together with the children, old men, and the faithful Negro slaves, they did what they could to harvest the crops and keep things going. The lack of manufactured articles, foodstuffs, and money called for adaptation to a poorer standard of living. Domestic industries were of necessity revived, and great ingenuity was shown in the making of clothes, shoes, and articles of household use. The diet of the people naturally changed. Since ordinary drugs for sickness were wanting, vegetable-type "home remedies" were widely developed. Heavier and heavier taxation, the collapse of banking and currency, and the breakdown of the various transportation systems made conditions progressively worse. Yet in the face of these burdensome difficulties life went on much as it had before.

By means of his wife's letters Polk kept in close touch with the work of the farm. "How are you progressing with ploughing &c?" he asked. "Has [*sic*] your sheep increased any? . . . Write to me about your . . . wheat, corn, cane, cotton, fowls, garden, stock. . . . I am glad to hear that you are getting on so well with your fodder [and] *pigs*. . . ." In his own letters he described with enthusiasm the excellent diversified agriculture of Virginia and gave detailed advice concerning the slaves and crops at home. He also sent some tomato seed, saying that the ripened fruit is

---

[11] Polk to Mrs. Polk, Sept. 9, 1862, March 26, Oct. 2, 1863, March 27, June 30, 1864; Diary, April 16, May 7, 1864.

"very large & fine"; and some "Yankees beans," explaining that he did not know "when or how to plant them" but he knew they were "splendid *cooked*." [12]

Like all armies, the Confederate Army had to travel on its stomach; and often its pace was slow. A "scanty supply of fresh beef with frequently no salt, and hard tack, and generally a half pound of rancid bacon per week, to the man," served as a typical ration in the Forty-third Regiment. Of course such a ration was supplemented at every opportunity. For example, near Richmond the men enjoyed meat, bread, coffee, sugar, and molasses captured from the enemy. At Charlottesville the townspeople generously gave the soldiers bread, pies, cakes, milk, ice cream, and also matches and tobacco. Around Warrenton turkeys, opossums, partridges, rabbits, and a red fox were all taken without firing a gun; "when surrounded by a regiment of yelling rebels," wrote Polk, "they seemed to be utterly helpless." A more surreptitious foraging endeavor, in Kinston, failed to be completely successful: "Some body went out night before last & stole 7 hogs & 30 chickens from an old lady, & now we have to drill 3 times a day, & have roll call 5 times a day." In a letter to the *Argus* Polk wrote on the subject of balanced diet.

> We hope our friends at home, will raise largely of potatoes, onions, &c., the latter especially being easily kept and transported, and very desirable for soldiers. In the meantime we hope they will save *largely* of *dried fruit*—an article of food which is considered healthy and an invaluable luxury in camp. Better send their apples and peaches to us, in this form, than convert it into brandy, for which their sons, brothers and husbands have but little use, especially at the exceedingly moderate price of from $40 to $50 per gallon.[13]

The problem of rising costs and depreciating currency bulked

---

[12] Polk to Mrs. Polk, Sept. 9, 1862, March 8, June 20, July 16, 1863, April 24, June 27, 1864; *Ansonian*, Sept. 20, 1876.

[13] *Argus*, May 21, 1863; *Ansonian*, June 7, 28, 1876; Polk to Mrs. Polk, March 27, June 4, 1864; Diary, June 17, 1864.

as large to the soldier in the field as to his family at home. In the essential particulars of food, clothing, and shelter he frequently endured considerable hardship. "I am nearly naked," Polk complained in the spring of 1863, "& my money cannot clothe me decently & feed me . . . to live on crackers & bacon & to buy a coat & pants costs over 2 months wages. . . . We are now paying $1.10 per pound for meat & everything else in proportion. It will cost us not less than $60. to live this month & economise as much as we can." His new suit cost $100; a box from home was a "rich treat" that "would have brought $75"; board in Raleigh, whither he went on a mission to procure clothes for officers, amounted to $16 a day—and no profit was made at that. As cool weather approached he asked: "Sallie how will you make out for shoes for yourself & family? I hope you have enough leather. Ordinary shoes are selling in V^a markets for $50 pr. . . . You had better have the boys making pegs to make their winter shoes. . . . I hope you will not have to buy anything from heartless speculators."[14]

Leonidas was happy to learn that Sallie looked well and wore her earrings again. "I am glad to hear it, & hope when I come home from the rugged scenes of War, to meet *all my little girls,* with cheeks flushed with the rosy tint of health. I am also glad to hear that my wife is proud enough to keep nice, & I wish I could say as much for myself. I go as decent as circumstances will allow but not as I wish to."

He was twenty-six in 1863 and thought he would "reach near 160 pounds." As to his own appearance, he wrote, "I have whiskers all over my face, & look rather saucy. . . ." One of those whiskers, a dark brown specimen six inches in length, he enclosed in a letter to her (and there it remains today, a singular item in the L. L. Polk Collection!). Perhaps in extenuation, he said that he had "a lively temperament & the happy faculty of

[14] Polk to Mrs. Polk, Sept. 9, 1862, April 6, 25, May 12, Sept. 1, Nov. 17, 1863, Feb. 13, March 1, 16, 1864.

looking 'on the bright side of the picture.'" And, he added, "It is fortunate for me that it is so, for a man devoted to his family, as I am, should have something in his nature to counteract the depression, which a long & painful separation produces."[15]

The lieutenant experienced some moments of elation during the war and thoroughly enjoyed relating them to his wife. When in June, 1863, his regiment invaded Maryland and Pennsylvania with Lee, Polk wrote: "We have destroyed *millions* of public property. . . . We have captured about 6 or 8 thousand cattle— the finest I ever saw, & I suppose 3 or 4 thousand of the very best of the Black Dutch horses. Nearly all our boys have new clothes & shoes, hats. We buy calico 50 cts, everything cheap. If I ever get back I will try to bring something to you." At the camp on the Rapidan in the fall of that year he remarked: "Our pickets & theirs exchange papers, talk, & seem to be more of neighbors than enemies. One of them told our boys yesterday that they were expecting a supply of winter clothing in a few days, & that we ought not to fight them until it was received, as we would be sure to get it all from them. Our boys cross the river in full sight of them, & gather beans, peas & corn." Perhaps the period of highest elation followed the fall of Plymouth Fort in April, 1864, when Polk wrote:

> I am seated in an old field, surrounded by men flushed with hope, & success, & dividing out their captured spoils. I write to you on Yankee paper, with a gold pen, & Yankee envelope, with Yankee ink smoking Yankee cigar, full of Yankee sugar coffee &.c. with a Yankee sword navy repeater & other "fixins" buckled about me. We had an *awful* time. . . . I did not get anything myself. The boys gave me what I got, except a few things I bought. They gave me 3 prs kid gloves for you slightly damaged. For the children a round comb a piece. I bought a pair of shoes for Lula. . . . I will send my tricks to you the first chance. . . . The boys gave me a fine spy glass,

[15] Polk to Mrs. Polk, Sept. 9, 1862, May 25, July 27, Dec. 4, 1863.

a very fine pipe, & the pen with which I write, just like the one at home. . . .

I *did my* BEST to buy you a dress—shoes or *something* but could get nothing. . . . I wish I could write a dozen letters tonight but the moon is far up the heavens already & the shortness of my candle admonishes me that my time is running short. We have prayer meetings every night. Enjoying ourselves finely over our spoils. . . . May you sleep & dream sweetly this lovely night. . . .

And the next morning:

Last night as the moon had climbed high up the star-gilt curtain, & gave to the slumbering camp a stilly sadness, with its mellow rays, I was seated on the ground writing by a dim light to my dear Sallie. *To-day* I am twenty seven . . . .[16]

Yet the feeling of depression engendered by the separation from home and by the war itself remained powerful and persistent. There were greater hardships—and greater dangers. He was "not yet well of the itch"; he "slept in line of battle all night, among the charred bodies of friend—foe—raining"; he "stood by a small tree to shoot, & 9 minie [*sic*] balls pierced it" no higher than his head; near Strasburg a bullet struck his heel and his leg was "deadened for a while"; at Bunker Hill a shell passed "about a foot" in front of his breast, just above his horse's neck, and exploded "about 10 feet" away. "I cant see how I escaped," he marveled after a very close call, "—only that God was my shield. . . . I declare I hate to send you such a letter as this but I can't really do any better." He wrote from Kinston: "I am depressed and dispirited, but probably without a just cause. Yesterday I had to witness the execution of two deserters. Last night we got the sad news that Gen Jackson is dead." Even after a visit home he had to apologize for his moodiness while there; he was think-

---

[16] Polk to Mrs. Polk, June 28, Sept. 28, 1863, April 20-24, 1864; Diary, April 20-23, 1864; *Argus,* May 5, 1864.

ing of the unhappy military situation created by the investment of Vicksburg. Though peace was "all the theme" in camp in 1864, the soldiers felt that an armistice would come only through further "blood and carnage." Soon Polk burst out, "As to this horrid war I am sick of practising it, sick of writing it, sick of thinking of it, sick of seeing it. . . ."[17]

The war was not of *his* making; he had fought against its coming as long as he possibly could. Then he had attempted to do his duty by serving his state and section as a soldier. Now, largely if not mainly for the sake of his wife and children, he wanted to leave the army and go home.

His taste for politics and public office had been whetted by his service in the legislature, and Governor Vance had led him to believe that a better position was in store for him. But here too he was doomed to disappointment. When Vance made Daniel G. Fowle adjutant general, Polk was bitter: "He forgets, like the most of his race, PROMISES. *Twice,* now have I been highly complimented for conduct in battle, but what does it avail me? *I was one of the old* UNION *men.* Little do I value their caresses or scorn, I am living for *you* & *my children,* & my greatest ambition is to leave them a name unsullied by any dishonest act as a man, or wrong as a husband & father. With this I am content." The war would end some time, he hoped, and then he would "ask none of them for favors." Though he saw Vance occasionally, he took care not to let the Governor think he would "boot lick" him. He felt that Vance had "acted very badly" toward him and had treated him "wrong." Nevertheless, Polk infinitely preferred Vance to Holden in the gubernatorial election of 1864 and soon forgot his earlier resentment.[18]

Polk was unwilling to bear the stigma of hiring a substitute, as he said Ed Liles had done, but he would have given Thomas

[17] Polk to Mrs. Polk, Dec. 24, 1862, May 12, June 17, Nov. 17, 1863, May 17, July 22, Aug. 30, Sept. 18, 1864; Diary, May 12, Aug. 25, 1864; *Ansonian,* Jan. 10, 1877.

[18] Polk to Mrs. Polk, March 21, April 19, Aug. 6, 1863, March 23, 26, 30, 1864.

S. Ashe a thousand dollars, "freely," if Ashe had procured a position for him, preferably one in the North Carolina state troops. This could not be done. Polk was also attracted by a position in the ordnance department. "If I could get it," he said, "I would rank as 1st L^{t} be on a Gen's staff, have a horse to ride, be out of the mud, & bullets, bombs &.c. & always be as comfortable as I could be in the Army. It is one of the easiest, safest & best positions in the service. Isn't it worth trying for? . . . I shall strive for it for my own and your sake." He intended to get testimonials from Ashe, Vance, General D. H. Hill, and Colonels J. T. Jones, J. R. Lane, and R. T. Bennett. Polk stood an examination for the place, but neither he nor any other North Carolinian could win it; the job went, "as usual," to a Virginian. "I should consider it the best strike of my life if by some unforeseen visit of fortune I could slide out of this war," he wrote his wife.[19]

Until such fortune should arrive, however, the young lieutenant resolved to make the best of his situation. He demonstrated distinct and commendable qualities of leadership, and before his service ended he had filled several regimental posts. At various times Polk was paymaster, enrolling officer, acting adjutant, judge advocate of a court-martial, provost marshal, and acting company commander. As provost marshal he had the use of a comfortable little office and could borrow books. He became acting company commander at a time when the first lieutenant was sick and the captain was not "in a proper state of locomotion." He also helped to frame the constitution of the Christian Association organized in the regiment. Once when a soldier had been condemned to be shot, Polk became so deeply impressed with the injustice of the sentence that he asked his colonel to draw up a petition for the man's reprieve. The request was granted, and the man was saved. Polk seems to have been popular with the men and to have won their confidence. "They say when we go into a fight they want me to lead them. And when I am detailed for any

[19] Polk to Mrs. Polk, May 9, 12, June 28, July 16, Dec. 12, 1863, April 6, 1864.

purpose they all want to go with me." He asserted that "they are *all* very much attached to me, & say they would be ruined if I were to leave them." Several times Polk was praised for his conduct in battle. "I hope I show no egotism or vanity to you," he wrote Sallie Polk, "when I say that I can fill a higher position with as much credit as the one I now hold." [20]

A "higher position" promptly captured Polk's thoughts when in March, 1864, he learned that the men in his regiment wanted him to run for the House of Commons, and Sheriff Threadgill of Anson wrote him that his name was frequently mentioned in the county. Polk confidently expected strong support in the army if he were nominated. The greatest task would be to attract votes back home. "If I run my *friends at home must* WORK," he declared. "I want to go to the Legislature & if my *friends* will *work* I *can go.*" [21]

At a meeting on April 8 the voters of the Anson companies adopted resolutions stating that they felt "deeply impressed with the idea that one of our next Representatives in the General Assembly of North Carolina should be a man from the army." They therefore unanimously nominated Lieutenant L. L. Polk and heartily recommended him to their "comrades in arms" and "friends in Anson county" as a "suitable person for the position." On being chosen, the nominee said, "I am now almost like 'Major Jones' was in New York when the woman gave him a baby to hold." But he had been sure of getting the nomination and was naturally delighted to make the race. "If I can only get through the bullets & ballot box wont I be fixed?. . . If defeated I will be no worse off than now. If elected it would be worth everything." [22]

So far as the county was concerned, Polk had to conduct his canvass *in absentia,* relying upon the reports of Sheriff Threadgill,

---

[20] Polk to Mrs. Polk, Jan. 27, March 17, April 19, 25, May 12, 16, Sept. 5, 10, 1863, March 27, May 20, June 4, 1864; Diary, May 18, June 10, Sept. 1, 7, 1864.
[21] Polk to Mrs. Polk, March 30, April 2, 6, 1864.
[22] *Argus,* April 14, 1864; Polk to Mrs. Polk, April 9, 24, May 2, 1864.

father-in-law Joel Gaddy, and various friends for information as to his prospects. The Forty-third Regiment was engaged in its great thousand-mile campaign from the time that Polk received the nomination, at Kinston, until the soldiers voted on July 28 at Martinsburg, (West) Virginia. Again he emphasized to his wife that friends at each home precinct must work for him and "play the agreeable." As for himself, he remarked waggishly, "your old man is on the carpet 'all smiles, soft talk & a sharp quantity of the agreeable.' "[23]

To advertise his stand on the issues of the day, Polk sent the customary political card to the Wadesboro paper. In it he declared that he favored upholding civil rights, that he opposed the sweeping character of the exemption law, and that he was against a convention or the withdrawal of North Carolina from the Confederacy. He was "for Vance against any other man in the State"; and "for the independence of these Confederate States." He believed that his own special appeal lay in the fact that he well understood the needs of the soldiers.[24]

In the race for the two seats Polk had five competitors, including his colleague of 1860, Edward R. Liles. The strongest "home candidate," A. J. Dargan, led the ticket with 461 votes. Polk, the "army candidate," received 331 votes to run second. The Anson County soldiers contributed over a third of their nominee's total, and, as in 1860, his strength in the county was broadly distributed. Liles, with 302 votes, failed to place, as did the other three men, with individual totals of 193, 160, and 70. In the fine flush of enthusiasm at the time of his election, Polk said: "I have always been unfortunate in some respects but . . . I shall never again complain of ill luck, but do my utmost to do my whole duty, to my God, my country, my family & myself."[25]

---

[23] Polk to Mrs. Polk, April 6, 9, 13, 24, May 5, June 16, 24, July [17], 25, 1864.
[24] Polk to C. W. Fenton, May 7, 1864; *Argus*, July 7, 1864.
[25] *Argus*, Aug. 11, 1864; Polk to Mrs. Polk, July 28, Aug. 2, 1864; Diary, July 28, 1864; *Ansonian*, July 5, Nov. 22, 29, 1876.

Little did he realize how soon this noble resolution would be put to the test. He was elected early in August, but not until December 4—two weeks after the legislature had convened—was it possible for him to leave his regiment. Delay in receiving the official certificate of his election due to wretched mail service, copious red tape in connection with his resignation, further dangerous fighting, illness, arrest, and court-martial—all these things vexed and tried him during those four months.

As early as July 17, even before the soldiers voted, Polk referred to the desirability, if he were elected, of getting from the Anson County sheriff as soon as possible a properly authenticated certificate. That important document did not arrive until September 18. Polk had previously applied for a leave of absence, in the hope that he might be allowed to visit his home before the opening of the legislative session. The application was returned to him "disapproved" because the certificate failed to accompany it. Soon he sent up both papers, but now a much more formidable obstruction loomed up to block his departure.[26]

On September 19 the Forty-third Regiment was ordered to Winchester for combat. When battle line formed Polk went to Brigadier-General Bryan Grimes to inquire whether, as a representative-elect who had given up his command, he ought to go into the fight. Grimes replied affirmatively, explaining that if Polk did not there would be "a great deal of talk." The lieutenant's impression of the entire conversation was that his superior had left the course of action wholly up to him. Polk then entered the battle, led his men in a charge, and conducted himself gallantly in "the thickest of the fight."

In the *mêlée* Captain Robert T. Hall fell wounded and asked Polk, whom he believed was under no obligation to be in battle, to take him to the rear. The Confederates were falling back at the time, there was no one else to help him, and Polk "fully

[26] Polk to Mrs. Polk, July 17, Aug. 19, 23, 30, Sept. 11, 18, Oct. 2, 1864; Diary, Sept. 18, 1864; Polk to James A. Seddon, Sept. 7, Oct. 1, 1864.

expected" that the Yankees would capture his friend. He therefore carried Hall to the hospital in Winchester and at the Captain's insistence remained there with him. When the enemy approached the town, according to Hall, Polk seized sword and pistol and rushed out to fight. After the battle, however, Polk was arrested. The charges preferred against him by General Grimes were "misbehavior before the enemy" and "absence without leave."

"It is done only to detain me, & keep me from coming home," Polk asserted. Yet this arrest was a small item on the Grimes agenda. The battle at Winchester, in which the Confederate troops "did not behave with their usual valor" and were routed, made September 19 the "most trying day of the war" for the General. And the ensuing weeks were harassing and exhausting weeks of movement and reorganization. Convinced that "the only salvation for this army and the country will be to inflict severe punishment on all who fail to discharge their duty," General Grimes attempted in that period to correct abuses which had crept into the ranks during the hard campaign. Firmer discipline became the goal.

With his arrest, Polk abandoned perforce all thoughts of going home. "As it is," he wrote his young wife, "I would not come if I could, until this thing is settled, for I love the name & character of myself, my wife & my children too well, to forfeit them . . . I feel that your pride & judgment will endorse my stay in order to vindicate myself against false charges." Indeed Polk longed for a trial, as he felt sure that the men of his regiment and brigade would sustain him.

As he waited, his situation did not seem bad, in spite of Grimes. Aside from a few days of chills and fever following the fight at Winchester, he maintained comparatively good health and spirits. In the fall of 1864 the regiment enjoyed good water and good food—chicken, eggs, butter, beef, apples, and apple butter. And not the least of the compensations of his detention was the fact that it kept him out of combat. Still, Polk remained under arrest for over two months before receiving an official copy of the charges against him. This chafing delay served to underscore certain opinions he had already expressed regarding army law. "I cannot forget," he once wrote, "that before I became a *slave* to military rule ... I had something of the spirit of a man, & however much they may cramp me they cannot extinguish that spark of independence which should burn in the bosom of all who claim to be freemen." [27]

Bluntly, the charge against Lieutenant Polk was that he had skulked in battle. Before the coming court-martial he would deny the accusation as vigorously as he had previously denounced dark rumors in Anson County to the same effect. As early as July, 1862, when he belonged to Zeb Vance's Twenty-sixth Regiment, Polk wrote his colonel from Wadesboro saying that reports were going the rounds that he had turned tail in battle. These he termed downright lies. During the engagement in question, he declared, he was sick but fought and followed orders anyway. He called upon Vance to investigate the matter, to punish him or let the thing rest as he saw fit. No charge was ever pressed. Again after Gettysburg, Sallie Polk informed her husband of similar whispers. "When I read your letter my blood boiled," said he, "& yesterday I sat down & wrote a *very plain* letter to the Argus, in which I denounced the authors of those reports as wilful, knowing, & malicious liars. ... give me the points & I will do the fighting."

He accused *"parlor warriors"* of circulating the slanders that he skulked at Gettysburg and that he was reduced to the rank of private for going home without a furlough. In turn he scored those who hired substitutes and wangled army contracts in Raleigh. Dramatically he declared that he was doing his duty, and that such "shafts of venom" fell harmlessly at his feet. In further

[27] Polk to Mrs. Polk, Jan. 29, July 27, Nov. 4, 1863, Sept. 24, Oct. 2, 9, 19, 28, Nov. 6, 17, 1864; Polk to Lt. A. Green, Sept. 21, 1864; Polk to Maj. —— Moore, Nov. 1, 17, 1864; sworn statements of Capt. Robert T. Hall, undated; Diary, Sept. 19-23, Oct. 8, 1864; Grimes, *Letters*, pp. 65-88.

refutation, he included a brief extract from a letter of Colonel Thomas S. Kenan to J. R. Hargrave. "I do not like for censure to rest upon the shoulders of Polk, when he does not deserve it," Kenan stated, adding that the young lieutenant "was justly entitled to and did receive my commendation for his brave conduct." To give such comfort as he could to his indignant little wife, Polk wrote with quiet conviction and true prophecy: "I do hope dear Sallie that you will not allow these things to trouble you, for I expect to have enemies as long as I live." [28]

Polk had been court-martialed once before. Late in October, 1863, he was arrested on the petty charge of attempting to straighten his battered canteen by exploding a blank cartridge into it. Soon released, he wrote the commanding officer, Colonel W. G. Lewis, that he was "deeply impressed with the belief" that he had been "treated with injustice." Officers, he said, were usually only censured, and not arrested, for "light offenses." Others, moreover, had committed the same act but had not been punished. No order had been issued to cover the case. Why had *he* been arrested? To his wife Polk asserted that he was too proud to submit to this "tyranny," and that he was the first officer who had dared oppose Lewis. In the opinion of the commanding officer the letter was "disrespectful and insubordinate"; Polk was immediately arrested again and held for trial.

Adjutant Drury Lacy, Jr., testified that Polk's letter, which passed through his hands, "excited surprise" because of the lieutenant's previous good record and was not inspired by any ill will toward his superiors. In his defense Polk declared that the canteen was his own and the cartridge was not wasted. Censure would have pained him enough, as he always strove to do his duty; but arrest, implying irregularity and tending toward mortification and loss of influence, was serious. Apparently, said he, Colonel Lewis had mistaken the meaning of the letter, for

---

[28] Polk to Vance, July 25, 1862; Polk to Mrs. Polk, Aug. 9, 1863; Polk to C. W. Fenton, in *Argus,* Aug. 20, 1863.

in it he stressed his sense of obedience and his fidelity to duty. He assuredly did not intend disrespect or insubordination. After boldly making the point that he was "of the opinion that there is, to some degree, a courtesy & respect which should be reciprocal, particularly between commissioned officers," he cheerfully rested his case. The judges then rendered the verdict that Lieutenant Polk was "honorably acquitted of the charge." [29]

When Polk faced the court-martial late in November, 1864, for alleged misconduct during the battle at Winchester, he at least had had sufficient experience in defending himself. He confidently predicted a successful defense. "I shall certainly come off *all right*," he said. His argument was detailed and cogent. Polk showed that, by General Grimes's own testimony before the court, he had been in the right and General Grimes had been inconsistent in arresting him. He proved that he had fought a good fight that day and had led a gallant charge. After all the evidence had been duly deliberated, the judge advocate of the court-martial wrote Polk: ". . . I have the honor to inform you, that you have been *honorably* acquitted of the Charges and Specifications preferred against you." [30]

To Polk it was the *"grandest triumph imaginable"*—a clear vindication of his character. *"Everybody* (except 'Father Grimes' of course) was very proud of my victory. . . ." The way home now lay open. On the evening before his departure by stage, his fellows paid him a compliment, as this diary entry for December 3 succinctly shows: "Am tonight serenaded. Whole Reg^t call me out. Band discourses sweet music. Have good time." From the front of his tent he gave them a talk, and they in return gave him three hearty cheers. Unknown to him, a meeting of the

---

[29] "Proceeding of trial at Morton's Ford V^a": MSS. including a statement of the charge and specification against Polk, an undated copy of Polk's letter to Col. W. G. Lewis, the testimony of Adjt. Drury Lacy, Jr., and Polk's defense (dated Nov. 16, 1863). Also, Polk to Mrs. Polk, Oct. 23, 28, Nov. 4, 17, 21, 23, 1863.

[30] Polk to Mrs. Polk, Nov. 24, 1864; Polk's defense, Nov. 30, 1864; "Testimony of Brig Genl Grimes," undated; R. C. Badger to Polk, Nov. 30, 1864; various official and private documents relating to the trial, dated and undated.

officers took place later, and the following resolutions were adopted:

> Camp 43ᵈ N C Regᵗ New Market Va. Dec 5ᵗʰ/64
> Whereas, our brother officer, Lt L L Polk, having been elected to the Legislature of North Carolina, and having left us to take his seat in that honorable body, therefore
> Resolved 1ˢᵗ That while we are highly gratified at the honor thus conferred upon him; we deeply regret that in future we are to be deprived of his association as a Christian gentleman, and his aid and example as a gallant officer.
> Resolved 2ⁿᵈ That his gentlemanly deportment, his upright and moral conduct, together with his gallant bearing as an officer, have won for him the esteem and confidence of the officers and men of the 43ᵈ N. C. Regt.
> Resolved 3ʳᵈ That we hope his conduct while serving his country in her Legislative councils, may be marked by the same honesty of purpose, patriotic devotion and unfaltering courage, that characterized it while serving her on the field of battle.
> Resolved 4ᵗʰ That a copy of these resolutions be sent to Lt L. L. Polk, and also the Raleigh Confederate for publication. . . .[31]

With this testimonial glowing before his eyes and the cheers of his friends still ringing in his ears, Representative Polk set out for Raleigh. He intended first to present his credentials and be qualified, then to obtain leave of absence to visit his home briefly. "I will be sure to come soon," he wrote his wife, "as I cannot stay in Raleigh after *my shirt gets dirty*." He took his seat on December 7 and remained only long enough to help elect his good friend Thomas S. Ashe a Confederate senator.

Returning in ten days, he plunged at once into the concern that interested him most—the lot of the common soldier. He introduced a resolution requesting the Governor to correspond with the authorities at Richmond in reference to a general order which frequently imposed great hardship on sick and disabled soldiers.

---

[31] Polk to Mrs. Polk, Dec. 1, 6, 1864; Diary, Dec. 3, 4, 1864; MS. copy of resolutions; the Rev. E. W. Thompson to Polk, Dec. 26, 1864.

Under the order such men, many with limbs maimed or lost, were obliged to travel long distances to report to their commands for the purpose of extending their furloughs and the like. Often they suffered the humiliation of being conducted under guard with "deserters and other degraded characters." Polk would rescue these unfortunates by permitting them to make their applications nearer home or by proxy. Another resolution he introduced requested North Carolina's senators and representatives in the Confederate Congress to attempt to amend existing laws so that transportation would be allowed privates, non-commissioned officers, and officers of the line on furloughs of indulgence. Both resolutions were quickly ratified. As a member of the House standing committee on education, Polk also reported on a bill to establish camp and garrison schools.[32]

Aside from the work of pushing and elucidating his own measures, Polk found most of the session slow and dull. "Resolutions against arming the slaves, & for negotiations for peace, are the most important matters before us," he wrote, "& they could be disposed of in one day, but the mania for speech making seems to have seized the members & we are destined to stay & see them through their *labor* & *delivery*." He revealed that the General Assembly was doing "nothing at all" but costing the state's taxpayers $10,000 a day. The most attractive question under discussion seemed to be when to adjourn. "It is a great trouble to be one of the *people's* favored few sometimes," said Polk, "but still not as much trouble as *some* positions I wot of." Toward the end of the tedious session, which at length adjourned on February 7, 1865, the young veteran wearily wrote his wife: "I am well but most awfully *bored*."[33]

Two months later, Lee surrendered to Grant.

[32] *North Carolina House Journal, 1864-'65,* regular session, pp. 103 (Dec. 7), 108-11 (Dec. 8), 175 (Dec. 19), adjourned session, pp. 25 (Jan. 24), 58 (Jan. 30); *Public Laws, 1864-'65,* reg. sess., public resolutions, p. 73, adj. sess., public resolutions, p. 31.
[33] Polk to Mrs. Polk, Jan. 21, 25, 31, Feb. 2, 1865.

Chapter V
A CHAPTER IN RECONSTRUCTION

FELLOW CITIZENS, *we are going home.* Let painful reflections upon our late separation, and pleasant memories of our early union, quicken our footsteps towards the old mansion, that we may grasp hard again the hand of friendship which stands at the door, and, sheltered by the old homestead which was built upon a rock and has weathered the storm, enjoy together the long, bright future which awaits us.

So spoke Edwin G. Reade, president of the convention called for the purpose of restoring North Carolina to the Union, on October 2, 1865. Meeting in the somewhat shabby chamber of the House of Commons, the members took the oath to support the Constitution of the United States and speedily set about to restore their state to its normal relations with the federal government. All of them were sincerely anxious to do so. These duly elected representatives of the people were predominantly old-line Union Whigs, middle-aged, conservative, not above the average in either ability or experience. Though a Northern reporter discovered, "with proper amazement," that Whig and Democratic party spirit still was lusty, the members of this convention were united on the great issues which had brought them together. By a vote of 105 to 9, they repealed the ordinance of secession and declared it "null and void from the beginning"; an ordinance prohibiting slavery in North Carolina unanimously passed, 109 to 0. The minor tasks of the convention—election of state and county officials, judicial and administrative measures, creation of congressional districts for the approaching national election—they performed with equal dispatch. At the insistence of President Johnson and Governor Holden, they repudiated entirely the state war debt. And in adjourned session during the late spring of 1866, the members undertook the task of constitutional reform.[1]

L. L. Polk appeared as one of the younger members of the convention. Because he had been a rising Union Whig and had twice served in the legislature, the loyal citizens of Anson County perhaps naturally chose him again as their representative. During the adjourned session, with Jonathan Worth now Governor, Polk introduced three resolutions: first, that the convention confine itself to constitutional reform unless the Governor recommended otherwise; second, that the *per diem* and mileage of officers and members of the convention be reduced so as to save the state $275 a day; and third, that evening sessions be held. The resolutions suffered a sad fate. In Polk's own words, the first was "rejected," the second "killed outright," and the third *"smashed."*[2] He also belonged to the committee whose duty it was "to inquire what is necessary to be done to restore the State to the Federal Union." After the convention's brief sitting had ended, Polk returned home to face the tremendous task of adjusting himself to the new conditions—personal, economic, and political—of a post-war world.

It is difficult to imagine a greater contrast than that between the enthusiasm of the South in 1861 and the dejection of the South in 1865. The story of the demobilization of the Confederate soldier at Appomattox, and his return to a devastated land, has often been told. It should suffice here to say that this individual tended to accept the situation and to begin at once the arduous work of personal rehabilitation. The problem of adjustment, particularly that faced by the women, seemed truly gigantic. Immediately after the war the average Southerner was far more

[1] Constitutional Convention of 1865, *Journal*, pp. 6, 7 (Oct. 2), 22-24 (Oct. 6), 27-29 (Oct. 7), *passim;* Sidney Andrews, *The South since the War*, chs. xv-xviii.
[2] MS. "Resolutions introduced by Mr. Polk Adjourned Session of Convention of 1866."

concerned with his own fortunes than he was with the political problems of Reconstruction.

So it was with Polk. Anson County had escaped actual invasion until March, 1865. Then, only six weeks before the war ended, the dread blow fell. Kilpatrick's cavalry, part of the left wing of Sherman's army, struck through the county in a northeasterly direction. The whole region was "at their mercy" and was left "a complete wreck," the Wadesboro paper reported. "We cannot particularize or individualize, as all were more or less sufferers." A familiar pattern seems to have been followed. Dwellings, smoke houses, corn cribs, and other buildings were pillaged, and some were burned; Negroes were taken, property was destroyed, and stock was driven away; women were offended and valuables were seized. The force remained in the vicinity until Hampton and Wheeler threatened it.[3]

The Polk homestead lay in the path of the invader and suffered like the rest. Their farm stripped of food and forage and most of their Negroes gone, the Polks had to turn their backs on the past and begin their life anew. Before that poverty-ridden crowd at Winfield, Kansas, twenty-five years later, Polk recalled those stern times as he said:

> When I returned ... at the close of the war, I found my home desolate and ruined. My little wife said, "If you can find anything to cook I will cook it." Remember she had never cooked a meal of victuals in all her life. She had been raised in true southern style. Her little fingers had done nothing but touch the keys of the piano or the silvery strings of the guitar. But she rolled up her sleeves and slapped those little hands into the face of the world, and said, "I for one will accept the situation." (Applause) I would have been less than a man, I would not have been worthy of the name of man if I had not rolled up my sleeves and dug for that little woman. I did do it. (Applause)[4]

[3] Wadesboro *North Carolina Argus*, March 30, 1865.
[4] Winfield *Courier*, July 10, 1890.

For eight years after the war, Polk devoted himself almost exclusively to the redevelopment of his farm. During his late twenties and early thirties, a contemporary biographer wrote, Polk "toiled early and late, working in the fields with such assistance as he could get, and doing himself everything required to be done on a farm, from making a horseshoe to building a house."[5] By the middle 1870's he could look upon his labor with justifiable pride. His land holdings were valued at $1,142, and a third of his 653 acres were under cultivation. Beneath the undulating surface of the land, the sandy and red clay soil was rich enough to produce a great variety. The cotton yield was 500 to 1,000 pounds per acre; and in bushels per acre, corn ran from 10 to 40, wheat from 8 to 25, oats from 12 to 25, and rye from 12 to 20, depending upon location and the seasons. The climate was good, the water abundant, and all kinds of vegetables and fruits grew well. A new and larger house arose to accommodate a family that had doubled in size since the war; the Polks were now the parents of six daughters.[6] Outside the labor on the farm, only an occasional glimpse of Polk can be had during these difficult years—serving as a magistrate, distributing Southern Relief supplies, being elected a vice-president of the "Agricultural Club of Anson County," addressing a political meeting "in his usual forcible style," making a speech in behalf of a soldiers' monument.[7]

The year 1873, however, marked a great change in the activities of Polk and in the life of his immediate region. The Railroad was coming to Anson County. Construction of the Wilmington, Charlotte, and Rutherford, a line connecting North Carolina's chief city and seaport with the whole southern border of the state, had been interrupted by the Civil War, but in the 'seventies progressed rapidly. The road was designed to tap a dozen well-settled

---

[5] [Charles Robson], *Representative Men of the South*, pp. 356-57.
[6] Land Registry form, Polk Papers.
[7] Const. Conv. of 1865, *Journal*, p. 20 (Oct. 5); W. H. Bagley to L. L. Polk, Feb. 28, April 2, 1867, in Jonathan Worth, *Correspondence* (J. G. deRoulhac Hamilton, ed.), II, 906, 929-30; *Argus*, May 27, July 15, 1869; MS. "Speech . . . delivered . . . May 21st 1870 by Leonidas L Polk."

and productive counties all the way from the coast to the mountains. Realizing the potential economic importance of the railroad, both Wilmington interests and citizens along the route strongly supported the project. Anson County alone subscribed $120,000 as its share.[8]

Polk's home in the western part of the county occupied the center of a region that was well-peopled and fairly prosperous for those days. Eight miles west of Wadesboro, the county seat, and approximately three-quarters of the two-hundred-mile distance between Wilmington and Charlotte, it stood near an east-west post road over which a considerable amount of traffic flowed. The new railroad, just renamed the Carolina Central, was to push its track directly through Polk's farm. As he listened to the distant whistle of a locomotive one day, Polk had a powerful, appealing idea: he would turn his farm into a town.

He quickly laid out his land in lots on either side of the C.C. line. He had already petitioned for a post office to be called "Luneville"; as the railroad came nearer, however, the name of the proposed village became "Polkton." There was only one house, to be sure, but it was a fairly large one, and Polk made it serve its purpose as a nucleus very effectively. He converted one room of his residence into the post office and another into a small store. Later, in the room above the post office, he set up a printing press. With characteristic energy and persuasiveness Polk induced a number of people to settle. Bit by bit, he sold his land to the newcomers. The better to advertise Polkton, he launched a weekly newspaper. He told of the good farming country, where corn, cotton, rye, oats, wheat, and hay flourished; of the soil that was adapted to the successful cultivation of potatoes, melons, apples, pears, peaches, and grapes; of the fine water and healthful climate; and of the abundance of all kinds of lumber and stone for building purposes.

Within a year thirteen families had permanently located, and

---

[8] Robert Somers, *The Southern States since the War*, pp. 33-34; Charlotte *Southern Home*, Jan. 23, 1872.

more planned to come. Furthermore, there were now three general stores, a drug store, a shoe and boot shop, a wagon and carriage manufactory, a steam saw mill, a school, a Baptist church, and the prospect of a Methodist church. An act incorporating Polkton was ratified by the General Assembly on March 19, 1875. The town, whose corporate limits were one half mile square with the store of Gaddy and Williams as the center, was to be governed by an intendant and five commissioners. Another year, and the number of general stores had increased to twelve; there were also a "first-class country hotel," a blacksmith, two brickyards, and another saw mill; and the Methodist church had become a reality. When Polk deeded his lots, he provided that no spirituous liquors should be sold on the property. He then felt able to boast that Polkton had "more good water and less mean whiskey than any place in the State." The census of 1880 credited the little town with a population of 183.[9]

With the rapid growth of Polkton, Polk's own varied business activities expanded. For three or four years prior to the creation of his town, he had operated a little country store in partnership with his wife's brother, Risden Bennett Gaddy. It was one of the thousands that sprang up in the South after the war. The great slaveholders of ante-bellum times had bought goods for their retinue from the nearest large city, but when the slaves were freed they of course became independent purchasers. Thus goods suited to small farms rather than large plantations came into demand. To many small farmers, both white and black, Polk and Gaddy sold all kinds of supplies in exchange for cash, produce, or cotton. Though the volume of their business was comparatively large, their profits were quite small.[10]

During the early days of Polkton the firm was dissolved, for sufficient reasons, and Polk determined to manage a store of his

[9] Raleigh *Farmer and Mechanic*, July 29, 1880; "Grantor Index to Deeds, P-Q-R," Anson County courthouse, Wadesboro; Polkton *Ansonian*, April 16, 1874, March 25, 1875, April 12, 26, 1876.
[10] Polk and Gaddy ledgers, receipts, etc.

own. Upon returning from buying trips to Wilmington and Baltimore, he stated his case in the following advertisement:

> At last! The undersigned is enabled to announce to his old customers and friends that he is now receiving one of the most complete and cheap stocks of goods ever offered in this section, and in selling them he intends to test fully and fairly the truthfulness of the old adage: "a nimble sixpence is worth a slow shilling." He offers a splendid line of ready-made clothing. And gents' underwear. Hats, boots, shoes, saddlery, hardware and cutlery. Guns and pistols. Woodenware, crockery, tin ware, stoves, plows, bagging, ties, twine, tobacco, segars, notions, confectionaries, flour, bacon, salt, molasses, fish, cheese, and everything else usually kept in a first class store. He has a fine stock of pant and coat goods, of all grades. Brown sheetings, tickings, plaids, linseys, calicoes. He endeavored to select such goods, and at such prices as would suit the farmers of the country, and if by fair dealing and short profits he can secure it, he hopes to share largely the patronage of the people. He will take great pleasure in showing and pricing his extensive stock to his friends. Be sure to favor him with a call when you come to Polkton. L. L. Polk.—Highest market price paid for cotton and all kinds of country produce at the Farmer's Cheap Cash Store. L.L.P.

He also manufactured his own candies for all who were "willing to buy at Northern prices"; acted as agent for "THE 'DIXIE PUMP,' *The best Wooden Pump now Made"*; and urged the use of his "Land Plaster" on one's clover patch.[11]

No one doubted that "Colonel" Polk was the mainspring of Polkton. He not only conceived and founded it but played the leading role in its early growth. At one time or another during the brief four years he belonged to it, he was farmer, merchant, express agent, postmaster, editor, juror, Mason, Sunday School teacher, holiday and commencement speaker, town commissioner, mayor, and politician. He appeared with his daughters in charades

[11] *Ansonian*, April 23, Oct. 15, Dec. 10, 1874, Feb. 11, 1875, May 17, 1876.

and tableaux staged by the "Polkton Literary and Social Club." He "fussed" editorially with persons who had borrowed books from him and had failed to return them. When he was called to a wider field in 1877 his fellow-townsmen were conscious of losing one of their "noblest, best citizens and most energetic working men." [12]

Polk's weekly newspaper, which he named the *Ansonian,* did not operate merely as a vehicle for the advertisement of Polkton. Anyone even slightly familiar with Polk's deep interest in agriculture and government knew that. He was also a writer, and one with emphatic notions. He fully appreciated the community value of a lively local paper that would entertain and amuse as well as educate. The *Ansonian* first appeared on April 16, 1874. A typical country weekly in content and make-up, it was edited for a year by Polk before the "heavy pressure of business" compelled him to relinquish his charge. He intimated, however, that he would resume the editorship as soon as it became practicable. Two Polkton merchants, F. O. Hawley and C. D. Gale, managed the paper while Polk was engaged in his multifarious activities. Many of his readers missed him. "Why rusteth in idleness Col. Polk's versatile and brilliant pen?" asked his friendly rival from across the county, Ed Liles. *"He* rail-roadeth around, maketh speeches (good ones too) eateth dinners and skedaddleth back to Thermopylae; why thundereth he not through the Organ?"[13] Polk did return in April, 1876, and for a second year edited the *Ansonian,* this time until he finally left Polkton.

"Fearlessly the right defend—impartially the wrong condemn." That was the motto of the *Ansonian* and the goal Polk set for himself in the discussion of matters both moral and political. His stated aim in those days of Reconstruction was to protect and to advance the best interests of North Carolina and its people. The

---

[12] *Ansonian,* 1874-1877, *passim; Argus,* May 27, 1875; Wadesboro *Pee Dee Herald,* March 15, 1876; interview with Mrs. Bettie Beachum, Polkton, N. C., Feb. 24, 1938.

[13] *Pee Dee Herald,* Feb. 2, April 12, 1876.

paper's opposition to men and measures, he declared, "shall be characterized by proper courtesy, honor and manliness, and whenever we strike we shall aim *breast high*." As a newspaper editor he always sought to foster a spirit of friendliness and co-operation with other members of the press, so that he and they might exchange opinions freely and perhaps achieve an effective unity in their treatment of state problems.[14]

The newly-formed North Carolina Press Association was an organization which embodied this same idea. Polk became a member and attended its annual convention of 1874, held in Raleigh. There the Association concentrated upon some of the business problems of a newspaper: "the custom of gratuitous advertising in the shape of local notices," the danger of spurious advertising, the question of uniform rates, and the matter of accepting advertising from agencies. Forty-five papers were represented. Although his *Ansonian* was less than a month old, Polk served on the committee to prepare business for the convention, and he participated in the debates on advertising practices. His views on a resolution against accepting advertising from agencies were reported as follows: "Mr. Polk was tired of being dictated [to] by agencies.... his people advertised in the Ansonian for their benefit, and not so much to aid him, but he was disposed to always favor his own people. If we favor anybody, let us favor North Carolinians. The resolution should pass as a protection to the press of North Carolina. Let us stand square up to it. It is a measure for our protection; we will get just as many advertisements as we now get and more dollars, too."[15]

During the convention the members of the Association were taken on an educational tour of the state capital. They visited a new cotton factory, the Edwards and Broughton printing house, the State Geological Museum, the penitentiary, the insane asylum, the colored institution for the deaf, dumb, and blind, and the city's

[14] *Ansonian,* April 16, 1874, April 5, May 31, 1876.
[15] North Carolina Press Association, *Historical Records, 1873-1887,* pp. 12-18.

three schools for young women. At St. Mary's School the gentlemen of the press were greeted with the singing of "The Old North State Forever," and upon leaving were "waved out of sight by a little forest of handkerchiefs...." At Peace Institute they were entertained by the "calisthenic exercises" of the young ladies, and by Miss Tate, the Greensboro prima donna. The editors also paid their respects to Governor Caldwell and posed for a group photograph on the capitol grounds. Everywhere they were welcomed with "handsome speeches" and "splendid collations." Upon the invitation of Colonel Thomas M. Holt, industrialist and president of the State Agricultural Society, the members journeyed by special train to Durham, site of the Dukes' infant tobacco industry, and to Haw River, where the Holts were pioneering in the development of North Carolina's cotton mills.

The press convention in Raleigh was the focal point of a "swing around the circle" for Polk. He traveled from Polkton by way of Wilmington and Goldsboro, taking note all the while, as a journalist should, of political developments, new building enterprises, and farm conditions. His visit to Raleigh was his first in eight years. While in Durham, he recalled that he had passed through in 1865; that he had "stepped into a house near the station, over the door of which was painted, in dim colors, 'Durham Tobacco,' and purchased a parcel." From the interesting factory at Haw River he moved on to Winston for a "grand Temperance Celebration," and to Charlotte, where he was a delegate to his Congressional District convention.[16]

This extended trip, and a number of lesser ones, served to reacquaint Polk with the state as a whole. Sharply focused in his mind now was a challenging contrast: North Carolina's burden of economic distress and political corruption, and the bright hope of the state's undeveloped natural and human resources. To Polk the economic problem seemed the more important. Yet he realized that the political problem was the more pressing and

[16] *Ansonian*, May 14–June 4, 1874.

that its solution would be a necessary prelude to any stirring of the state's potentialities.

Through War and Reconstruction Polk remained a Whig at heart, though the exigencies of the late 'sixties and early 'seventies made men either Radicals or Conservatives. As late as 1868 he would have rallied "with renewed zeal" to the standard of "the old Whig party as led by the immortal Clay." The "good of the country," however, demanded that he and others like him join their old Democratic opponents in support of the Seymour-Blair ticket and the New York platform.[17] Old Whigs and old Democrats thus became Conservatives in protest against the Republican-Negro coalition that was Radicalism.

The great task ahead, Polk and his friends agreed, was the redemption of state and section from Radical rule. Polk's editorial voice mingled with the Conservative chorus which cried out in condemnation of the vindictive spirit of their oppressors. "I am by birth, education, habit, thought, feeling, and interest—a Conservative," said he in the first issue of his paper. "I claim, that under the organic law of the country, I have some of the prerogatives of an American freeman, yet left me, and as one of the Representatives of a Free Press, I shall exercise the right to combat error, in whatever form it may present itself, and from whatever source it may emanate."

The legislation of the Radical Congress respecting the Negro, beginning with the Fifteenth Amendment and culminating in the Civil Rights Bill, Polk regarded as "the *most stupendous farce* ever enacted in the name of Republicanism, if not the *greatest crime of modern times.*" He felt that "the great body of whites" wished to see the Negro's newly-granted citizenship protected. But the Reconstruction measures, forced upon a prostrate South, menaced state rights, ignored all justice and common sense, and were of fundamental social danger. Nevertheless, he counseled, "let us not boil over with rage and passion" or resort to violence, out-

[17] Polk to Col. R. T. Bennett, Sept. 3, 1868.

lawry, or mobocracy of any kind; let us just *"keep cool"* till polling time.

When the Conservatives finally wrested control of North Carolina from the Radicals in 1876, Polk made a promise on behalf of the victors. The Negro, said he, has been taught to hate Democrats and Conservatives and to vote against them. One of our first duties, then, is to allay his fear of being oppressed by us. There should be an impartial protection of the laws. "We intend," Polk stated, "to make good our promises and declarations, and thus prove to the negro, that the white men of the South are his very best friends." If this were done, and if the expected response were received, then the much-feared Negro suffrage would become the "great conservative element" of Southern politics, and would soon result in the total overthrow of Radicalism.

To make the victory of 1876 complete, it appeared that Tilden had won the Presidency; Hayes, however, was certified by the Returning Board, and the South resigned itself to more trouble. Yet after the inauguration Polk reminded his readers that, after all, this government is *our* government; we should support Hayes when he is right, oppose him when he is wrong.[18]

In state and local politics Polk was quite active, especially during the hot campaign of '76. Usually in the dual role of delegate and reporter, he attended all the important political conventions—township, county, district, and state. He organized, and by acclamation was elected president of, the Lanesboro Township Tilden and Vance Club, which was provided with constitution and by-laws, other officers, a "Working Committee" of twelve, and a regular time for meeting. The members were required to take a Conservative pledge. As evidence of thoroughness and zeal, the club listed the names and addresses of all voters in the township. The editor of the *Ansonian* wrote many editorials, made many speeches, and talked with many people in support of the Conservative cause.

[18] *Ansonian,* June 4, 11, 1874, Feb. 11, 1875, Nov. 15, Dec. 6, 1876, March 14, 1877.

Polk was rather widely and favorably known by 1876, and during the campaign friends put his name in nomination for the state senate. Saying that he was "no aspirant for political or official honors" and that "the office should seek the man," Polk apparently did not campaign openly for the post. He emphasized the necessity of harmony in this important year and declared that if any man in the district could poll a stronger vote against the Republicans than he, then it was the "plain duty" of the people to turn to him. Again his chief opponent was Ed Liles. On the first ballot for the Democratic-Conservative nomination Polk received 1,240 votes, Liles 1,158, B.I. Dunlap 186, and J.A.Leak 150—no majority. The result of the second ballot was: E. R. Liles 1,371, L.L. Polk 1,365.

Though Polk had insisted that he was not seeking the senate seat, his defeat, particularly the closeness of it, stung him. He felt called upon to make some explanation. In an *Ansonian* article entitled "PLAIN ENGLISH" he pointed out that he had made no effort to get himself nominated, had not disparaged his opponent, and had not employed ring tactics. He was aware that the kind of misrepresentations he had had to cope with in previous years had been circulated against him again in this campaign. He pleaded guilty to being a Baptist and a Granger. He admitted that he was "not very decided" in his position on the usury law. But that he sympathized with Radicalism was a charge so patently false that he need not reply to it; "the true Democrats of this township will say that no man in Anson has done more to break the back bone of Radicalism, than myself, in this section." As for the war record, that all-important criterion of a man's political fitness, he had only to print in full the resolutions with which his fellow-officers had honored him when he left the army in 1864. "I carry no free passes on Rail Roads in my pockets," he added for good measure. "I bow to no man, or set of men, as my master."[19]

To lead the Democratic state ticket to victory, just one man was in sight—Zeb Vance. In the first issue of the *Ansonian* over

[19] *Ansonian,* April 19, Aug. 30, Sept. 6, 1876.

two years before, Polk had praised Vance as "our *first choice* for Governor" in 1876. During the campaign Polk's editorial and oratorical support was as vigorous as he could make it. Since the 'sixties his admiration for North Carolina's great war governor had increased with occasional personal contact. With a whoop the state convention nominated Vance on the first ballot, and he prepared to fight it out with his Republican opponent, the able and clever Judge Thomas Settle. Their joint campaign, the famous campaign of '76, ranks as one of the three or four most colorful and exciting in the history of the state. To the wild delight of Conservatives and Democrats, their nominee won the governorship by a majority of 14,000 votes, and most North Carolinians looked forward eagerly to better days ahead.

When the first surge of jubilation spent itself, a more serious note sounded. What of the future of North Carolina? How could the freedom and security of its people be guaranteed? How could those better days ahead be attained? The clear-thinking editor of the Raleigh *Observer* put it in these words:

> North Carolina is to-day ignorant and poverty-stricken, and ere long, without some exertion on our part, she will be helpless. Our lands will not increase in value; how can they, unless brought nearer to market? Each succeeding generation of children will grow up in greater ignorance. Instead of a tide of immigration to our borders, the fever of emigration to other lands will seize all our young men, who feel within them a desire for different and more enlightened surroundings.... To stand still is ruin. Every man must see this. We have now a golden opportunity. Let us seize it and make the most of it....
>
> The Democratic party is responsible for the future of North Carolina. Let it take care that it does not sink under it. That it will so sink if it lacks either the brains or the nerve to perform its plain duty, we have no doubt.[20]

No man felt the challenge more than L.L. Polk.

[20] Raleigh *Observer*, Feb. 7, 1877.

Chapter VI

GENESIS OF A DEPARTMENT OF AGRICULTURE

NORTH CAROLINA during the Reconstruction years was poor—desperately poor. Amid the political, economic, social, and spiritual turmoil of the time, it seemed utterly impossible that the state should ever recover its old-time stability and prosperity. Even when the rest of the South began to evidence signs of revival, poverty remained the rule in North Carolina.

The destruction wrought by four years of war, the most obvious cause of economic distress between 1865 and 1877, was staggering to comprehend. Homes, barns, fences, crops, warehouses, stores, shops, railroads, and public property were damaged or destroyed, and farm animals were seized. Most of the men who returned to repair and rebuild were weary and disillusioned if not crippled or sick. And so many of the state's finest citizens—young men, always the hope of the future—did not return at all.

The war left North Carolina with few banking facilities and practically no capital. Investments in stocks and bonds had generally become worthless. The repudiation of the state's war debt liquidated the banks and wiped out many private fortunes. Money was scarce, interest rates were high, and debts simply went unpaid. Taxes, county as well as state, were as burdensome as they had ever been during the war. The federal tax of ten per cent on state bank notes effectively prevented the revival of the prostrate state banks. Because of the amount of capital it prescribed for the establishment of a national bank, the act of 1863 was of little assistance. National banks, moreover, were forbidden to lend money on the only security which the South had to offer—land. In the whole state of North Carolina during the period there were only six banks, all of them national, with a combined capital of less than $1,000,000.

A succession of poor crops in the disorganized years immediately following the war was accompanied by an inevitable decline in agricultural prices. Production and prices of all crops, with the exception of cotton and oats, fell off sharply. The high federal tax on cotton seemed bad enough; but between 1866 and 1869 the state property tax increased ten-fold, and so many farmers were forced to sell that land became a drug on the market. Land values of course depreciated tremendously, and thousands of acres were sold for taxes at pitifully low prices. Perplexing also since emancipation was the two-sided problem of securing dependable Negro laborers and dependable white employers. To the native white majority the great question of "Negro rule" in politics presented itself.

In kind and degree, the adversities of North Carolina differed little from those of the other Southern states. War and Reconstruction wreaked the same havoc on them all. All felt that they had the same heavy cross to bear. Soon it became apparent that fundamental changes in the South's society and economy would result from the new conditions. With the disruption of the old order, a marked leveling of the various social classes took place. The old plantation system gave way to the new tenant system, with its rent, its credit, its crop liens, and its small supply merchants. Owing to the practice of decades and to the high prices just after the war, cotton continued to be the one big money crop, and the raising of home-grown food supplies was still neglected.

By the 'seventies the darkest days of the post-war period had passed, and the South, like a convalescent, began slowly to improve. In spite of defeat and despair, poverty and ruin, bitterness and suffering, distinct indications of hope and progress brightened the Southern skies. The native white majority, represented by Conservatives and Democrats, was beginning to break the grip of the "carpetbaggers," "scalawags," and Negroes. Agriculture had become better organized and more productive. The development of manufacturing was a hopeful trend. There were even encouraging signs of a cultural and educational revival. The picture of the 'seventies is not so black as it has usually been painted. North Carolina's recovery lagged behind that of the South as a whole, yet even in North Carolina evidences of progress could be seen: towns were growing, more money was in circulation, and the lot of the small farmer was somewhat better. In 1878, for instance, fairly good cotton land would bring from five to twelve dollars an acre. Census reports at the beginning and end of the decade revealed a noticeable increase in the state's population and in the number of North Carolinians gainfully employed.

The labor problem created by the Negro's transition from slavery to freedom loomed as a momentous one to all classes. The groups most immediately concerned—former masters, former slaves, and the poorer whites—were greatly disturbed by it, and there existed a considerable feeling of mutual distrust. As to the capability and reliability of Negroes many white farmers were scornful and pessimistic. Yet a brave new agricultural monthly, established in the "black belt" of eastern North Carolina in the midst of Reconstruction, analyzed the matter with enlightened reserve:[1]

> A new era has dawned upon us agriculturally as well as politically. The slave of yesterday is the freeman of today; a citizen by the laws of the country and the consent of the Southern people. It behooves us, then, to accept the present condition of things, to turn to our use and profit, if possible, the result of a revolution, the most noted of this century. We must recognize the colored laborer in his new light and rights, deal fairly and honorably with him, elevate him in the human scale, and make him an honest Christian tiller of the soil. We must adapt our planting operations to the new order of things.
> We were once rich and proud in a system of contented

[1] Tarboro *Reconstructed Farmer*, I, 18, 19 (May, 1869).

laborers; we are at present poor and proud with a system of discontented and unreliable laborers. . . .

What must be done to bring about the desired reconstruction?

In the first place, we must conform to the new order of things, and no longer look back to the "flesh pots" of slavery, for this will in no wise advance our prosperity . . . we must learn to respect our former slaves as freedmen, and deal with them as honestly in all our transactions as if they were white.

The writer went on to advise less dependence upon Negro menials and more dependence upon ourselves; less idling and more hard work by everybody.

No one denied that the handicaps of the emancipated slave were formidable indeed. Few denied that his conduct after the war was much better than had been expected. Notwithstanding his genuine progress, however, the conviction was general that more efficient, more dependable laborers were badly needed.

The great immigration campaign began only a few years after the war. In 1869 there was incorporated the North Carolina Land Company, an organization composed of "a number of intelligent, enterprising and respectable gentlemen of the States of New York and North Carolina," whose purposes were to aid in the transportation and location of Northerners or Europeans who would immigrate to North Carolina, to advise those who wished to invest money in the state, and to sell any kind of land that might be needed. They asserted that since the end of the "rebellion" the inducements of the Southern states were "vastly superior" to those of the Northwestern states and territories, and that substantial settlers were "everywhere hailed with joy." To advertise North Carolina the company printed and distributed a 136-page *Guide to Capitalists and Emigrants*. The publication detailed, county by county, the geography, population, resources, and advantages of the state and included extolling letters on these subjects by such prominent natives as William B. Rodman, W. E. Pell, Thomas L.

Clingman, Jonathan Worth, D. M. Barringer, W. W. Holden, W. C. Kerr, and R. S. Mason. In recognition of the company's activities, the General Assembly made its president, George Little, state Commissioner of Immigration (without salary).

Bannister, Cowan and Company, supported by the names of Zebulon Vance, Thomas Bragg, W. A. Graham, and Asa Biggs of North Carolina, Horatio Seymour of New York, and J. Drexel of Philadelphia, was a similar organization founded in 1869. Within four years the legislature had also incorporated the Railroad Immigration Association of North Carolina and the North Carolina Immigration Society. The aim of the former was to secure the co-operation of the various railroads of the state in attracting new settlers, in reducing fares for *bona fide* immigrants, and in sharing the profits of immigrant travel and shipping. Impetus came from the other side, too. An agency in Birmingham, England, urged North Carolina officials to advertise to the fullest in Great Britain. In 1875 the new state Board of Immigration, Statistics, and Agriculture, in the pages of a booklet much like that of the North Carolina Land Company, issued again a plea for "the hardy, the intelligent and moral of every land to till these grounds, to occupy these vacant places." North Carolina's endeavors to reinvigorate itself with new energy, new skill, and new capital found close parallels in the other Southern states.

Still, the wave of immigration would not roll. Only a disappointing trickle of newcomers had entered the state by the middle 'seventies, and they were faring none too well. Many of them, in fact, had been shamefully swindled by land companies. The government officials, business men, editors, and railroad owners who were the strongest backers of immigration became greatly puzzled and increasingly apprehensive. Good land was certainly cheap enough and rich natural resources were merely awaiting development; yet few able, energetic settlers came. To many thoughtful North Carolinians there seemed to be grave danger that without outside assistance even a partial recovery of the state would be long delayed.[2]

One of those deeply concerned over the immigration question as it affected the future of the commonwealth was L. L. Polk. He had observed the efforts of the land companies, the railroads, and the immigration societies, and had noted their failure. He agreed with them as to the practical necessity of new people and more capital, but upon the methods of getting these he matured some novel ideas of his own. Principally in a letter to the *State Agricultural Journal,* organ of the Grange, and in a series of five articles in his own weekly *Ansonian,* he laid his interesting and well-received argument before the public in 1875 and 1876.[3]

Like most men of his race and class, Polk was unwilling to commit the agricultural future of North Carolina to the Negro. In his opinion, the "negro experiment" had failed badly. We could not hope, he asserted, to develop our state's magnificent resources or to establish crop diversification with the Negro as a share tenant. The problems connected with emancipation and Reconstruction, however, persuaded the Negro to work only on the share system, and then pretty much in his own way. "Guided, directed and controlled by the intelligent white man," said Polk, "he has no equal in the world, as a field laborer. But under the wild delusions with which emancipation staggers and beclouds his feeble mind, he assumes that with his freedom, came the foresight and capacity to manage farms, as well as governments." In this light, we could only wonder why he did no worse. "The question with us," Polk went on, "is not so much the final issue of an experiment . . . affecting the negro race . . . as [it is] to ascertain some method by which we may escape the ruin, which threatens to engulph all the material interests of our State and section." At this the

[2] George Campbell, *White and Black: the Outcome of a Visit to the United States,* p. 293; Edward King, *The Great South: a Record of Journeys . . . ,* p. 468.
[3] Polkton *Ansonian,* May 7, 1874, June 23, Oct. 20, 1875, April 5–May 3, Sept. 6, Nov. 29, Dec. 6, 1876; Raleigh *State Agricultural Journal,* Sept. 1, 8, 1875.

"demagogical howl of 'Equality' " would doubtless be raised—notwithstanding our stated belief that Southern whites would be the firmest defenders of equality before the law—but it was a duty to our own race and to the state as a whole to take this attitude.

For the material development of North Carolina and the South we had to have thrifty, ambitious, and hard-working white immigrants from Europe and the North. Why didn't they come? Polk thought that "the laboring white man, throughout the Northern States and Europe has been educated to believe that in the South, labor was and is regarded as degrading [and] that a man who was compelled to labor, thereby forfeited his claims to respectability, and was ignored as a component of Southern society." The white laborer's mind was thus prejudiced; he feared that he would be forced to live on equal terms with former slaves, that he would be looked upon as no better than a Negro. Also, before the war the slave-supported South, for obvious reasons, made no real effort to attract immigration. At the same time the alluring Northwest, with the support of the federal government and the press, drew the stream of white laborers in that direction.

Soon, however, the picture changed. Negro labor was no longer profitable. Land actually burdened those who owned it. The land companies proved to be unsatisfactory and in many cases corrupt. North Carolina's resources were advertised, but few prospective settlers saw the literature; and the inducements offered were in no tangible form. This, coupled with the fact that the state's enormous debt tended to frighten away working capital, possibly explained why there was no large immigration. The General Assembly, "composed for the most part of non-landholders and politicians," offered little hope. The handbook prepared by the Board of Immigration, Statistics, and Agriculture, which he read "with peculiar interest and pleasure," seemed to be a "life like and attractive" presentation. Yet it did not bring immigrants to North Carolina. How, then, could this be done?

It was the obligation of the landowners themselves, stated Polk. Their task should be to adopt a liberal policy that would attract permanent settlers and "banish their apprehensions of social and political ostracism." Owners should immediately register their land with an agent who would persuade immigrants to buy and to settle. Each owner should reserve the amount of land he actually needed, then divide the remainder into lots of, say, twenty-five acres each. Let the agent be given full power of attorney to sell, and to investigate all would-be purchasers. The new citizens might bring with them their own artisans, and their ministers, school teachers, and family physicians. They should be cordially received by the white people of the state and protected against "forced social contact with the negro." If this were done, in ten years values would be enhanced, land now almost worthless would be sold, and the whole community would benefit from the influx of new blood and new energy.

Such a wonder could be worked if the landowning farmers of North Carolina would only co-operate; and they could best secure such co-operation by joining that worthy agricultural order, the Patrons of Husbandry, or Grange. "The first essential step in this great undertaking," Polk declared, "is for the State Grange at its next meeting, to establish, at some central point in the State, PERMANENT HEAD QUARTERS and in connection therewith a Patron's State Museum." That would "give to the Order tone, character and dignity," and would "commend our Grange to the confidence and respect of the people of every class. . . ." The town of Greensboro, for example, would gladly erect and furnish a suitable structure. This building ought to be two stories in height: the lower floor to house the museum, the upper to be used as a meeting hall and library. The offices of the state organization's secretary and treasurer would also be there. All over the state subordinate granges could collect and send specimens of their products to the museum, where they would then be carefully arranged by counties. The various counties and granges might compete with one another in preparing the best exhibits. Perhaps the railroads would agree to ship the specimens free.

A display of this kind would be of great educational value to natives as well as immigrants. And this much, Polk emphasized, could be done without spending a hundred dollars of the Grange's money. The salaries of the secretary and the treasurer should be raised, however. One of these men should be designated state agent for the sale of lands, and to each subordinate grange he should send forms on which the members would enter the amount of land they had to offer, together with a full description, their terms of sale, and the like. With the museum and this information centrally located, it should be an easy matter to advertise North Carolina and its resources.

These were Polk's views on immigration. The kind of people he most desired, of course, were those who would diversify the economic life of the commonwealth; those who would help develop manufacturing, mining, lumbering, and improved agriculture. To settle our vacant lands, he said, "we want a class who can grow something besides cotton . . . we want them to cover our hills and plains with their vines, fruits, flowers, vegetables, Corn, Wheat, Oats, Rye, Barley, Clover and all the grasses . . . we want fine horses, cattle, hogs, and sheep." None the less, the diversification of agriculture was a duty which devolved chiefly and squarely upon the native farmer, and Polk knew this.

He never forgot a picture that met his trained eye on the way to Gettysburg in 1863. Of the Valley of Virginia, he wrote at that time: "There is one attractive charm inseparable from, & peculiar to, this section. The lands when once brought into cultivation are not turned out to wash into deep gullies or to grow up in old field pines, but there is a rich, uniform, covering of green verdure all through summer. If not sown or planted, the whole earth as far as you can see, is hidden by a carpetting [sic] of clover & grass, which grows luxuriantly upon the highest knobs.... The finest stock, especially cattle, I ever saw. Everyone has his milk house, through which pours, in abundance, the clear water that gushes from the heart of the mountain above, as cold, almost, as ice...." That was the work of the native farmer.[4]

"Brother farmer," began Polk's leading article in the first issue of his *Ansonian,* "light your pipe, and be seated. We want a plain, little talk with you." The subject was "Bread and Meat vs. Cotton." In 1873, said he, the South produced four million bales of cotton, which at an average price of twelve cents a pound brought the growers $240,000,000. "What has become of the bulk of that large sum? It has gone to pay for almost every single implement used on these cotton farms, from an axe handle to a wagon—it has gone to pay for mules and horses from the Central States—it has gone to pay for hay, corn, flour and bacon from the Western and Northern States." Suppose the $240,000,000 had been received for only two million bales at twenty-four cents a pound. That would have meant half the land in other crops, and a vast saving to the farmers. "The difference," stressed the editor, "is that what you make on your farms *will then belong to you.* Millions of dollars worth of cotton is mortgaged annually to commission merchants, for supplies, before even a seed is planted." The policy the South should adopt to relieve itself of dependence upon other sections was simply this: raise its own bread and meat. So long as the South followed the ruinous practice of "all cotton," its struggle for better times would be in vain.

Again and again Polk returned to this theme, reiterating the sound arguments against the one-crop system and the financial and psychological benefits of diversification. "Don't," he warned, "leave North Carolina, and go to Texas or Arkansas to grow rich raising cotton. If by producing ten bales here, you lose money, you will lose more if you produce one hundred there. Don't look to any other source than the ground for help. Go to that

[4] Polk to Mrs. Polk, June 20, 1863.

for bread and meat, make it at home, live at home, if you would rid yourself of hard times."

A well-to-do neighbor of his illustrated the truth in the gospel of diversification. Because he raised his supplies at home, this farmer had bought only thirty-five bushels of corn in forty-five years and had produced but two bales of cotton in his life. Another man came to Polk about a money matter one day. "Col.," said he, "that little debt I owe you is the only one I have fallen behind on, since I have been keeping house." "Well," Polk answered, "I presume then, you raise your own bread and meat?" "Yes, I always try to do that." "Of course, he is not often troubled with debt," Polk remarked to the readers of his paper. With the approach of spring in 1877, Polk asked: "Farmers are you preparing to plant a full crop of cotton, that will cost you 14 cents per pound and for which you will receive, perhaps, 10 cents, and will you rely on buying corn at $1.25 per bushel, that you ought to produce at 60 cents? And will you still complain of hard times?"[5]

He offered this homely illustration of the two types of farmer:

> The man who buys his supplies, of course, has to give a mortgage. He buys all along through the spring and summer on that mortgage, labors in nothing but his cotton patch, and in the fall he brings his cotton to market, drives his cart up to the yard of the man to whom it is mortgaged and rolls the cotton out. He then walks into the counting room and remarks to the cotton buyer: "I have a bag of cotton out here, what are you going to allow me for it?" He is compelled to take whatever price is allowed him. On the other hand, here is the man who raises his own supplies, and what cotton he makes is extra. He gives no mortgage, and always pays cash for what he buys. When he drives his load of cotton to town he stops in the street and says: "Say, come out here, examine this cotton and tell me what you are paying for

[5] *Ansonian,* April 16, 1874, April 12, May 24, 1876, March 7, 1877; N. C. Department of Agriculture, *Report on the General Condition of the Agricultural Interests of North Carolina,* p. 6.

it." "Well," says the buyer, "cotton is a little dull today." "It don't make any difference," says the independent farmer, "if you don't give me my price you can't get it; I am able to hold it." And if they can't agree on a price the independent farmer hauls his cotton around to a warehouse and stores it. This is the difference between the man who raises his supplies and the man who buys them.[6]

"Every table in North Carolina," declared Polk, "should be supplied with bread, bacon, beef, mutton, fish, molasses, cheese, rice, butter, milk, wine, fruits and vegetables, produced in North Carolina. North Carolinians should drive North Carolina mules and horses, to plows, buggies, carriages and wagons made in North Carolina. North Carolina cotton should be spun and wove in North Carolina. Every man, woman and child in North Carolina should wear in winter shoes and clothing made of North Carolina leather and North Carolina wool. North Carolina farms should be cultivated with North Carolina implements and fertilized with North Carolina lime and marl."[7]

The economic and social conditions of the 'seventies caused many North Carolina farmers to look with favor upon the activities of the Grange. This organization was conceived by Oliver Hudson Kelley, a clerk in the Agricultural Bureau at Washington, following a three-months' fact-finding journey through the South early in 1866. Struck by the poverty and conservatism of Southern agriculture, Kelley, who was a Mason, concluded that a nationwide secret order of farmers would go a long way toward furthering the economic reconstruction of the South and advancing rural interests all over the nation. His idea gradually took hold. When that first great wave of post-bellum agrarian discontent reached its height between 1872 and 1874, the number of granges and Grange members increased with tremendous rapidity.

The fundamental reasons for agrarian unrest throughout the country—the decline in the value of farm products, the corrupt

---

[6] Raleigh *News and Observer*, May 8, 1881.
[7] N. C. Dept. of Agr., *Monthly Crop Reports* (July, 1877), pp. 4-5.

practices of the railroads, the prosperity of merchants and manufacturers at the expense of farmers, the iniquities of high finance, and the disturbing political and social conditions of Reconstruction—applied in varying degree to North Carolina. Several thousand Tar Heel farmers, like most farmers traditionally individualistic, came to believe that, in order to better their status and to make themselves heard, they would have to organize. "The great principle of cooperation," said Dr. Columbus Mills, first Master of the State Grange, "is essentially the practical thought of the times. No question is more important to the Grange welfare and none so little understood. Our duty is to study it, discuss it, and learn it." [8] The Grange motto pointed the way: "In essentials, unity—in non-essentials, liberty—in all things, charity."

North Carolina's first subordinate grange seems to have been organized in Guilford County in the spring of 1873 by Colonel D. Wyatt Aiken of South Carolina. The first annual meeting of the state body was held early in 1874, and a year later, on February 20, 1875, the organization was incorporated by the legislature as the "North Carolina State Grange of Patrons of Husbandry." So rapid was the growth of the Grange in North Carolina that by the time of its incorporation it had already reached what proved to be its maximum strength—approximately 500 lodges and 15,000 members. Only in South Carolina and Georgia among Southern states had the order made greater headway. After 1875, however, the Granger movement suffered a marked decline. "Natural reasons," the farmer's disappointment in the lack of tangible gains, the power of the middleman and the vested interests, the failure of the Grange co-operatives, and business depression, all contributed to the loss of membership and influence, and to the ultimate collapse. [9]

Nevertheless, the Grange left behind it a number of substantial

---

[8] North Carolina State Grange, *Proceedings, 1875*, p. 7.

[9] Raleigh *Observer*, Feb. 4, 1877; *N. C. Private Laws, 1874-'75*, pp. 524-25 (ch. 76); State Grange, *Proceedings, 1875*, pp. 11-12, 13, *1876*, pp. 9-10, 15; D. A. Montgomery to Polk, Dec. 14, 1879.

benefits. By increasing the social intercourse of isolated farm families, it was able to promote a greater spirit of tolerance among persons of different political parties and religious denominations. For the tiller of the soil himself, the organization provided an invaluable kind of business training.[10] Though the idea of agricultural co-operation did not come to full flower until some ten years later, in the 'seventies it had at least germinated. In North Carolina and the South the political influence of the Grange was not nearly so strong as it was in the West, but in the social and economic fields the results of the Granger movement were indeed salutary.

The considerable amount of business activity in which the North Carolina State Grange engaged was responsible for some varied experiences. To the farmer's advantage, the organization arranged to obtain fertilizers at reduced prices and to supervise the establishment of a Patrons' Mutual Aid Society. The state body also joined the Direct Trade Union, a co-operative founded to aid all Southern grangers, but saw the enterprise fail. Local co-operative stores and associations, however, formed on the Rochdale plan—the plan of dividing profits among members in proportion to their purchases—were reported to be successful in North Carolina. In the effort to make the farmer's dollar go as far as possible, the Grange, besides supporting the co-operatives, would sometimes endorse certain commercial firms. One of these was Farley and Company of New York, which North Carolina and Mississippi made their Grange agent. In spite of the fact that O. H. Kelley, the founder of the Grange, and others had recommended the firm, it was discovered to be entirely fraudulent. Yet the North Carolina State Grange reimbursed its members for their losses and presented claims to the National Grange at its annual session of 1875; the national body, however, did no more than resolve to exercise strict care in the future. After the Farley episode it was natural for members of the Grange to lose con-

[10] State Grange, *Proceedings, 1876,* p. 16.

fidence in the order and especially in its national officers. This painful experience was undoubtedly one factor in the decline of the Grange in North Carolina.[11]

That the Grange was deeply conscious of certain social responsibilities even during its declining years is a significant fact. It was one organization that early appreciated the state's great need of popular education. Captain Sydenham B. Alexander of Charlotte, Master of the order in 1878, declared: "The most distressing sign of the times is the lack of interest taken by the agricultural and mechanical classes in educating their children. . . . Let us awake from our lethargy. The Grange must foster education. . . . North Carolina can only prosper in proportion as her agricultural and mechanical classes are educated."[12] Heeding his words, the State Grange recommended that primary and even high schools be established and supported by county and local granges whenever possible. A number of these did exist in North Carolina; for example, in the Northampton County village of Potecasi a Professor Picot conducted a flourishing grange high school of some sixty scholars.[13] For the enlightenment of adults, Captain Alexander urged the subordinate granges to form libraries and subscribe to agricultural newspapers, which many of them did. In addition to these formal efforts, obviously the business meetings and the sociables of the Grange had considerable educational value. As one paper said: "Many an old clod hopper, 'rude of speech' has found out that he could talk, rise to a point of order, and venture a few remarks. This is education. Many an uncouth country boy, and coy lassies have learnt something of the social graces and amenities of life. And this too is education."[14]

Although he sympathized fully with their aims, Polk did not at first join the Patrons. In the summer of 1875, however, he be-

[11] Solon J. Buck, *The Granger Movement*, pp. 252-53, 257, 265, 273; North Carolina Grange Papers, 1873-1875, Duke University Library, Durham.
[12] State Grange, *Proceedings, 1878*, p. 7.
[13] Buck, *Granger Movement*, p. 291; R. I. Beale to Polk, March 1, 1880.
[14] Raleigh *Farmer and Mechanic*, Feb. 21, 1878.

came a member of Pond Mill Grange, No. 471, three miles from Polkton. In due time he was its Master and rapidly rose to positions of Grange leadership in the county, district, and state. He started a "Grange Department" in his newspaper and was often a featured speaker at Grange picnics and other functions. "Leonidas is always *thar* when there's any *grangeing* to be done!" said Ed Liles, his editor neighbor.[15]

At his first state meeting in 1876, Polk served as a member of the committee on the order of business, and, as a result of his constructive interest in the problem, was made chairman of the committee on labor and immigration. Here he presented, in the form of a resolution, his cherished plan: the establishment of permanent headquarters for the State Grange, with a Patrons' State Museum and a Land Registry Office connected therewith. He also offered a resolution concerning the better organization of the Grange in North Carolina. At this meeting Polk was appointed Deputy Organizer for the Fifth District, which comprised the counties of Harnett, Cumberland, Moore, Richmond, Montgomery, Anson, Union, and Stanly.[16]

It was the duty of deputies to organize and encourage subordinate granges and to furnish information respecting them to the state officers. For organizing a lodge a deputy received $10.00, and for visiting one already established, $5.00; the sums were paid by the individual granges out of their collected dues. As Deputy of the Fifth District (and also as Lecturer of the Anson County Grange), Polk traveled all over south central North Carolina in the cause of agricultural organization. His Stanly County itinerary for the week of October 16-21, 1876, provides a good sample. It included successive days of "grangeing" at Stony Hill Church, Bethel Church, Prospect, Bodenheimer's Store, Locust Level, and Big Lick—names redolent of that Piedmont countryside. In ad-

---

[15] *Ansonian*, June 4, 1874, and 1875-77, *passim;* Wadesboro *Pee Dee Herald*, Jan. 26, 1876.

[16] State Grange, *Proceedings, 1876*, pp. 17-20, 25-26, 44-45.

dition, Polk became a member of the State Grange executive committee for two years. His membership in the Grange continued for some time longer, but on account of more important activities he resigned from the committee in 1879 and gave up his close connection with the organization.[17]

The climax of the Grange's career in North Carolina, and a cause to which Polk devoted himself thoroughly, was the establishment of the state Department of Agriculture. As early as 1860 Governor John W. Ellis, in his message to the General Assembly, had recommended "the establishment of a Board of Agriculture, with the power to divide the State into agricultural districts, and to make suitable provisions for the giving of instruction in this branch of science." War was approaching then, however, and the project was passed over in the excitement. At the height of the immigration campaign after the war, the legislature in 1874 did set up, as an appendage to the Secretary of State's office, a Bureau of Immigration, Statistics, and Agriculture. But this agency paid only perfunctory attention to agriculture, and farm leaders were far from satisfied.

Through the Grange they resolved to do something about it. At the state meeting in March, 1875, James R. Thigpen, who had been an editor of the progressive *Reconstructed Farmer* of Tarboro, asserted that "there ought to be a Department of Agriculture, as in Georgia and many other States and countries less exclusively agricultural than North Carolina." A few months later Thigpen and Colonel Thomas M. Holt discussed the matter before a "Cotton States Agricultural Congress" in Raleigh. Holt was not only a well-known cotton manufacturer but was president of the North Carolina Agricultural Society as well. In September the State Grange presented a memorial to the constitutional convention then in session. Under the leadership of W. F. Strowd, of Chatham, and G. Z. French, of New Hanover, an

[17] *Ansonian,* Sept. 27, 1876, and *passim;* Potecasi *Roanoke Patron* supplement, Jan. 16, 1882.

ordinance to amend the state constitution so as to require the General Assembly to establish a Department of Agriculture passed overwhelmingly in response to the clear need of the farmers.

When Governor Vance took office in January, 1877, he called the attention of the legislature to this provision in the constitution of 1875. Vance had no definite plan of his own in mind, but he spoke of the importance and desirability of a Department of Agriculture and recommended that the members soon create one.

As the lawmakers sat during January and February the Grange, the State Agricultural Society, and the State University all intensified their activity in behalf of the new department. Kemp P. Battle, president of the University, called a joint meeting of representatives from these three to discuss in some detail "the best means to accomplish the good desired for the farming community." The emphasis was placed upon the regulation of commercial fertilizers, and particularly upon the establishment of an agricultural experiment station at Chapel Hill. The leaders of the group—Professor W. C. Kerr, State Geologist, Dr. Columbus Mills, Master of the Grange, General R. F. Hoke, Battle, and Polk, who was a vice-president of the Agricultural Society as well as a member high in the councils of the Grange—were appointed a committee "to mature the details of the proposition" and to lay it before the legislature.

More important, however, was the annual meeting of the Grange. Over one hundred members, a tenth of them women, gathered in Goldsboro convinced that this session was the most vital ever held by the order. In the approving presence of visiting committees from the State Agricultural Society and the General Assembly itself, they enthusiastically adopted the report of their own "committee on the establishment of the agricultural department." The committee report recommended that a Department of Agriculture be located at the state capital; that the Geological Survey become a bureau therein; that a Bureau of Immigration, Land Agency, and Statistics be created; that an experiment station, connected with the department and with the University, be erected at Chapel Hill; that a Board of Fish Commissioners be appointed; that the legislature make a liberal appropriation for the department's support; that a license tax of not less than $1,000 be assessed upon each brand of fertilizer sold in the state; and that rigid dog laws and fence laws be passed for the benefit of the counties that desired them. Wary of possible political control of the proposed agency, the Grange "respectfully but most earnestly" suggested that the management of the department be entrusted "strictly to agriculturists." [18]

This committee report was essentially the handiwork of Polk, who had been one of the first men in the state after the war to agitate for the establishment of a Department of Agriculture. He advocated his plan before the Goldsboro meeting after first submitting it to Vance and winning the Governor's approval. Now the Grange endorsed Polk's ideas fully and charged him, as chairman of a committee, to present the plan to the General Assembly. This he did in the Yarborough House, Raleigh, at a large meeting presided over by Representative Montford McGehee. The important people present, including Governor Vance and other distinguished citizens, received the proposition most favorably.[19]

The bill to establish a Department of Agriculture was introduced by Senator W. C. Troy, of Cumberland, who guided its legislative career. As an able joint committee of Senate and House began consideration of the bill, Polk was summoned to aid in framing it, as were Kerr, Battle, Vance, Attorney-General Thomas S. Kenan, and others. Various plans were proposed at the conferences, but that of the Grange was followed for the

[18] *Observer*, Feb. 7-9, 1877; MS. report of committee.
[19] Raleigh *North-Carolina Farmer* extra, Feb. 19, 1883; *Ansonian*, Feb. 14, 1877.

most part, and Troy and Polk were appointed a subcommittee to make the final draft. The legislative committee then recommended Senate Bill 668 for passage, believing that the creation of the Department, "in the promotion of the great farming interests, is paramount to all other questions now before the General Assembly."

Both houses of the predominantly Democratic legislature appeared to be sympathetic. Yet some strong opposition was inevitable. Professor Kerr feared that North Carolina was "not ready, by a generation or two, for this sort of thing"; that "the great aim of a large no. of the members is (& has been in the past too), to see that not a dollar is spent for anything...."[20] Polk, however, declared that he was more hopeful for the future of the state than he had been at any time since the war. His optimism seemed justified. The Senate, whose fifty members included seventeen farmers and five more part-time farmers, passed the bill by a vote of twenty-nine to twelve, and the House concurred, forty-eight to twenty-nine.

At several stages the struggle had been quite difficult, but the efforts of Senators Troy and Holt and Representatives McGehee and Roberts helped greatly in pushing the bill through. After it was all over, Troy wrote Polk, who had returned to Polkton: "I have at last gotten our bill through, but it has been a great deal of trouble.... The Senate ran over me rough shod in adopting House amendments—I afterwards by hard fight got it reconsidered and struck out two amendment[s] that were very objectionable—& today I got through a supplemental bill changing another amendment they put in. So it is now a law...."[21] The Raleigh *Observer* believed this to be "the only instance in the history of the State in which the farmers, as a body, have come before the Legislature for aid and protection...." The paper added that the lawmakers deserved credit for promptly

[20] W. C. Kerr to Polk, Jan. 20, 1877.
[21] W. C. Troy to Polk, March 8, 1877.

giving the farmers all that they had asked for, "though not exactly in the shape proposed by them." [22]

The act "to establish a Department of Agriculture, Immigration and Statistics, and for the Encouragement of Sheep Husbandry" provided that a seven-man Board of Agriculture should exercise general control and supervision. The board consisted of the governor as *ex-officio* chairman, the state geologist, the president of the University of North Carolina, the master of the State Grange, the president of the State Agricultural Society, and two agriculturists appointed by the others. The working head of the department, however, responsible to the board, was the commissioner, who had to be an agriculturist. Ideally, said the *Observer*, he should be an experienced, practical farmer, of liberal education, of indomitable energy, and [with a] thorough knowledge of agricultural chemistry." [23]

In view of his labors in behalf of the new agency, his plans for the agricultural future of the state, and his confidence in his own abilities, it is not surprising that Polk wanted the job, or that most of his associates wanted him to have it. He certainly stood first in line. Still, the politics of the legislature, as well as the preferences of the board, had to be taken into consideration. Ed Liles, who had won his state senate seat by a margin of six votes over Polk, wrote Polk: "Your friends, Holt, Kerr, Austin, *Scarborough* and (if you'll believe it) myself are working quietly, but I think effectively for you. Yesterday I had to contradict a report, circulated around here, that you are neither now—nor ever were a *farmer*. You may readily surmise where it originated. Holt says you ought to be here and Kerr was about to telegram [*sic*] you to come; but we concluded it was hardly necessary." [24]

[22] *Observer*, March 11, 1877.
[23] *Public Laws, 1876-'77*, pp. 506-16 (ch. 274), 562 (ch. 291); *Observer*, Feb. 27, 1877.
[24] Edward R. Liles to Polk, March 9, 1877; Thomas S. Ashe to Polk, Jan. 31, 1877; Thomas H. Robinson to Polk, March 5, 1877. C. Austin was a member of the House from Union County; John Scarborough was State Superintendent of Public Instruction.

Shortly after the department bill became law, the Board of Agriculture met to organize. Vance, the Governor, Kerr, the State Geologist, Battle, the President of the University, Alexander, Master of the Grange, and Holt, President of the Agricultural Society, first appointed the two agriculturists required. They were Captain James R. Thigpen, of Edgecombe County, and Major Jonathan Evans (a friend of Senator Troy), of Cumberland County. The full board then convened. Most of the members were Polk's close friends, and to a man, apparently, they favored him. They elected North Carolina's first Commissioner of Agriculture on April 2, 1877.

Three weeks before his fortieth birthday, Polk got the job.

CHAPTER VII

MR. COMMISSIONER

WHEN L. L. POLK took the helm as North Carolina's first Commissioner of Agriculture in April, 1877, he was embarking upon an uncharted sea. His new office, in the Briggs Building on Fayetteville Street, Raleigh, was empty; and he had no model to guide him in his work, for the North Carolina Department was, in many respects, unlike any other in the United States. But he did have some strong convictions regarding the basic needs of the state—and the sanguine belief that somehow those needs could be met. He wrote:

> We want capital—we want a more reliable labor—we want skill and energy and enterprise—we want manufacturies [sic]—we want our unoccupied lands improved—we want our mines of wealth developed—we want our vast water-power utilized—we want our educational system put on a firm and prosperous basis—we want the credit of the State restored—we want our people to be independent. . . .[1]

> We want more State pride—we want a true North Carolina policy—we want this grand old Commonwealth to rise and shake off the accumulated dust of an age of apathy and inaction. We have everything beckoning us on to enjoy the rich reward of active, energetic co-operation.[2]

North Carolina must arouse from her lethargy and keep step with the progress of the age. An aristocratic nobleman, broken in fortune and wrapped in the folds of a tattered old

[1] Polkton *Ansonian*, Nov. 15, 1876.
[2] *Ansonian*, Jan. 17, 1877.

velvet gown, and relying on the prestige of departed wealth to secure a perpetuation of his former high position, might excite our sympathy, but certainly would not inspire us with that hopeful energy and buoyant spirit so essential to success in life. With our new surroundings, we have not only much to learn, but much to *unlearn*. . . .[3]

During the . . . years of humiliation and suffering through which we have passed, what have we learned? . . . Under oppression have we learned patience? In adversity have we learned perseverance? In poverty have we learned self-reliance and self-esteem? Under misgovernment have we learned patriotism? In our weakness have we learned the true source of strength and power? . . .[4]

Now was the time for action. The general objects of the Department were six: to compile and distribute statistical and educational information pertaining to agriculture, to analyze soils and fertilizers, to restock streams with fish, to encourage sheep husbandry, to induce immigration, and to foster new industries.[5]

In order to carry out the ambitious program, it was of course necessary that the Department establish some medium of direct communication with the farmers. Polk's first act, therefore, was to organize a corps of trustworthy correspondents, chiefly farmers, in all the counties—and in almost all the townships—of the state. On forms furnished by him, they reported monthly on the condition of crops, livestock, weather, and the like in their respective localities. The Commissioner then incorporated the data into

[3] N. C. Department of Agriculture, *Report on the Work of the Dept. of Agr.*, p. 25.
[4] Henderson *Gold Leaf*, June 8, 1882.
[5] The next several pages, covering for the most part the Department's first two years (1877-78), are based chiefly upon the following Department of Agriculture publications written by L. L. Polk: *First Quarterly Report* (July 17, 1877); letter "To the People of North Carolina," Raleigh *Farmer and Mechanic,* Jan. 3, 1878; *Third Quarterly Report* (Jan. 15, 1878); *Fourth Quarterly Report* (April 16, 1878); and "Report . . . for 1877 and 1878," *North Carolina Public Documents, 1879,* No. 8. See also *Farmer and Mechanic,* Jan. 10, 1878. The Polk Papers are voluminous for this period.

circulars and crop reports and distributed some 5,000 of them each month during the growing season.

So that he might benefit fully from the experiences of others, Polk also corresponded with the Department at Washington and with those of the various states. By exchange and otherwise he was sent many of their publications, and these soon came to constitute a useful little agricultural library of over three hundred volumes. His office likewise received twenty-seven agricultural weeklies and nine monthlies from other states and twenty-eight weekly and daily newspapers published in North Carolina. Among the periodicals received were *Scientific Farmer, Maryland Farmer, American Farmer, Planter and Farmer, Semi-Tropical, American Agriculturist, Farmer's Friend, Turf, Field and Farm, Kansas Farmer, Prairie Farmer,* and *Home and Farm.* The North Carolina press, it should be stated, gave the Department of Agriculture and its Commissioner almost unanimous support from the beginning.

One of the most important functions of the new Department was the regulation of commercial fertilizers. The "fertilizer situation" had become quite serious. An investigation made in 1876 revealed that preparations of one kind or another were being used on no less than thirty-five per cent of North Carolina's cultivated area. Their use had so expanded the acreage of lands suitable for cotton growing that there ensued a heavy increase in cotton production—with all its "one-crop" implications. In perhaps most cases the use of fertilizer was wise because the need for it was great, but farmers were showing a deplorable tendency to depend entirely upon this to the neglect of good stable manure. North Carolinians paid about $3,000,000 a year for the various brands. Many of them were distinctly poor and some were absolutely worthless. Ignorant purchasers suffered great imposition, and a large amount of hard-earned money was being wasted.

The act establishing the North Carolina Department of Agriculture sought to protect the farmers in two ways. A privilege tax of $500 annually was imposed upon the maker of each brand of manipulated guano, superphosphate, or other artificial fertilizer offered for sale in the state. And an agricultural laboratory under the supervision of a skilled chemist, Dr. Albert R. Ledoux of New York, was set up at Chapel Hill for the purpose of analyzing samples of all fertilizers, soils, marls, waters, and minerals submitted to it and recording the results for publication in Department circulars. Together these measures soon succeeded in driving the bad brands from the state and in bringing about various degrees of improvement in the others. Within a few months' time the number of commercial fertilizers on the North Carolina market dropped from over one hundred to only twenty-nine. A group of Baltimore manufacturers who bitterly opposed the law—two-thirds of North Carolina's fertilizer came from Baltimore—tested its constitutionality and found it unshakable. The better manufacturers eventually became friendly to the act, for it served to eliminate their less scrupulous competitors. By 1880 the number of licensed brands had increased gradually to forty-eight.

It is not surprising that the farmers enthusiastically supported the law. They felt that Dr. Ledoux's analyses helped teach them the importance of scientific agriculture, that costly frauds were exposed, that the quality of commercial fertilizers was improved, and that the preparation of home fertilizers was stimulated. At the end of four years, it was Governor Jarvis's opinion that: "If nothing else had been done, the protection given to the farmers against worthless fertilizers, has more than ten-fold over compensated for the labor and expenses of the department."[6] Moreover, it is highly significant that the revenue from the fertilizer tax was the Department's sole means of support, since the General Assembly had made no direct appropriation for the purpose.

Fish culture received due attention. Hatcheries were established

[6] *Public Documents, 1881*, No. 1, p. 16.

at strategic points in the state, and artificial propagation was presently begun. During the first season more than half a million young shad were released in the Tar, Contentnea, Neuse, Cape Fear, Yadkin, and Catawba rivers, and eggs of the California salmon were hatched at Swannanoa Gap in the hope that the species would adapt itself to the cool mountain streams of western North Carolina. At the same time, the Department made an effort to stir up public sentiment in favor of strengthening and obeying the fish and game laws, especially with regard to stream obstructions. Lack of respect for these laws, as well as poor enforcement, had seriously depleted the supply of fish and game and threatened to nullify all the benefits of conservation and restocking. Co-operative legislation with Virginia was discussed. In this connection, a Virginia correspondent stated a truth that Polk could well appreciate: "The hardest work we have to do is to fight the Legislature, for pelt-hunters and fish destroyers are *voters*." [7]

Unfortunately for the encouragement of sheep husbandry, dog owners were voters too. Polk's correspondents reported that sheep could be raised profitably in almost every county of the state but for the presence of sheep-killing dogs. They listed one dog to every three sheep, and declared that more sheep were killed by dogs than by disease. No one would discuss the matter in public, said Polk, but he was convinced it should be discussed. In his first speech as Commissioner of Agriculture, and in most of those that followed, he "raised the black flag" against these "worthless curs," advocating that their number be reduced by taxation and by killing so that sheep husbandry might become practicable. Some success in this line was attained, for the state auditor's report in 1880 recorded a total of 582,648 sheep in North Carolina, a substantial increase over 1870. Polk's attack on the dogs came to be a part of his speeches that audiences anticipated with much relish. "Your visit to Pender was a glorious success,"

[7] John Ott to Polk, May 25, 1878.

one friend wrote him. "Dogs gone and sheep coming." "At the name of Polk," another said, "every dog in the neighborhood is heard to howl most pit[e]ously, and every sheep blates with joy." [8]

A new fence law was another agricultural reform Polk championed. The practice of decades had been to fence in crops and allow stock to roam at large, but modern conditions demanded that the stock rather than the crops be enclosed. The new plan had been tried in Mecklenburg County with encouraging results. In Polk's eyes, also, the familiar zigzag rail fences were not worth their high cost. Building and repairing them not only stripped the forests, to leave barren, gullied fields, but consumed the time and energy that farmers might better employ in preparing manure, or pastures, or forage crops.

Then there was immigration. It goes almost without saying that the Department was keenly interested in promoting this pregnant cause. A large majority of Polk's county correspondents, in answer to his questions, stated that the freedmen were not improving their condition, that lands under their management deteriorated, and that a good class of white immigrants was ardently desired. The Land Registry and State Museum which Polk had first urged in connection with Grange headquarters he now set up within the Department of Agriculture. By October, 1878, approximately 200,000 acres of land, representing farming, mining, and water-power opportunities in different sections of the state, had been registered for sale. Polk insisted that the owners send him specimens of their garden and field products, so that prospective buyers might see tangible evidences of North Carolina's wealth in natural resources. The Commissioner was glad to forward tags and shipping instructions; and mailing the specimens to Raleigh would cost nothing.

The advantages of advertising the state by means of a con-

[8] W. M. K[ennedy] to Polk, undated; D. A. Montgomery, in *Farmer and Mechanic*, March 7, 1878.

venient bird's-eye view of its products spurred Polk to attempt to get every county represented. Having ensconced the Museum in a large hall adjoining his office, he had neat cases built for each of the state's ninety-four counties, and arranged them alphabetically. The contents of the Museum increased gradually, until most of the counties were at least partly represented. Catawba, a well-exhibited county, co-operated fully by sending specimens of rye, oats, German millet, timothy, feather and orchard grass, flour, corn, Fultz and Boughton wheat, Irish potatoes, white, black, and whippoorwill peas, dried apples and peaches, chinquapins, leaf tobacco, sheetings, copper ore, and alum. Polk also displayed such products before the large crowds at the annual State Fair. And he was responsible for the North Carolina Exhibit at the Paris Exposition of 1878; he shipped eight cases of material to Washington and was highly complimented by Commissioner of Agriculture William G. LeDuc.

A British traveler who visited the State Museum observed that Commissioner Polk seemed to be "an active man," and that his agricultural collection was "very good." [9] About the same time, Mrs. Cornelia Phillips Spencer of Chapel Hill wrote Polk: "I am pleased to hear such a good account of your Museum as my daughter brings me—but I must confess I have the impression that she admires *Col. Polk* even more than she does his collection!" [10]

In planning for economic progress, North Carolina leaders confidently expected immigration. The capital, the mechanical skill, and the energy of white settlers from the North and Europe were, in their minds, so obviously desirable for the elevation of the South that they did not wish to contemplate the failure of immigration. One editor expressed the common view when he wrote: "The only hope under Heaven of fully and honorably settling the State debt is by bringing in new men, new money,

[9] George Campbell, *White and Black,* p. 301.
[10] Mrs. Spencer to Polk, Jan. 7, 1879.

new enterprise and vigor, and raising the taxable value of the State property, and thereby distributing the burdens over a greater number of shoulders, while at the same time developing those matchless resources which if properly handled would render the debt a mere bagatelle, payable any day before breakfast." [11] But this was an "iridescent dream." Though the campaign continued on into the 'eighties, immigration and capital were not forthcoming. Those who dreamed passed too lightly over the psychological impact upon the North of certain political-sectional questions. The North, moreover, had its own problems to solve —its own Reconstruction. Money and energy were needed first at home, and most of the surplus went to the West. New industries, ranching and mining, and the extension of the railroad empire proved far more attractive to the North than investment in the South, where poverty and unsettled political and social conditions prevailed. By 1880 the more prescient leaders of North Carolina and the South were convinced that the immigration campaign was fruitless, and that the advancement of their state and section was their own problem, and theirs alone. As Professor Paul Buck well says: "No lesson was more valuable or more thoroughly learned than that the section's redemption would have to be achieved through the efforts of Southern people. Yearnings for easy escape were frustrated." [12]

Polk's faith in immigration was profound, and he never fully relinquished it; but fortunately his faith in the people of North Carolina was even more profound. Despite the apathy and ignorance of so many of the farmers, as Commissioner of Agriculture he performed a remarkable amount of labor in their behalf. He maintained the office of the Department, supervised the Museum, carried on a voluminous correspondence, made quarterly reports to the Board of Agriculture and a biennial report to the legislature, prepared periodic crop bulletins and miscellaneous circulars, fur-

---

[11] *Farmer and Mechanic*, Jan. 16, 1879.
[12] Paul H. Buck, *The Road to Reunion, 1865-1900*, pp. 150-53.

nished material to the press, and delivered numerous speeches to crowds of farmers in all parts of the state. To assist with much of the work, the Board of Agriculture provided a junior clerk and its own secretary—first Thomas J. Robinson, and after his death Peter M. Wilson. Though the Board held meetings, Dr. Ledoux analyzed fertilizer, and the secretary and clerk looked after routine, none the less, under Polk, running the Department of Agriculture was largely a one-man job.

At the end of the first year, the Department had made its existence known to the world. It flattered state pride to know that Virginia, South Carolina, Georgia, Mississippi, and Louisiana were each considering the adoption of a law, similar to that passed in North Carolina, creating a Department of Agriculture and featuring a fertilizer tax.

It was natural that Commissioner Polk should frequently forsake his office and carry his message to the people personally. He journeyed to every section of the state to tell the farmers about North Carolina's resources and capabilities, the origin and purposes of the Department of Agriculture, his own work, and his need for whole-hearted co-operation. Halifax, Cumberland, Wilson, Catawba, Alamance, Iredell, Pender, Orange, Cherokee, Buncombe, Anson, Bladen, and many other counties heard his two-hour speeches and received them most favorably.[13]

His visits to Chapel Hill and Asheville in 1878 were especially successful. At the invitation of President Battle, Polk spoke to the 379 students of the summer Normal School and the citizens of the University village on the subject, "What Are the Demands of Our State and How Shall We Meet Them?" It was reported that not only was he applauded "more frequently and more warmly" than any other speaker the students had heard, but that after his speech he "turned songster." Accompanied by Professor Charles Wilson, he rendered "with much effect" the popular "Ho, for

---

[13] *Farmer and Mechanic,* Feb.–Sept., 1878, *passim.*

Carolina!"¹⁴ Polk's address to the mountain farmers at Asheville was described by one editor, who disclaimed any desire to flatter, as the best he had listened to since the days of Edmund Ruffin. "It was purely an agricultural speech, intended for the ear of the farmer," this editor wrote, "and aside from its entertaining and instructive value, breathed such lofty patriotism that our heart yearned toward him. . . ." As head of the Department of Agriculture, he added, "we have been fortunate in securing a man not only of great ability, but one whose whole heart is in his work." Another editor declared that when the Commissioner appeared before the people of the west, he was perhaps "the first man who had ever come from east of the Blue Ridge to address them upon matters of public concern who did not come to seek their votes, and whose personal interest in their immediate welfare did not cease as soon as their votes were deposited in the ballot-box."¹⁵

One of Polk's greatest assets in the conduct of his work was the full support of Zebulon B. Vance. Peter M. Wilson, who was close to both men, wrote in later years: "Governor Vance liked him, saw his usefulness to himself and to the state, and made him one of his 'pets'— the name given to those who were in the governor's inner circle by those who were on the outside. The governor informed the Board of Agriculture of his wish that Colonel Polk be commissioner and—by singular chance—the Board found itself quite in agreement with his wish."¹⁶ Vance and Polk occasionally shared the same speakers' platform, and their thought on agricultural subjects was very much alike.

Irvin S. Cobb once said: "What North Carolina needs is a press agent. She has practically everything else."¹⁷ Polk believed this in his day, and while Commissioner of Agriculture he attempted in several ways to fill the role himself. To portray the state to natives,

---

¹⁴ *Farmer and Mechanic*, July 25, 1878.
¹⁵ Asheville *Citizen* and Asheville *Pioneer Republican*, quoted in *Farmer and Mechanic*, Aug. 29, Sept. 5, 1878.
¹⁶ Peter M. Wilson, *Southern Exposure*, pp. 159-60.
¹⁷ Irvin S. Cobb, *North Carolina*, p. 11.

visitors, and possible immigrants, he prepared a comprehensive *Handbook of North Carolina*. He compiled the contents in three months and published the book in March, 1879, timing it to appear while the General Assembly was in session. Copies were distributed to the counties on the basis of their white population, and many were sent to other states and countries.

The *Handbook* contained a mass of interesting and useful information in convenient form. There was a brief historical sketch of the state from Sir Walter Raleigh to the convention of 1875, with lists of governors and other officials for the whole period; a section on political and social conditions in which the government of North Carolina, race relations, natural resources, and "Our Future" were discussed; a full account of the University, the denominational and military schools, and the institutions for women; a list of native North Carolinians prominent in other states; and the roll of Tar Heel inventors. There were pages devoted to towns, railroads, mills, churches, asylums, and newspapers. Professor W. C. Kerr, the State Geologist, contributed a physiographic description and a detailed map of the state.

One of the most valuable sections was that on the counties. For each county, information was given as to the date and manner of its creation, its geographic location, the county seat and its distance from Raleigh, a brief description of the surface, products, fruits, timbers, lands, schools, and manufactures of the region, and the names of the county's Department of Agriculture correspondents. Writing to Polk, a teacher said of the *Handbook*: "I take it to school and require one child each day to read a history of one county, and then we discuss it ... one little fellow of eight summers said 'Oh! Miss Sallie we have just learned a heap, and did not have to read much.' I know you will appreciate the compliment from the little school boy. You certainly have given us a good history of the State in a condensed form."[18] Prominent also, of course, were the chapters dealing with agriculture—statistics on

[18] Sallie Robinson to Polk, Feb. 28, 1880.

crops, production, use of fertilizer, and farm animals, notes from correspondents regarding outstanding achievements in agricultural production, and accounts of fish culture, silk culture, beekeeping, and fruit growing.

The *Handbook,* based upon many different sources, was one of the best fruits of the Department's first two years. In spite of various errors, gaps, and imperfections, it proved to be very popular and so much in demand that it stimulated the production of similar publications in the 'eighties and 'nineties.

The great object of the Department of Agriculture was to benefit the mass of North Carolina farmers. To reach them, however, through circulars and correspondence and speeches was difficult at best. Therefore, shortly after the work was well begun, it was determined that a weekly agricultural journal, "entirely disconnected with politics," should be established to keep the farmers in touch with the Department's activities.[19] The paper was to be a commercial enterprise. The Department would provide the publishers with a ready-made list of probable subscribers in return for free access to the paper's pages, while the farmers who subscribed would receive more and better reading matter than the rather expensive circulars could ever give them. If the venture were successful, all parties concerned stood to gain. The 8-page, 48-column paper which appeared every Thursday was named the *Farmer and Mechanic* and was regarded primarily as the organ of the Department of Agriculture. Its managing editor was a Confederate hero and experienced journalist who had asked for the job, Randolph Abbott Shotwell.[20] The contributing editors included Professor Kerr, Dr. Ledoux, Mrs. Spencer, John D. Cameron, John S. Long, C. B. Denson, and Nat. A. Gregory. October 10, 1877, was the date of the first issue, and immediately the *Farmer and Mechanic* became a constructive force in North Carolina journalism. The typography and make-up were unsurpassed in the state, and the paper seemed saturated with a spirit of intelli-

[19] Raleigh *Observer,* Sept. 18, 1877.
[20] Shotwell to Polk, Sept. 15, [1877].

gence and service. Most of the paper was devoted wholly to agricultural matters, but a good deal of space was also given to state and local news, personal items, the "Ladies' Department," and advertisements. The section on the work of the Department of Agriculture was of course edited by Polk.

After a year or two it was possible to estimate the value of the Department. To do so necessarily meant to pass judgment upon the Commissioner as well. Peter Wilson, who as Secretary of the Board of Agriculture was closely associated with Polk in his work, has written:

> ... [The Commissioner] conformed to no pattern save of ... [his] own cutting.... L. L. Polk, although a state official, was really the spokesman for a class; for a class which at that time needed an advocate and which [Walter H.] Page described in his imperishable phrase, "the forgotten man.".... By nature, he was a stirrer-up of friendly strife. There was nothing vicious about him, but he was entirely upon his side of the fence and was honestly convinced that all others were trespassers. So, in the ten years succeeding flagrant and honorable warfare, when he saw or thought he saw that the land owner and tiller had an inferior position in the economic scheme, his indignation magnified the injustice....[21]

Of his personality and accomplishments, another contemporary wrote:

> Col. Polk comes nearer being a steam locomotive than any man we know in official station. With a keen analytical brain, a restless, nervous temperament, an eye that is always dancing like a racehorse, and a ... spirit of *push* and go aheadativeness in him, he keeps every one around him moving at fiery speed. The work which he has already accomplished ... is marvelous. Going against wind and tide, with a new and difficult system to organize, with unexpected obstacles meeting him at every step ... he has nevertheless made great strides on the road to success.[22]

[21] Wilson, *Southern Exposure*, pp. 158-59.
[22] John S. Long, in *Farmer and Mechanic*, Jan. 24, 1878.

These statements express fairly the feelings of friends and associates. The establishment of the Department and the appointment of Polk to head it won genuine popular approval, and both press and public were in sympathy with the labors of the first two years. Ex-Governor W. W. Holden, that provocative personage, wrote Polk as follows: "Dean Swift says that 'he who makes two blades of grass to grow where only one blade grew before, is worth the whole race of politicians put together.' The work in which you are engaged is of prime importance, and I trust your efforts may be crowned with entire success . . . the administration of Gov. Vance deserves much praise for the attention it is giving to Education and Agriculture. . . . May God bless and protect the old ship of State, no matter who may hold the helm!" [23] Solid support likewise came from the Grange, which maintained a paternal interest in Polk and the Department.

Beginning in 1879, however, dissenting voices arose in some quarters. A forceful gentleman of Greensboro, D. W. C. Benbow, doubted whether the Department of Agriculture—with all Polk's energy, Kerr's knowledge, and Ledoux's skill—was of much practical benefit to the mass of poor and ignorant North Carolina farmers. Most of them, he asserted, knew nothing of the Department's work and could not read Polk's circulars even if they should receive them—and few did. The printing of these costly circulars should stop. Instead, the Department should publish at its own expense a weekly newspaper for distribution among the agricultural classes. There was the *Farmer and Mechanic,* to be sure. Yet many farmers were either unable to pay the subscription price, were just plain stingy, or else were stubbornly prejudiced against "book farming." In spite of his reluctance, said Benbow, the farmer *must* be educated and enlightened. He should be told in specific terms how to farm, when to plow and seed, what fertilizer to use, and so on.[24]

[23] Holden to Polk, July 18, 1877.
[24] Benbow to Polk, March 29, 1878, Jan. 20, 27, Feb. 13, Nov. 30, 1879.

Further opposition to Department policy came from a startling source: Randolph Shotwell. The editor of the *Farmer and Mechanic,* an individualist and a man of strong feelings, broke with the Department of Agriculture in August, 1879. He announced then that the paper would no longer be the official organ of the Department, but that with himself and J. W. Dowd as publishers it would become truly independent. "The department has ignored the use of its pages," he explained, "preferring to spend large sums for printing circulars elsewhere, which nobody cared to read."[25] The burden of Shotwell's attack was "extravagance." He pointed to the good salaries paid the Commissioner and the Secretary "for the mere duty of answering letters of inquiry." He charged that the cost to the taxpayers of printing Polk's *Handbook* and Kerr's *Geological Survey* was $4,000 and $5,000 respectively, and that the money spent by the Department during its first three years amounted to $77,000, exceeding its fund on deposit in the State Treasury. Polk answered, of course, and Shotwell headlined his letter *"Polk once More Penning in Behalf the Salary Bureau."* The Commissioner protested that neither the Department nor the Treasury was financially responsible for Kerr's report; that the three-year expenditures of the Department came to only $61,000; and that the account in the Treasury had never been overdrawn. State Treasurer John M. Worth corroborated each of Polk's statements. At this, Shotwell was forced to hedge; he concluded the exchange by telling his readers, "You will see how near we came to the facts." He argued that, in any case, the whole Department could be run successfully on $6,000 a year, an amount then being received in salaries by Polk, Kerr, and Ledoux alone.[26]

Positive that the *Farmer and Mechanic* "must cease to be an 'organ' or die," Shotwell transformed it into a political paper, reducing the size and type, changing the material and make-up, increasing the amount of general news, and stamping it indelibly

[25] Charlotte *Southern Home,* Aug. 15, 1879.
[26] *Farmer and Mechanic,* March 4-25, 1880.

with his own personality. His war memoir, "Three Years in Battle, and Three in Prison," was a serial feature. During the campaign of 1880, when Shotwell hoped to win the Democratic nomination for state auditor, the paper became overweighted with the details of petty politics and lurid "outrages"; but from that year until 1885, when the *Farmer and Mechanic* merged with the *State Chronicle,* it was lively and clever. In this later period, incidentally, Shotwell was quite friendly to Polk—so friendly, in fact, that Polk's eldest daughter asked him playfully, "What do you pay Shotwell a week for the puffs he gives you?"[27]

Echoing the criticisms of Benbow and Shotwell were a number of editors and anonymous letter-writers. One called upon the legislature to "stop that *'rat-hole,'* the Agricultural Department . . . and by all means cut down the salaries of persons employed therein."[28] Another, who demanded to know just what good the agency had done since its beginning, asserted: "We do not want to be told of the museum, of the mammoth pumpkins, potatoes and other lusus naturae. We are tired of hearing of these, and of being told how many tobacco seed, or fish spawn, have been sent out. We do not want to hear any more about Prof. Ledoux's skill as an analytical chemist. . . ."[29] A third declared: "I am convinced that the whole Department—Agricultural, Chemical, Fish Hatchery, and whatever else may be attached to it,—is a * * * * * * on the farmer, and I enter my protest against it."[30] Others attacked the printing of circulars, the establishment of the *Farmer and Mechanic,* the operation of the fertilizer law, and the employment of an immigration commissioner.

These critics passed strictures upon Polk, also. Because of his driving executive activity, they called him the "Military Commis-

---

[27] Lula Polk Harris to Polk, Feb. 25, [1882].

[28] Raleigh *Protest,* quoted in Raleigh *North-Carolina Farmer,* III, 248 (March, 1879).

[29] Raleigh *Signal,* March 10, 1880.

[30] *Farmer and Mechanic,* Sept. 17, 1879.

sioner," and his system "Military Agriculture." According to them, he said often that he labored solely in the interest of the farmers, yet he received $2,000 and clerk hire for wasting their money on fish and printing and other non-agricultural matters! He was not a real farmer at all, but a Democratic officeholder with political ambitions. One anonymous writer avowed that the principal part of the Commissioner's work consisted of "blowing a Jeems-(k)-Polk horn." [31]

It was no accident that the opposition to the Department of Agriculture, particularly with respect to expenditures, reached its height while the General Assembly of 1879 was in session. This Legislature, meeting with the memory of what the Democratic majority called "carpetbag finance" still vivid, made the watchword "retrenchment and reform." Stringent economy in state finance and the consequent crippling of needed social services were the unfortunate—if perhaps necessary—results of the Southern reaction to Reconstruction. In this atmosphere there was reason for friends of the Department to fear that it might be injured, and indeed for Polk to fear for his very place. Another looming factor was the change in governors. After serving half of his four-year term, Zeb Vance resigned during the early part of the session to go to the United States Senate. His support of Polk and the Department had been a strong sustaining influence. He was succeeded by Lieutenant-Governor Thomas J. Jarvis, about whose sympathies there was some question.

As had been expected, several changes were made. This General Assembly of 1879, which Professor Hamilton has described as "a hardworking, serious body and one of the best legislatures in the history of the state," first abolished the position of State Geologist held by W. C. Kerr. Then the Department of Agriculture was divided into three equal sub-departments, filled by Polk, the Commissioner, Kerr, the Geologist, and Ledoux, the Chemist.

[31] Raleigh *News,* June 3, 1880.

Finally, Polk's monthly reports were dispensed with and all his clerical assistance was eliminated.[32]

Thus hamstrung in the name of economy, the Department's usefulness was reduced; and the influence of Polk's position was immeasurably lessened. In the months that followed the legislative session, a perturbing conviction fixed itself in the minds of Polk and his friends. It was that Governor Jarvis and President Battle, two of the three members on the executive committee of the Board of Agriculture, were attempting to reorganize the Department to serve certain ends of their own. Jarvis, they said, was intent upon building a political machine, with his eye on 1880 and beyond, while Battle was trying to augment the University by weakening the Department of Agriculture. And both, by their tacit hostility, hoped to drive the sedulous Polk from office and substitute a more congenial man.[33]

Previous to becoming president of the University of North Carolina, Kemp P. Battle had been a lawyer, a business man, and state treasurer. His contacts were of the best, and his political influence surprisingly strong. When the evidence pointed to him as the moving spirit behind the reorganization of the Department of Agriculture, Polk asked him to clarify his position. Polk explained that when the legislature took away his clerk it necessarily closed the greater part of his correspondence with the farmers and worked great hardship in the conduct of his office; he wondered if the Board could not find a way to give him clerical assistance. Battle replied as follows:

> ... I know that the Gen. Ass^y *intended* to cut off your clerk. They passed an Act to that effect, understanding what the Act meant.

[32] Kemp P. Battle to Polk, Jan. 15, 1879; James R. Thigpen to Polk, Jan. 22, 1879; Polk to J. I. Scales, Jan. 27, 1879; James W. Albright to Polk, Feb. 1, 4, 1879; J. G. deRoulhac Hamilton, *North Carolina since 1860*, p. 199.

[33] Sydenham B. Alexander to Polk, March 17, 1879, Sept. 14, 1880; Jonathan Evans to Polk, Aug. 2, 1879; D. McN. McKay to Polk, June 12, 1880; Josephus Daniels, *Tar Heel Editor*, p. 296.

Now I believe it is *illegal* for us to give you a clerk. Moreover I feel sure that if we evade it, the dep^t will be crippled, if not abolished, at the next session. . . .

I wish I could see how to give you aid as clerk. But I see no way to do it without breaking the law and incurring the danger of injury to the Board, *and to you.*

I am aware that you & perhaps others think that my mind is bent towards aggrandizing the Univ^y. The record of facts show[s] that this is not correct. All I want to do is to carry out the law. . . . My position has never been illiberal towards other branches of the Agr. work. Several times I waived my own opinion in deference to yours. . . .

In a second letter, Battle declared that he was not trying to cripple the Department and that he harbored no personal feeling against Polk. Remarking that his course at Board meetings had always been consistent, he urged that strict economy be observed or else the legislature would hurt everybody. He assured Polk that he would do anything *legal* to help. Actually, as he revealed later in his *Memories,* Battle looked upon the Commissioner as "a visionary, unpractical man." [34]

There was no encouragement for Polk in Battle's attitude. Governor Jarvis was sitting still. The other members of the Board—Thomas M. Holt, W. C. Kerr, James R. Thigpen, Jonathan Evans, and W. H. Cheek, who had succeeded Sydenham B. Alexander as Master of the State Grange—were seemingly partial to Polk, yet could do nothing to improve the situation. The legislative temper was ominous. With these storm signals flying, Polk knew that sooner or later a squall would strike. After three years of operation and the expenditure of $61,000, the Department was expected by the public to continue forward; but with the scope of the work now so severely curbed, it was difficult to see how much could be accomplished. "Thus reduced," said Polk, "what remained to justify paying a Commissioner a salary of two

---

[34] Battle to Polk, July 17, 21, 1879; Battle, *Memories of an Old-Time Tar Heel,* p. 248.

thousand dollars to hold the office?" So his ambitious plans for immigration and crop diversification and agricultural education, springing from a love for North Carolina and the promise of a new day, were wrecked on the rocks of "retrenchment and reform."

Polk resigned as Commissioner of Agriculture on May 24, 1880. Immediately afterward he joined the daily Raleigh *News* as corresponding editor, in which capacity, he said, "the Department and all the great interests it represents shall continue to have my faithful and earnest support."

The Raleigh papers expressed regret at his resignation and appreciation for his services and were echoed by the press and people of the state in large numbers. *"I don't want to give you up,"* wrote Jonathan Evans, and the Raleigh *State Journal* growled, "The wit[l]ings who have incessantly prated of 'military agriculture' are perhaps now happy." James W. Albright was incredulous: "What is the matter? Has somebody made you mad? Have you gone crazy—found a gold mine—drew a prize in a lottery—or WHAT?" Randolph Shotwell stated: "We have said more complimentary things of Col. Polk than of any man during our whole journalistic career, Gov. Vance excepted. And we have also censured some features of his conduct; some management of his office. In doing so we invariably qualified our criticisms by admitting that others were in a sense responsible for the action complained of, and that perhaps no man in the State could have done so much for the Department as the gentleman in question. . . ."[35]

After Polk's resignation, Secretary Wilson carried on until the election of a new commissioner. The Board's first choice was Sydenham B. Alexander. This substantial Mecklenburg farmer was popular in both agricultural and political circles, but he declined to serve. Apparently his analysis of the situation was too

[35] *News,* June 6, 8, 1880; *Observer,* June 6, 1880; Evans to Polk, June 3, 1880; *State Journal,* June 8, 1880; Albright to Polk, June 8, 1880; *Farmer and Mechanic,* June 10, 1880.

much like Polk's for him to find the position promising. In October, 1880, the Board picked Montford McGehee, of Person County, who occupied the place for the next six years. He was one of those who had helped push through the bill establishing the Department of Agriculture, and he seemed to fit the requirements of Jarvis and Battle exceptionally well. According to Josephus Daniels, who as a young editor made a detailed investigation of the Department in 1886, McGehee was "a classical scholar who had lost three fortunes trying to farm." He had "married a daughter of Judge [George E.] Badger, had influential friends, and was elected Commissioner of Agriculture to give him a salary. . . ."[36] In 1880 also, Dr. Ledoux resigned as State Chemist and was succeeded by Dr. Charles W. Dabney. Professor Kerr stayed on as State Geologist.

Many people throughout the state were surprised at Polk's resignation and manifested deep concern over the future of the Department. In answer to their queries, Polk made public a letter in which he had discussed the subject. It was wrong, he wrote, for the General Assembly and the Board of Agriculture to cripple the Department as they had. By taking away the Commissioner's clerk, dividing the agency into sub-departments, and discontinuing the monthly reports, they had weakened it beyond the point of real usefulness. Yet the Department should not be abolished, as some were advising. It should by all means be strengthened. North Carolina, Polk argued, was an agricultural state, and its farmers desperately needed the enlightenment and inspiration that such a Department should provide. It had been created for that purpose. In only three years, while in the process of organization, it had saved the farmers over $200,000 on fertilizers alone, and the masses of the people were not taxed a cent for its support. If it was to be of genuine service to them, however, the Board of Agriculture had to undergo a thorough reorganization.[37]

Following his experience as Commissioner, Polk became con-

[36] Daniels, *Tar Heel Editor*, pp. 296, 318.
[37] Polk to W. M. Kennedy, in Raleigh *News and Observer*, Jan. 21, 1881.

vinced that there were fatal defects in the make-up of the Board. As originally constituted, this body included the governor, the geologist, the president of the University, the master of the Grange, the president of the Agricultural Society, and two practical farmers. Sponsors of the bill setting up the Department of Agriculture had felt that it was necessary to have the influence of Vance, Kerr, Battle, Alexander, and Holt in order to get the bill through. Now Polk firmly believed that the Board of Agriculture, dominated by the three or four members who were not agriculturists, was the greatest single hindrance to the development of a progressive Department.

Randolph Shotwell, one of Polk's strongest allies during the early 'eighties, agreed with him. The present arrangement, Shotwell wrote, "makes the Board a 'close corporation' (chosen to serve *indefinitely*) composed of the Governor (a politician), the President of the University (a teacher), the chief of the Grange (a secret society with only a few hundred members), the State Geologist (whose conduct, work, and money matters are all supervised by the Board of which he is a leading member,—so that he helps to investigate himself!), the President of the State Fair (who may be a Lawyer, or a Manufacturer), and finally *two* farmers, who are *elected by the other members,* and you know that people usually select their friends." Of the seven members, furthermore, two were from Edgecombe County and four resided within a short distance of Raleigh. [38]

Contrary to general expectations, no important legislation affecting the Department was passed by the General Assembly of 1881. Probably the change of commissioners had satisfied the political leaders. In 1883, however, the movement to reorganize the Board made considerable headway under the leadership of Polk, Shotwell, J. H. Enniss, editor of the monthly *North-Carolina Farmer,* and others. As the best-qualified critic of the Department during the 'eighties, Polk was twice called before the joint

[38] *Farmer and Mechanic,* Feb. 14, 1883.

committee on agriculture to present his views. His second appearance followed discourses by Jarvis, Holt, Evans, McGehee, and Dabney which clearly showed the members of the Board and the officers of the Department wedded to the *status quo*. Replying to Jarvis in particular, Polk in his speech advocated the plan that the reformers favored most.

The proposed change, said Polk, would have the Board of Agriculture composed of nine members—one from each congressional district—elected by the General Assembly. The burden of Governor Jarvis's argument seemed to be that "fitness rather than locality should govern in the selection of the members of the Board." This, Polk asserted, begged the question, for *"locality is one of the essential elements of that fitness."* In each district there was not only one man but there were scores of men who were at least as well qualified as, if not better qualified than, the present Board members. In North Carolina this representation by congressional districts would assure the adequate representation of all the leading agricultural interests of the state. No member of the present Board was identified with any of them. The proposition was a fair one, and would win popular support. It should be remembered that the Department of Agriculture was created for the farmers, who constituted seventy-two per cent of the state's population, and they certainly needed a full voice in its management. Personal considerations should be ignored; it was the whole people that the state had to serve. So Polk urged that a sound patriotism rule. "In this matter," he said in conclusion, "I have no axe to grind—no selfish purpose to subserve, but [I speak] as one, who, throughout his whole life, has been identified with the industrial classes of our people...." [39]

Though the incumbents opposed the new plan bitterly, the General Assembly of 1883 passed legislation in line with the suggested reforms. What the more conservative officials thought of Polk at this time could be seen in an article written by Com-

[39] *North-Carolina Farmer* extra, Feb. 19, 1883.

missioner McGehee. Purporting to be a full history of the Department and its work, the long account nowhere mentioned Polk's name. There was much about the beginnings of the Department, but sole credit for the accomplishments of the early years was given to the Board, to which McGehee assigned many virtues. Nothing was said about there having been a former Commissioner.[40]

In 1881 the Department of Agriculture moved its quarters from the Briggs Building to the newly-purchased National Hotel property, and the chemical station was transferred from Chapel Hill to Raleigh. All through the decade the Department for the most part followed the tack set by Polk with respect to land registry, immigration, handbooks, fertilizer analyses, geology, fish, and the rest.

This agency of the state government should have touched the lives of the farmers closely and beneficially. Yet during the 'eighties it was not popular. Progressives like Polk and Josephus Daniels gave voice to the dissatisfaction of the people when they rebelled at the conservative management of the Department, its political cast, its aloofness from the masses, its energy-wasting concern with non-agricultural matters, and its financial extravagance. Polk proposed that the December meeting of the Board of Agriculture be thrown open to properly qualified representatives of the farmers for free discussion, and that the Commissioner of Agriculture be elected either by the legislature or by the people.[41] Daniels, the twenty-three-year-old editor of the Raleigh *State Chronicle,* recommended in his bold and independent exposition that the funds of the Department come directly from the State Treasury on an appropriation basis rather than from the more variable fertilizer tax.[42] Even the Raleigh *News and Observer,* commonly an apologist for the Board, admonished: "Let us have

[40] Dept. of Agr., *Bulletin,* May, 1883, pp. 1-10.
[41] *Progressive Farmer,* Feb. 10, 1886.
[42] Raleigh *State Chronicle,* Jan. 14, 1886.

done, for a time at least, with far away things and let the energies of the department be devoted to building up agriculture here at home." [43]

In 1887 Montford McGehee, whom the reformers thought archaic, was succeeded as Commissioner by John Robinson, Board member from Anson County, whom they regarded as equally unsatisfactory. It seemed to them then that the Department was doomed to remain in its old rut for a long time to come. At this same time, Syd Alexander received an appointment to the Board. He wrote Polk: "I have not accepted the place on the Board of Agriculture, as yet. But the more I think of it the more I think I ought to accept, for if any damn thing ever needed a friend, it does now." [44]

Polk's profound interest in the Department of Agriculture did not cease with his resignation as Commissioner in 1880. He remained a sympathetic but trenchant critic of its work until he moved to the national scene in 1890. The following sentence, written in 1882, offers excellent insight into his whole attitude: "I may, in my great anxiety to see our old State move off, overestimate the value & utility of the Dep^t but I sincerely believe if it were run on the proper track, it would & could do more for N. C. in ten years, than has been done in all her past history." [45]

Nevertheless, Polk was keenly aware of the most formidable impediment to progress: The "Bourbons" were in the saddle.

[43] *News and Observer,* Jan. 24, 1886.
[44] Alexander to Polk, June 23, 1887.
[45] Polk to Edward A. Oldham, Dec. 30, 1882, misc. MS. file, Duke University Library, Durham.

CHAPTER VIII

THE EARLY 'EIGHTIES

To ITS READERS on May 20, 1880, the Raleigh *News* made an interesting announcement. Colonel Thomas M. Holt, the prosperous cotton mill owner, and John Gatling had just bought the paper. They and the editor, Peter M. Hale, now formed the *News* Company, with the Edwards and Broughton printing house as business manager. "For once," the announcement read, "abundant means, business capacity, knowledge of the printing business, and newspaper training are combined upon a Raleigh daily newspaper." This seemed like a fortunate circumstance indeed at a time when the life-expectancy of daily newspapers in the South was somewhat short. The paper proposed to follow the same policies that had made the Raleigh *Observer* of Peter M. Hale and William L. Saunders the finest daily in the state during its brief career in the late 'seventies. The *News* will be a "North Carolina Democratic newspaper," wrote Hale. "These four words tell all that a column of explanation could convey."

It was four days later that L. L. Polk wrote his letter of resignation as Commissioner of Agriculture for North Carolina, and three weeks later that he actively began his work with the Raleigh *News*. He became corresponding editor and part owner. In the capacity of a roving reporter he visited the different sections of the state and described their industries and possibilities. At the same time, he introduced the *News* into these areas in an effort to win new subscribers. The other owners felt that Polk's fresh and thorough knowledge of the state's needs and resources, plus his well-known energy and enthusiasm, would be of great value to the paper and its readers. Polk himself, when he had come to regard his position as Commissioner untenable, was thankful for the opportunity. The new work enabled him to continue his agitation for the vigorous development of the state's material interests, which now appeared to be his ruling passion. In the course of his roving, it should be added, he also managed to conduct a column on practical agriculture and to report such events as college commencements and political conventions.

Eighteen-eighty was an important political year. The Democratic South, certain that Tilden had been cheated out of the Presidency in his contest with Hayes four years before, fervidly hoped for the election of Hancock over Garfield. Fully as momentous in North Carolina was Governor Jarvis's bid for victory against his Republican opponent, R. P. Buxton. After serving the last two years of Vance's term, Jarvis now desired four years as governor in his own right.

Polk was called upon to report the speeches of various candidates—principally Jarvis—during the campaign. He traveled from one end of the state to the other on his assignments and in the meantime made several rousing speeches of his own. His reporting was far from impartial. The *News* was stanchly Democratic, and so was Polk. Following a joint debate between Jarvis and Buxton at Kenansville, Polk wrote:

> Governor JARVIS was bold, aggressive and incisive, and his strong argument and eloquent appeals to the people to stand by good government and rebuke with defeat the corrupt party that had burdened them with taxes, defrauded them of the privileges of education for their children, preached discord instead of peace, emptied the treasury, and added neither material prosperity nor honor to the State, were applauded with enthusiasm.
>
> Judge BUXTON made a mild reply that was weak in matter and manner and gave comfort to the Democrats and dealt dissatisfaction and distrust to his friends. It is no injustice

to say that his plausible platitudes are not the sort of stuff that will gain him votes, and . . . that is what his party needs. . . .

Both men were in truth poor platform speakers. The full text of their exchange, nevertheless, reveals that each made a good, careful speech, and that Polk's comments were prejudiced.[1] In those days, unbiased political reporting was all but unknown; the duty of the trusty correspondent was to emblazon the magnificent efforts of his paper's candidate while belittling the feeble pains of his opponent. Even so, Polk's partisanship in this campaign seems excessive.

Governor Jarvis won out in a rather close race, and the Democrats retained their control of the state. Some inroads upon Democratic strength in 1880 were made by the national Greenback movement, but these were not extensive enough to affect the result of the election materially. The "Liberal Democratic" movement of two years later was something else. This purely local phenomenon grew out of a coalition of anti-prohibition Democrats, Greenback Democrats, and dyed-in-the-wool Republicans formed to fight the "Bourbon," or regular, Democrats. In the early 'eighties the dominant Democrats split over the prohibition issue, and some Republicans made overtures to other dissident groups in an effort to drive the wedge deeper. Condemning prohibition, a county government law, the internal revenue system, and sectionalism, the "Liberals" endorsed the federal Blair Bill, a moderate tariff, and "equal political rights to all." They were strong enough in 1882 to reduce Democratic majorities and to elect one of their number to Congress. In 1884, however, the now united and harmonious Democrats overwhelmed the Republican-Liberal ticket. When the movement had thus collapsed, most of the Liberals became straight Republicans.

Polk, a regular, scorned the bolters. Speaking as a leading member of a Raleigh political club, he declared before a rally in 1882

[1] Raleigh *News*, Aug. 4, 5, 1880.

that he and his associates would "resist the payment of a single farthing of the fraudulent [Reconstruction] debt," that they were "opposed to the entire internal revenue system," that "the present white man's government" was "good enough" for them, and that they did not want any "nickle-plated [*sic*], weak-kneed, independent Democrats" in their club. It was reported that these declarations were greeted with "continued cheers."[2]

No matter what Polk may have thought of Jarvis's actions and attitudes regarding the Department of Agriculture, he thoroughly sympathized with the Governor's politics and with the central theme of his inaugural address. That arresting text was: "NORTH CAROLINA, THE DEVELOPMENT OF HER RESOURCES AND THE EDUCATION OF HER CHILDREN." Jarvis asserted that the commonwealth's most urgent need was popular education and that the need for advertising, immigration, and initiative remained as great as ever. Steady progress in both directions followed during his term. Jarvis, a practical and upright man with a strong sense of executive responsibility and leadership, took rank as the ablest governor of the state between 1865 and 1900.

In a concentrated attempt to make North Carolina inviting to possible immigrants, elaborate exhibits were prepared for the "International Cotton Exposition" of Atlanta in 1881 and for the "New England Manufacturers' and Mechanics' Institute Fair" of Boston in 1883. The Atlanta Exposition, under the guiding genius of Henry W. Grady, proved to be a powerful stimulus to the building of cotton mills all over the South. Many North Carolinians, including Polk, visited the Exposition and were impressed by what they saw.

Correspondence between Edward Atkinson, Boston economist, and Charles W. Dabney, State Chemist of North Carolina, paved the way for the North Carolina exhibit at the Boston Fair. The cotton, silk, cereals, minerals, woods, and other products of the state occupied the center of the huge exhibition hall and were

[2] Raleigh *News and Observer*, July 18, 1882.

viewed by a large number of people. To Boston, Governor Jarvis himself led a sizable visiting delegation from North Carolina. "He carried the good will and the hopes of his people into New England, speaking without complaint and without reproach of the past," Peter M. Wilson has written. With the Governor were Montford McGehee, who "recalled his Harvard days," and L. L. Polk, "a soldier who could find comrades in courage here on the other side of the battlefield." These men, Wilson believed, "held the candle" for Henry Grady's famous "New South" address of three years later.[3]

The six-year term of Thomas J. Jarvis (1879-1885) witnessed the beginnings of industrialism in North Carolina. Following the defeat of Hancock in 1880, the South turned its prime attention from a national political victory to local internal development. A concerted campaign to build cotton mills commenced. When in the 'eighties these factories multiplied, a great migration from farm to mill ensued, giving rise to economic and social problems of the most far-reaching significance to both agriculture and industry. North Carolinians of every class welcomed and encouraged the new industries, for to a poverty-ridden state they represented hope for the future. In 1887, when the industrial movement was well under way, the state commissioner of labor statistics declared: "Prosperity in manufacturing means a greater prosperity in every other direction. . . . The weakness of North Carolina in the past has been peculiarly upon this point. The State has been too exclusively agricultural. . . . The wealth of the State must come through mechanical and manufacturing channels, and not through the products of the farm; the history of the past abundantly proves that fact. . . ." He admitted, however, that North Carolina was still overwhelmingly agricultural, and would remain so for years to come.[4]

Polk thought first, of course, of the farmer, and he approved

[3] Peter M. Wilson, *Southern Exposure*, pp. 141-46.
[4] Bureau of Labor Statistics, *Annual Report, 1887*, p. 50.

the new trend because he believed that it would benefit the farmer. He had always agreed with those who advocated many small, diversified industries for North Carolina. On reflecting that almost everything he ate, wore, and used came from the North, Polk stated: "It may be that we will yet learn that diversified industries is the surest foundation of prosperity, and that to increase these we must have less politics and give a little more time to business, talk less about Southern independence and work harder to bring it about."

Taking the old town of Fayetteville as an example, Polk showed how new industries could be made to flourish there. If, he said, the property-holders should agree to sell a part of their lots to actual settlers at nominal cost; if factory sites were either put on the market at a fair price or else subscribed as stock toward the erection of a mill; if property devoted to manufacturing were rendered tax-exempt for a number of years; if these inducements were widely advertised; then nothing could keep industrial activity from immediately forging ahead. In the light of Fayetteville's abundant water-power, substantial bank deposits, and extensive trade territory, all this could certainly be done—and Fayetteville was only one of many.[5]

In the fall of 1878, after he had been Commissioner of Agriculture a year and a half, Polk decided to move his family from Polkton to Raleigh and thenceforth to make the state capital their permanent home. Two of his daughters had already attended the Baptist Female Seminary there, and convenient educational and social advantages for the others was a consideration undoubtedly prominent in his mind. At this time his own future definitely seemed to lie in Raleigh. In December the eight Polks—the parents, and six daughters ranging in age from twenty down to four—occupied a handsome eight-room house on East Jones Street. Their new home, in addition to the usual rooms, contained an office and a library and was described as having "all modern con-

[5] *News*, July 16, 1880; *News and Observer*, Nov. 20, 1880.

veniences, such as bath-rooms, water-closets, hot and cold water and gas."

The Raleigh of that day was a "sleepy, delightful, shaded old place," in the words of Edward King of *Scribner's Monthly,* and Sir George Campbell found it "a pretty country place, with plenty of flowers and good vegetation."[6] The British traveler added: "The town of Raleigh is, as usual, very scattered, with broad streets quite unpaved, and a good deal of ornamental ground about the houses. ... There are many whiskey shops, and a good many churches." He noted that the cotton market was "very busy," and that the general market seemed "well supplied." In describing Fayetteville Street, the main thoroughfare, Walter H. Page wrote: "The treeless street seemed absurdly wide, making the business buildings on either side ludicrously squatty; for ... the Board of Trade, wishing to give the business part of the town a metropolitan appearance, had induced the aldermen to cut down the elms which fifty years had made beautiful. ... But the oaks in the capitol square yet stood, and the dignified little granite State House was impressive. . . ."[7] Ranking second in the state behind Wilmington in 1880, Raleigh numbered 9,265 people, about half of whom were Negroes. Architecturally undistinguished and poverty-stricken, the town seemed extremely lethargic.

By the time that Polk had resigned as Commissioner of Agriculture and joined the staff of the Raleigh *News,* he had become a full-fledged citizen of the state capital. When the *News,* in September, 1880, merged with the *Observer* to form the Raleigh *News and Observer,* Polk continued as corresponding editor on the new paper. The following February, however, he gave up this post in favor of two others he had just assumed. He had been elected secretary of the North Carolina Agricultural Society, and he was about to open an agricultural implement store. "Journal-

[6] Edward King, *The Great South,* p. 468; George Campbell, *White and Black,* pp. 293, 300.
[7] Walter H. Page, *The Southerner: a Novel, Being the Autobiography of Nicholas Worth,* pp. 112-13.

ism," explained one of his friends, "is honorable and useful, but not profitable."[8]

The weightiest responsibility that devolved upon the secretary of the State Agricultural Society was the general management of the annual State Fair, an enterprise which had been sponsored by the Society ever since its organization in the 'fifties. Naturally the fairs had been interrupted by the Civil War and its aftermath, but they revived in the early 'seventies. Polk, for several years one of the Society's numerous vice-presidents, had attended them all since the revival. Now, as secretary, he promised that the Fair of 1881 would be "a rattler, and no mistake."

Polk had the congenial task of advertising and organizing. He made speeches about the Fair, kept the event before the people in the press, invited prominent speakers, supervised finances, prepared the agricultural exhibits, and issued awards to the prize-winners. He also arranged for popular entertainment. At the Weldon Fair the previous year he had complained that "horse racing and other attractions" tended to "monopolize the occasion." Yet he fully, if reluctantly, saw the need for non-agricultural entertainment at the State Fair. To attract sportsmen, he procured "Captain Bogardus and Sons," the expert marksmen; and to lend color and dash to the scene, the cadets of the Bingham School. Besides all this, Polk staged a Confederate reunion, and as his reward was chosen secretary of the newly-formed State Survivors' Association.

People considered the Fair of 1881 a great success. In spite of the autumn drought and the competition provided by the Atlanta Exposition and the Yorktown Centennial, the Fair cleared some $1,500 above all expenses—the first time since the war that such a thing had happened. They gave Polk's efficient management most of the credit. The Polk name gained further distinction when Juanita, Colonel Polk's second daughter, won the Fair's "star premium" of $50 in gold, awarded to the young woman who should

[8] *News and Observer,* Feb. 6, 1881; Raleigh *Farmer and Mechanic,* Jan. 27, 1881. The remainder of this chapter is based chiefly upon these two sources and the Polk Papers, 1881–1885 *passim.*

exhibit the finest collection of products made by her own hands.

Early in 1882 Polk resigned the secretaryship because of the demands of private business. For a year he had operated an agricultural implement house, and now he felt he should give most of his time to it. L. L. Polk and Company, consisting of Polk, Colonel W. J. Hicks, and Major P. A. Wiley, dealt in farm implements, steam-driven machinery, and field seeds. First housed in the Adams Building on Wilmington Street, the firm soon needed more commodious quarters. Accordingly, it leased one of the largest store buildings in Raleigh. Located at the corner of Wilmington and Martin streets, it was owned by W. H. Dodd, a business man who later became mayor of the city. Dodd and Polk, trading as a separate firm under the name of Dodd, Polk and Company, shortly set themselves up as cotton factors and commission merchants and solicited the consignments of the farmers.

In addition to the main purpose of turning an honest—and perhaps shrewd—dollar, the complementary purpose of L. L. Polk and Company was to contribute in some measure to the improvement of Southern agriculture. Polk agreed with Henry Grady that Southern farms were "littered with ill-adapted and inferior implements and machines, representing twice the investment that, intelligently placed, would provide an equipment that with half the labor would do better work." Polk took advantage of his State Fair, as Grady did of his Atlanta Exposition, to "bring the farmers face to face with the very best machinery that invention and experience have produced."[9]

At the Fair of 1881 Polk's firm advertised its goods by erecting a building of its own on the grounds. Under the spacious roof two steam engines kept in motion the various types of machinery displayed. There appeared a cotton gin and press, a corn mill, an ensilage cutter, a wood saw, and several kinds of threshing machines and cutting knives. Among the farm implements could be

---

[9] Henry W. Grady, "Cotton and Its Kingdom," *Harper's New Monthly Magazine*, LXIII, 732 (Oct., 1881).

seen a great variety of plows, cultivators, harrows, fruit dryers and evaporators, and cider presses. Since Polk at this time occupied himself chiefly with his duties as secretary of the Fair, his assistant, David Anderson, had immediate supervision of the exhibit. Polk advertised on much the same scale at local fairs in Weldon, Fayetteville, and Tarboro, and at the State Fair again the following year.

It should not be necessary to add that on these and many other occasions he made speeches. He remained a popular favorite, especially with rural audiences, and much in demand. One old farmer said of Polk: "It is a pleasure to hear that man speak. He talks like he knows what he is talking about, and he talks sense."[10] During these months Polk did not neglect to urge his friends to buy improved implements and machinery for their farms, and also field peas. The latter he described as the best and cheapest of all natural fertilizers for the South at $1.75 per bushel.

Polk's business ventures, however, presently fell upon evil days. After a year Dodd, Polk and Company dissolved, though Dodd continued his cotton business in Polk's office. At the end of two years—in April, 1883—L. L. Polk and Company was forced to assign. Liabilities totaled $13,000, and assets $10,000, with most of the debts due Northern manufacturers. As an appointed trustee Attorney Richard H. Battle carried on the business. But on May 30 a clearance sale was held, and on June 2 a final auction. The *Farmer and Mechanic* believed that the failure, one of several about the city at that time, should be blamed upon "the unexpected decline in Raleigh's trade, resulting from the short crops, the low price of cotton, and the natural sequence of 'Railroadery' in politics. . . ."[11]

Polk was now forty-six. His life up to this time, except for war service, town-building, and politics, had been connected with agriculture in one or another of its various aspects. He had been farm owner, rural editor, Grange organizer, Commissioner of

---

[10] *News and Observer,* Aug. 29, 1882.
[11] *Farmer and Mechanic,* April 11, 1883.

Agriculture, Fair secretary, and dealer in agricultural implements. The early 'eighties, however, witnessed a strange interlude in his career: he became the manufacturer and salesman of a patent medicine.

The story began twenty years previously—in 1862. Polk was stationed with Zeb Vance's regiment near Petersburg when he wrote: "I feel very uneasy about my family, for I hear that the soar [sic] throat is raging, & in most cases, [is] fatal to children." [12] The dread diphtheria scourge caused him great concern, for his wife and two baby daughters lived alone in an isolated rural section. In 1862, moreover, the South was running short of ordinary drugs for sickness. Faced with this situation, the people of the Confederacy ingeniously began to develop vegetable-type "home remedies" on a large scale. The adeptness of country folk along this line has always been traditional. During the war and for many years afterward the Polks used a home-made concoction that proved definitely effective in the treatment of all kinds of throat ailments—from slight sore throat to diphtheria itself. It seems to have included such ingredients as herb extract, tannic acid, and turpentine.

Encouraged by the remarkable success of the remedy in almost a hundred cases, Polk determined to develop it commercially. While still Commissioner of Agriculture in 1879 he had it chemically analyzed (at the Agricultural Experiment Station in Chapel Hill) and arranged with Congressman Robert B. Vance to have it patented. He then obtained as many testimonials as possible from persons who had used the medicine, certifying that it was safe, effective, and reliable. Many of the endorsers were people well-known in North Carolina and included a number of doctors. Polk planned to put his remedy on sale in drug stores throughout the state, with Raleigh as manufacturing and distributing headquarters. A physician friend had suggested some possible names:

[12] Polk to Mrs. Joel T. Gaddy, Oct. 17, 1862.

"Polk's Diphtheria Cure," "Diphtheria Destroyer," "Polk's Diphtheria Alterative or Specific," "Diphtheritic Wonder."[13]

"Polk's Diphtheria Cure" was the name selected. The formula Polk did not make public. Yet hundreds of the little brown bottles containing the mysterious liquid sold for fifty cents each. The Raleigh newspapers which ran Polk's advertisements professed considerable interest and hoped that his "discovery" would help to end diphtheria's annual ravages. Neither Polk nor the newspapers nor the public regarded the Cure as a quack remedy in any sense, for its efficacy had been proved—against a particularly stubborn disease. As one paper remarked: "Col. Polk cannot afford to put his name to a fraud or humbug; neither could those whose names he presents."[14] The solution, primarily a specific for the throat, was to be applied to the whitish patches characteristic of early diphtheria in an effort to check the growth of the malignant false membrane that caused most of the trouble. The directions stressed local treatment, early treatment, and constant treatment.

For a while Polk sold diphtheria medicine and agricultural implements simultaneously. A few months after the failure of the implement house, he made the acquaintance of a young Mr. Holman, who offered to buy a half interest in the Diphtheria Cure. Holman, whom Polk probably met at the time of the Boston Fair, was the well-to-do son of a Baptist preacher of that city. With this capital support, Polk decided to set up headquarters in Boston. Though his remedy had succeeded to some degree in North Carolina and surrounding states, he believed that greater opportunities lay in the North. Bearing an impressive letter of introduction signed by Senators Ransom and Vance, Governor Jarvis, Mayor Dodd, and three other officials, Polk set out for New England. He got to work at once. His advertisement appeared on the

[13] Daybooks, ledgers, bills, receipts, business letters, advertisements, newspaper clippings, and similar material in the Polk Papers give detailed information on this enterprise of Polk's.
[14] Raleigh *Evening Visitor*, Sept. 12, 1882.

cover of 10,000 sheets of popular music; 250,000 pamphlets were circulated; a large "fancy picture" for drug stores was distributed. "These things," noted the *Farmer and Mechanic,* "take time, labor, and money; but they are absolutely necessary to success."[15]

From all evidence, the partnership of Polk and Holman was not a happy one. Holman withdrew within a year. Polk then organized a stock company and moved to New York. Attracted perhaps by a serious epidemic there, he established himself at 24 West 14th Street, "in the heart of the fashionable shopping region." Ever hopeful, he attempted to qualify for a $5,000 prize offered by the French Academy of Medicine and also wrote Senator Zeb Vance that if Congress would offer a reward of $100,000 for the discovery of a real diphtheria cure, *"the remedy will be forthcoming."*[16] This was the Gilded Age, when men made fortunes overnight, and stranger things had happened. As late as February, 1887, he was still advertising his solution and looking for capital to back it, but by that time the scheme had died a natural death. Even so, for many years after Polk's death in 1892 members of his family received numerous requests for the medicine. Though "Polk's Diphtheria Cure" was by no means a disastrous failure, its success was limited. Sales volume appeared to be comparatively large, but heavy expenses seem to have consumed most of the profits.

Obviously, the efforts to make money had ended in frustration. With Dodd, Polk and Company, L. L. Polk and Company, and "Polk's Diphtheria Cure" in mind, Josephus Daniels has written: "He went into business for which he had no training, perhaps no fitness. Naturally, success was not attained. . . . This generation has forgotten the days in the early eighties when Colonel Polk seemed to have failed, when his influence was well nigh negligible in the State."[17]

Was this failure, or darkness before dawn?

---

[15] *Farmer and Mechanic,* May 7, 1884.
[16] Polk to Dr. Edward Warren, April 18, 1883; Polk to Vance, Dec. 15, 1884.
[17] Josephus Daniels, in *News and Observer,* July 29, 1926.

CHAPTER IX

THE PROGRESSIVE FARMER

DURING THE 1880's the Civil War heritage of North Carolina often made the general outlook seem gloomy. The South had been defeated in battle and thereby had failed to win its independence. Four years of exhausting war and twelve more of confusing "reconstruction" had brought an unparalleled poverty to the region. Failure and poverty together accentuated a provincialism that already, since long before the war, had been fostered by ignorance and resentment of criticism. The race problem, of course, bulked most significant of all. Contemplation of the recent past tended to render North Carolina apathetic toward the immediate future. "Overmuch brooding," said Irvin S. Cobb, "made her slothful. She was like a desolated maiden who quits washing her neck and ears."[1]

The Democratic Party gained full control of the state government in 1877, the year that Federal troops were withdrawn from the South. By reflecting the popular abhorrence of "Negro rule," by appealing to the memory of the "Lost Cause," and by promising financial economy, the native white Conservatives and Democrats won the support of the majority of the people. Their leaders were the misnamed "Bourbons," whose dominance in the state lasted until 1890.

Contrary to widespread belief, the Bourbons were not restored ante-bellum planters or even their spiritual descendants. They constituted a new class entirely. They advocated reconciliation with the North and industrialization of the South, and Henry W.

[1] Irvin S. Cobb, *North Carolina*, p. 39.

Grady was their prophet. After the war, the center of economic and political gravity slowly shifted from country to town. Returning prosperity touched merchants, money-lenders, manufacturers, railroad promoters, investors, and lawyers long before it did farmers and planters. Consciously and unconsciously, federal, state, and local governments began to favor business at the expense of agriculture. All through the 'eighties and 'nineties the farmer fought a brave but losing battle against the powerful combination opposing him.

Politically, Bourbonism arose as the reaction to Radical Reconstruction. The main policies of the New Democrats were to practice financial economy and to guarantee white supremacy. Their government in North Carolina seemed generally clean and honest and had the effect of calming the state so that the industrial movement could get under way. Their economy—and timidity—relieved the people of heavy taxation but spread needed social services extremely thin. Support of public education was meager. Little social legislation was encouraged. As the years passed, the Bourbons concentrated so intensely upon keeping the Negro out of office and keeping themselves in, that they became deaf to all cries for reform, fearing a split in the white vote. Social and economic progress was thus gravely paralyzed.

Content with the *status quo,* the Bourbons failed to comprehend the problems of a changing age. Confident that recollection of the "Lost Cause" and dread of "Negro rule" would always rally the majority to their side, they felt their power secure. Radical Reconstruction had given the Bourbons the excuse that, in self-defense, they should try to win and rule by any methods they could. Eventually both Democrats and Republicans reached the crystallization point: neither argued real issues or looked intelligently to the future. "Nowhere," Professor Connor has said, "is there a better illustration of Jefferson's theory that a political thunderstorm is necessary in a democracy at least once every generation."[2]

[2] Robert D. W. Connor, *North Carolina: Rebuilding an Ancient Commonwealth,* II. 431.

Wise old Governor Jarvis had given fair warning in 1881. Speaking particularly to his victorious Democratic colleagues, he declared in his inaugural address: "You cannot, as a party, afford to stand still. The State must go forward, and if you will not seize this golden opportunity to guide and direct her progress, the people will look for leaders outside of your ranks. If you expect to receive popular support in the future, you must do so on works performed for the public good."[3]

When Polk in 1883 went to Boston and New York to engage in business, he had no intention of leaving North Carolina permanently. He merely wanted to make some money. Then he would return to such private enterprise and public service as he might choose. After two years afield, however, his fortune had not swelled as he had hoped, and there seemed to be little chance that it would. So he came back home. His roots lay deep in North Carolina, and his concern for its welfare no one questioned. His heart still appeared to be with the farmers. Traces of printer's ink remained on his fingers, too.

In 1885 L. L. Polk developed plans to establish a weekly paper devoted to agriculture and all its problems. He negotiated with a number of advertisers whose response was satisfactory. He also informed many of his friends of the project and felt heartened by their support. D. McN. McKay, an old friend, wrote him:

> With the *vim* I know you possess and your popularity with the farmers of the state, I can see nothing against your succeeding in the enterprise. The time *now* is auspicious. The material at hand to make an aggressive campaign in behalf of the defrauded farmers of N. C. is super-abundant. They *feel* their wrongs and they intend to have redress. Their neglect is too glaring, their impositions are too burdensome —too grievous to be longer tolerated. . . . Let us have the paper, let it be a genuine *advocate* of the farmer's rights, and have it so, exclusively. . . . there is a limit to silence even in the submissiveness of farmers. . . . If ever the farmers needed a paper it is now. It is true the editor of it, such as *you* must

[3] *North Carolina Public Documents, 1881*, No. 22, p. 13.

be, has to be a bold man, and, also, an independent one. . . . He must be prudent with all. . . . Hoist your standard, my friend, and let us on to victory! The skies are bright!! Vance said in his inaugural that, "There is retribution in history." When we farmers succeed in doing for ourselves what we contemplate, then I shall believe it.[4]

Syd Alexander advised Polk to edit his paper mainly on the eclectic plan; that is, subscribe to or exchange with as many reputable agricultural journals as possible, foreign as well as American, and make up most of the paper from their most useful material. In that way he could offer each week to the North Carolina farmer "the essence of the brains of the world." He urged Polk not to be afraid of rejecting all the commonplace articles sent him by "'unsophisticated' old boys who know they know it all."[5]

Polk originally planned to publish his paper in Raleigh. He found, however, that better business arrangements were possible in Winston. This lusty young town was experiencing at that time a commercial and building boom which had been stimulated by the rapid development of the tobacco industry and other industries in its vicinity. Located in the Piedmont county of Forsyth, Winston doubled and redoubled in size during the 'eighties. Its population, combined with that of the adjoining town of Salem, was approaching 10,000. Colonel Polk, with his family, moved to Winston with the intention of making this editorship his life's work.

He chose *The Progressive Farmer* as the name for his paper. From the office on Fourth Street the first number issued on February 10, 1886, and a remarkable journalistic adventure began.[6]

Naturally the *Progressive Farmer* showed the influence of the

[4] D. McN. McKay to Polk, Oct. 12, 1885.

[5] Sydenham B. Alexander to Polk, Nov. 14, 1885.

[6] John D. Hicks, in "The Farmers' Alliance in North Carolina," *North Carolina Historical Review*, II, 169 (April, 1925), has erroneously stated that Polk established the *Progressive Farmer* in 1866 and was later called to Raleigh to become Commissioner of Agriculture. The error has been repeated in Connor, *North Carolina*, II, 432, and other works.

three journals with which its editor had previously been associated. From the Polkton *Ansonian* came Polk's editorial personality, his devotion to the local community, his interest in state and national affairs, and his old slogan "fearlessly the right defend, impartially the wrong condemn." From the Raleigh *News* came the reporting of special events, the column on practical agriculture, and a motto. "As a citizen of the State," he wrote in 1880 and repeated in 1886, "our whole political creed may be embodied in this brief and simple platform: *The advancement of our educational and material interests should be paramount to all other considerations of State policy.*"[7] Chiefly, however, the *Progressive Farmer* derived from the early *Farmer and Mechanic*. In size, typography, general appearance, subject matter, departments, unpolitical character, and spirit of service, it bore a close resemblance to the paper which had been the organ of the Department of Agriculture from 1877 to 1879.

Above all else, the *Progressive Farmer* claimed to be a paper for the North Carolina farmer and his family. The first essential, therefore, was practical instruction in up-to-date farming. In the first two months appeared discussions of ensilage and silos, potato culture, beekeeping, egg production, and fruit canning. Also, since the paper stood in the center of a rich tobacco region, it presented a series of articles on how to manage tobacco—from the plant-bed to the warehouse. Polk followed Alexander's advice and included many excerpts from other farm journals on the subject of agricultural methods and policies.

That section of the paper headed "Correspondence" revealed that Polk found it possible to tap the talent of leading North Carolina farmers as well. Some of the *Progressive Farmer's* most valuable material came from this source. Writing from Enderly Farm near Charlotte, Syd Alexander himself sent in a series of articles on cattle-raising. Professor George F. Atkinson of the University of North Carolina contributed another series on in-

---

[7] Raleigh *News,* Sept. 1, 1880; *Progressive Farmer,* Feb. 10, 1886.

jurious insects. Other articles of the kind, appearing in 1886 and 1887, included: "Fruit Trees—Transplanting and Cultivating," "An Ideal, Yet Possible Acre of Corn," "Do Not Leave the Farm— Let Our Young Men Read and Ponder," "The Industrial Classes vs. the Vultures," "Oats," "Investigating the Causes of Depression," "Legislation the Farmer Needs," "Grass Culture," "Tenant Farming," "Hard Times, the Cause and Cure," "Neglected Schools," "Farming as a Business," "Capital and Labor," "A Farmer Boy Speaks," and "The Chemistry of Wine." Among them too was "Food, Its Preparation and Its Relation to Health," by Annie L. Alexander, North Carolina's first woman Doctor of Medicine.

These contributions reached a high level of merit for a publication of this kind. Perhaps the editorial standard expressed by Polk in the following words addressed to a correspondent provides a clue: "L.T.F.—Article too long. Besides you are too fond of theorizing. This is a practical age. Our readers want *facts*. If you have produced an extra yield of Potatoes, Corn, Wheat, Hay, Cotton, Tobacco, &c., tell us how you did it and stop. One such *fact* is worth ten columns of *theory* as to how it might be done."[8]

For the women members of the farm family the *Progressive Farmer* had much to offer in the way of recipes, special articles, and poetry. In the issues of the first year alone appeared recipes for such tempting preparations as cookies, plum pudding, chicken pie, "a good cup of coffee," ginger crackers, brown Betty, popovers, corn bread, one-egg cake, orange cake, smothered chicken, charlotte russe, apple pudding, beef tea, jelly roll, fried chicken, stewed steak, corn fritters, peach-water ice, tapioca pudding, roast turkey, mince pie, doughnuts, and fruit cake. Among the articles written especially to appeal to women were "Manners for Boys," "Bright's Disease," "Bathing," "Relief for Toothache," "Tact in Baby Management," "The Future Mrs. Cleveland," "Wisdom for Those About to Marry" (which included the admonition: "Never speak in loud tones to one another unless the house is on fire"),

[8] *Progressive Farmer*, Feb. 10, 1886.

"Uses of Ammonia," "Removing Objects from the Eye," "To Destroy Red Ants," "Advantages of Low Ceilings," "Our Presidents," "Hints to Housekeepers" (which ran serially), "Night Air," "Canning," "Breadmaking," "How Stoves Are Put Up," "How Looking-glasses Are Made," and "The Coming Girl." The poems printed or reprinted in the paper usually centered about such themes as mother, home, fireside, kitchen, love, work, and worship. "When the Cows Come Home," "Portrait of a Lady," "We've Always Been Provided For," "The Land of the Afternoon," and "The Old Mill" were typical examples.

"Flashes of Fun," a column containing jokes, puns, and riddles, was naturally one of the most popular parts of the paper. "Bill Arp" was also a regular feature. When this Georgia humorist, whose real name was Charles Henry Smith, visited Winston and other points in North Carolina, Polk gained the right to publish his amusing tales and sketches. In August, 1891, "Zeke Bilkins" made his *début*. A *Progressive Farmer* creation, Zeke was depicted as a shrewd old farmer with a persistent curiosity regarding public affairs. Each week he would call some editor or politician on the telephone, ask him questions, and debate with him. Zeke often seemed perplexed, but by the time the conversation had ended the other party was invariably discomfited. Such was Zeke's method of proving the soundness of his—that is, the *Progressive Farmer's* —point of view.

Polk likewise endeavored to keep the business standards of his paper high. After ten issues had come from the press, he wrote: "Readers of the PROGRESSIVE FARMER cannot have failed to notice . . . that there is not an advertisement of a questionable character in its columns; no swindles, no lotteries, no catches to cheat unwary people out of their money; nothing to harm or rob man, woman or child. And what is more, there never will be. . . . We shall publish a *clean* paper, which cannot be made the tool of fraud of any kind. . . ."[9] He carried out this promise faithfully.

[9] *Progressive Farmer*, April 14, 1886.

Most of his advertisements came from small business houses in Winston and Raleigh. There were Smith and Brown, druggists; the Winston Agricultural Works; George E. Nissen and Company, wagon manufacturers; A. C. Vogler, furniture and undertaking; S. E. Allen, hardware and crockery; J. W. Denmark and Company, booksellers; the North Carolina Home Insurance Company; Norris and Carter, general merchandise; J. W. Watson, photographer; the Piedmont Warehouse of Winston and the Parrish Warehouse of Durham; the Pomona Hill Nurseries; and many others. Newspapers, religious weeklies, and educational institutions also advertised in the *Progressive Farmer*. This policy, too, continued until his death.

In his new paper Polk resumed a campaign that he had begun in the *Ansonian* and had continued as Commissioner of Agriculture and as an editor of the Raleigh *News*. This was the campaign to persuade Southern farmers to diversify their crops and raise all their necessary food supplies at home. The passing of a dozen years had in no way altered his views as to the evils of the one-crop system. The situation now seemed even worse.

"It was a fearful mistake," Polk told the farmers, "when you made this trade with the North: 'Make everything in the world that we need and a thousand things we don't need—send them to us at your own price and we will take them. We will raise *one* crop with which to pay you and *you* may put *your price* on *that* crop.'"[10] Instead, said Polk, farmers should first raise their own bread and meat. Only when that was done should they undertake money crops like cotton or tobacco. If this rule were followed, the farmers would undoubtedly become self-sufficient and independent. Their security would no longer depend upon the vagaries of trade. If their money crop should fail or bring too low a price, they would still have something to fall back on and would thus avoid the clutches of the mortgage-holder. The one-crop system exhausted the soil and called for too much use of

[10] *Progressive Farmer*, Feb. 16, 1887.

commercial fertilizers; wise diversification protected and enriched the land with grass, clover, and natural manures.

A young farmer reported to Polk: "I don't know that I handle much money by the plan, but I always try to raise my own supplies at home. I took an old farm eleven years ago and could produce only two bales of cotton to the plow and thirty barrels of corn. Now I raise ten bales of cotton and sixty barrels of corn to the plow. I have not cleared an acre of land and use compost." "That man," declared Polk, "is a success as a farmer."[11]

The *Progressive Farmer* occasionally echoed other old Polk campaigns. One was immigration. Give us *"neighbors, not laborers,"* he said, despairing of Southern Negroes and Northern or European "riffraff" alike.[12] Another was better roads—to improve mail and market facilities. "We appreciate the value of railroads," he wrote, "in this day of speed and progress. But good country roads are of quite as much if not more importance than railroads."[13] In this connection Polk gave his opinion on the convict labor question. He held that convicts should be employed on public works such as road-building and repair rather than be leased to private concerns at purely nominal cost and thus compete with honest labor.

All these things—practical agricultural instruction, informative articles, recipes, poetry, humor, small-business advertising, and campaigns for diversified crops and better roads—might have characterized almost any farm periodical of the time. The *Progressive Farmer,* however, seemed to be without doubt the best agricultural paper ever published in North Carolina. Indeed, it took exceptionally high rank in the whole nation. Polk worked hard to keep it there. By maintaining it as a real organ of the farmers and by crusading with pen and tongue for the farmers' rights, he soon made it a power in the life of the state. In its editorial voice, in time to come, lay its greatest strength.

[11] *Progressive Farmer*, Aug. 11, 1887.
[12] *Progressive Farmer*, Oct. 6, 13, 1886, Dec. 11, 1888, Nov. 26, 1889.
[13] *Progressive Farmer*, Feb. 2, 1887.

The first number revealed that Polk intended for the time being to concentrate on two main issues. One was the reorganization of the state Department of Agriculture, a subject already noted in Chapter VII. The other was the establishment of a state agricultural and mechanical college, which will be discussed in the next chapter. Polk well knew that the achievement of these great objectives would require much more than editorials and speeches. The matter clearly called for the farmers as a body to make their weight felt politically. In recognition of this elementary truth, Polk determined, as a necessary preliminary, to organize farmers' clubs all over North Carolina.

Farmers' organizations were not new in the state. They had existed in some forms before the Civil War. It is not necessary, however, to go further back than the period of Polk's own manhood to notice examples of farmer co-operation prior to the founding of the *Progressive Farmer*.

In the Littleton community of Halifax County in 1858 a small group of farmers organized the "Pioneer Agricultural Club." They restricted the number of members to twelve, adopted a constitution, and held monthly meetings. According to the corresponding secretary, "the principal object we have in view, and the one by which we hope to profit most, is the monthly visit to the farm of some member of the Club, by the whole Club, where we propose to make a minute examination of his farming operations, his mode of cultivation, the condition of his team, hogs, farming utensils, wagons, carts, &c." This would be followed by discussion and helpful suggestions, and it was hoped that the result would be stimulation to greater individual effort. After attending a meeting by invitation in 1880, Polk called the Littleton group "a model farmers' club." He found the original organization unchanged and the members deeply interested in agricultural problems of all kinds.[14]

In 1868 the *Carolina Farmer* of Wilmington proposed that each

[14] Raleigh *North-Carolina Planter*, I, 235 (Aug., 1858); *News*, July 10, 1880.

county set up a central agricultural society composed of at least six neighborhood farmers' clubs. Going a step further, the "Farmers' Mutual Aid Association" of Mecklenburg County called in 1871 for a farmers' state convention—"for the purpose of a general and thorough organization." A state agricultural convention did take place in Raleigh the following year; nearly two hundred farmers assembled to discuss their problems and pass resolutions.[15] Efforts like these were not in themselves effective, but the spirit that provoked them was caught up in the Granger movement which swept into North Carolina in the middle 'seventies. For a time the Grange served as the greatest medium of agrarian discontent. Yet the Grange declined so rapidly after 1877 that during the 'eighties it was strictly a moribund organization.

By 1886 the field was thus clear. Such agricultural organizations as did exist were pitifully weak. Still, the causes of agrarian discontent had multiplied, and the need for co-operation seemed greater than ever before. Organization, Polk pointed out, was a trend of the times. In order to advance their respective interests railroad executives, steamship owners, bankers, merchants, and manufacturers all had organized. Consequently, control of rates, interest, loans, and tariff was passing into their hands, and the farmers were paying for it. Even laborers could unite successfully, as the growth of the Knights of Labor testified. Polk thought it high time the farmers organized for their own protection. The farmers of North Carolina, he said, should make a concentrated effort to impress their views upon the state legislature whenever that body debated any matter of special interest to farmers. The *Progressive Farmer* would back them to the limit.[16]

The foundation of the organizational structure would be the individual farmers' club, representing the township or school district. Here neighborhood agricultural problems could be dis-

[15] Wilmington *Carolina Farmer*, I, 52 (Dec., 1868), IV, 89 (March, 1872); Charlotte *Southern Home*, Nov. 28, 1871, Jan. 23, 1872.
[16] *Progressive Farmer*, March 10, 31, Nov. 10, 1886.

cussed, policies formulated, and the advantages of social intercourse and education enjoyed. The clubs should meet as often as possible. Polk suggested that they choose delegates to a county organization which would meet once a month. Then, after the counties were thoroughly organized, the county units could send delegates to an annual farmers' state convention. Eventually, the various state organizations might come together as a great national body of farmers.[17]

Polk started the ball rolling on April 10, 1886, when, with a speech at "Boyer's school house" in Forsyth County, he inspired the formation of a large club near Winston. Week after week during the following year the *Progressive Farmer* happily announced the birth and noted the progress of other clubs in various parts of the state. One of the strongest from the beginning was "The Farmers' Circle" of Trinity College in Randolph County. By September, enough neighborhood clubs had been established in Forsyth and Anson for these two to form county clubs, and other counties were soon ready to do likewise. A sizable number of North Carolina farmers, apparently, were in a mood receptive to the plea that they organize.

Taking as much time away from the *Progressive Farmer* office as he dared, Polk actively assisted others in laying the groundwork of organization. His engagements for a typical week—December 4-10—included six places in as many counties: Wake Forest College in Wake, Henderson in Vance, Wilton in Granville, Merry Oaks in Chatham, Pocket in Moore, and Lillington in Harnett. Prior to such a trip, he would announce in the paper: "I propose to discuss questions in which every farmer and every good citizen in the State is vitally interested. I would be glad to meet the young and old. Come out and bring your families and baskets and devote one day to your interests."[18]

As the leader of this agrarian movement, Polk had several

[17] *Progressive Farmer*, May 5, 1886, April 28, 1887.
[18] *Progressive Farmer*, July 7, 1887.

suggestions to offer the growing number of farmers' clubs. Above all, he wrote, a club should meet regularly, and its officers should be prompt and faithful. Some question of special interest to the members ought to be debated at each meeting. A good plan would be to have each member bring a written question to meeting and deposit it in a box provided for the purpose. Then a "query committee" could select a topic for the next meeting, together with affirmative and negative representatives to debate it. There were many interesting and important questions that could be discussed. For example:

—Is it wise to produce any one crop to the exclusion of others, and depend on buying farm supplies?
—What is the least price at which we can afford to raise tobacco or cotton?
—Is it wise or safe to give crop liens or mortgages?
—Should our public roads be worked better, and if so, how?
—Is the extensive use of commercial fertilizers, as now practiced by our farmers, a benefit or an evil to the agricultural interests?
—What is the best home-made compost for tobacco, and how is it made? What for cotton?
—What benefits can the farmers derive from organization? . . .
—Could sheep-raising be made profitable in our section? . . .
—How does the "stock law" benefit us?
—Would a county fair be beneficial to us?
. . . What constitutes the comforts of a farmer's home, and are they attainable? . . . What is the cheapest and best method of raising and fattening pork? What is the best method for reclaiming old wornout lands? What is the best method for making manure on the farm? . . . Does our tenant system pay? . . . What benefits do we derive from our State Agricultural Department? What may this club do to push forward the work of organization among the farmers of our county? What papers should farmers and their families read? [19]

[19] *Progressive Farmer*, May 12, 1886, May 5, 1887.

Mindful of the success of Littleton's "Pioneer Agricultural Club," Polk further suggested that club meetings, whenever practicable, be held at the home of some member, so that the other members might examine and discuss his premises, methods, crops, and stock. Also, it would be good if, once a year, the club would hold a picnic or other social gathering in which all the members and their families could participate. Finally, some plan should be adopted by which disputes and difficulties between members could be arbitrated and settled within the club, so as to avoid needless litigation and costs, and unfortunate feuds. Polk stood ready to mail forms of a constitution and by-laws to organizers and officers upon their request.

Women were welcomed into the farmers' clubs as honorary members. This was deemed desirable, not only because of the social benefits that accrued, but because farm problems of particular concern to women were sometimes discussed in the clubs. Among them were such superficially trivial yet actually important matters as milking, and the distance of the spring or woodshed from the house. Polk tried to look a little beyond the goal of economic betterment. He declared that farmers should not set out solely to make money but should strive to build pleasant and comfortable homes. The farm should be made more attractive to the boys and girls so that they would not leave it so readily. Their interests should be animated by giving them definite duties to perform, by showing them exactly how to do farm work, and by letting them have something of their own to raise and sell. In this, the women might well take the lead.[20]

It was not long before the clubs had made the farmers do a great deal of "thinking, talking and acting," as Polk put it. They had proved their educational value. Already many farmers had taken up new agricultural methods. The economic advantages of this practical education were soon demonstrated. The Mountain

[20] *Progressive Farmer,* March 10, Nov. 3, Dec. 8, 1886.

Creek Club of Richmond County, to take an example, saved its members about $1,000 on their farm purchases in 1886.[21]

Educationally, the regional farmers' institutes carried out the farmers' club idea. In North Carolina these followed closely the pattern of the teachers' institutes. At one such gathering held in Greensboro by the farmers of Guilford and adjoining counties, eighteen papers or addresses were presented during the two-day session. To list them would indicate the scope of a typical institute. They included: "Department of Agriculture," by Commissioner John Robinson; "Commercial Fertilizers," by Peter M. Wilson; "Agricultural Chemistry and Home Fertilizers," by Dr. Charles W. Dabney, State Chemist; "Clover," by Colonel Thomas M. Holt; "The Dairy," by D. W. C. Benbow; "Agricultural College," by Henry E. Fries; and, by farmers and teachers well-posted on their specialties, "Farm Education," "Does the Farm Pay?" "Stock Raising," "How Shall We Keep Our Boys on the Farm?" "The Orchard," "Tobacco Culture," "Ensilage, and Its Effect on Stock," "Special Crops," "Strawberries," "Cherries," and "Cooking."[22] A few of these later appeared as articles in the *Progressive Farmer*. Polk's address at this meeting was "Shall We Diversify Our Crops?"; at a Raleigh institute he spoke on "the needs of our agriculture"; and at Rockingham, on "the absolute importance of organization and co-operation among the farmers."[23]

By January, 1887—eleven months after the founding of the *Progressive Farmer,* and only nine months after the initiation of the farmers' club movement—a large number of North Carolina farmers were actually organized for concerted action on a state-wide basis. They had begun, moreover, to turn their backs upon the dead issues of the recent past and to turn their faces toward the living issues of the immediate future. They believed that North

[21] *Progressive Farmer*, Jan. 26, 1887.
[22] *Progressive Farmer*, May 12, 1887.
[23] *Progressive Farmer*, Nov. 10, 1887.

Carolina and the South needed "less of political claptrap and glory and more of sound statesmanship and dollars."[24] Polk was their leader and the *Progressive Farmer* their guidepost. "The farmers of North Carolina," Polk wrote, "may not get all they ask nor all they desire this year nor next year, but if they cling together and persevere it is but a question of a little time when they will get not only all they ask but they will be offered more than they have thought of asking. . . . They want the recognition they are entitled to in shaping the policy of the State. . . ."[25]

The time was ripe. The farmers' clubs were on the march. The first significant victory lay just ahead.

[24] *Progressive Farmer*, Oct. 20, 1887.
[25] *Progressive Farmer*, March 2, 1887.

Chapter X

THE FARMER BUILDS A COLLEGE

IN THE NORMAL COURSE of nature a new generation had grown up. Twenty years after the Civil War, in the middle 1880's, the *young* men appeared in the South—questioning, criticizing, hoping, planning, and dreaming. They chafed under the rule of the stodgy Bourbons. They wanted to throw off the chains of fear and timidity and retrospection fastened upon them by a reactionary oligarchy. They were ready to move on into the future.

Under the guidance of young men of ambition and initiative, the South was making striking material progress. Cotton mills and railroads were multiplying, and cities were growing up fast. There was, indeed, new hope in the New South.

Yet not all progress was easy. The forces opposing change were strong. The leaders of the people, given to Confederate hero-worship, strict orthodoxy in politics and religion, and keeping the black man in his "place," discouraged new ideas. Social and educational advances came very slowly.

In North Carolina, all the same, an interesting group of young men determined to press forward. Banding themselves together in May, 1884, as an informal association which they called the Watauga Club, they proposed to stimulate among their membership the freest possible discussion of the state's industrial, agricultural, and educational needs. This flexible discussion group was not large, and its members were virtually all under thirty, but it contained a high degree of intelligence and an abundant measure of enthusiasm. Its leaders were William J. Peele, brilliant and modest lawyer, and Walter H. Page, dynamic editor who in later life was best known as Woodrow Wilson's Ambassador to Great Britain. Politics was expressly avoided. The name "Watauga," chosen because it would signify little or nothing to outsiders, pleased the members on account of its derivation from the Watauga Association, which under John Sevier in pioneer days struggled to create a new state in the wilderness. "To have called it the Progressive Club," one of its members has written, "would have been like waving a red flag in the faces of the politicians." [1]

Meeting from time to time in Raleigh, their common home, these young men held many stirring "talkfests." They heard and said a great deal about developing North Carolina's resources, about training men to operate the state's new industries, about improving agriculture, about broadening educational opportunities, and about bettering the lot of the common man. Before undertaking any charge upon the Bourbon lines, however, they wisely decided to concentrate upon a single issue. In 1885, therefore, they broached the establishment of an industrial school.

The Watauga Club intensively examined the whole field of technical education. Then, through a committee headed by Arthur Winslow, a graduate of the Massachusetts Institute of Technology, and including Peele and Page, the Club petitioned the General Assembly as follows:

> 1st. To establish an Industrial School in North Carolina, which shall be a training place for young men who wish to acquire skill in the wealth-producing arts and sciences.
> 2nd. To establish this school at Raleigh, in connection with the State Agricultural Department.
> 3rd. To make provision for the erection of suitable buildings and for their equipment and maintenance.

The authors continued:

> Having given this subject our full consideration, after careful study, we further respectfully submit the following suggestions:

[1] Charles W. Dabney, *Universal Education in the South*, I, 182-88.

1st. That instruction at this school be in woodwork, mining, metallurgy, practical agriculture and in such other branches of industrial education as may be deemed expedient.

2nd. That the necessary shops, laboratories, etc., be erected adjoining the building of the Agricultural Department, and that, in addition, an Experimental Farm be established in the vicinity of Raleigh, which shall be properly equipped.

There followed a detailed explanation, written by Dr. Charles W. Dabney, of the advantages of such a school, the need for one in North Carolina, and the matters of location and cost.[2]

The Wataugans succeeded in arousing much interest in the project. With the particular support of certain legislators—sympathetic young men like Augustus Leazer, Thomas Dixon, and Robert W. Winston and older progressives like Sydenham B. Alexander, Willis R. Williams, and John Gatling—a bill soon passed. The bill directed the state Board of Agriculture to consider any North Carolina locality's inducements in the way of land, buildings, equipment, or money and to apply to the industrial school any funds that were not required for the regular operation of the Department of Agriculture.[3]

The great weakness of the "act to establish and maintain an industrial school" was that complete control was vested in the Board of Agriculture. The friends of the proposed institution conceived of it mainly as a school of technology. Agricultural education would be subordinate. Yet the Department of Agriculture was apparently the only state agency to which the school could conveniently be connected. A direct appropriation for an industrial school seemed at that time entirely out of the question. Experience had shown that this Board usually moved with all the dash and spirit of a glacier. So when months passed without any real progress, the Watauga Club, together with other inter-

---

[2] Watauga Club, *The Need of an Industrial School in North Carolina* . . . ; William J. Peele, "A History of the Agricultural and Mechanical College," *North Carolina Teacher*, VI, No. 1, pp. 12-21 (Sept., 1888).

[3] *North Carolina Public Laws, 1885*, pp. 553-54 (ch. 308).

ested citizens of Raleigh, staged a mass meeting for the purpose of prodding the Board to action.

"A GREAT SUCCESS," the Raleigh *News and Observer* called it.[4] At this meeting of November 11, 1885, a number of prominent men were warm in their endorsement of the industrial school idea. Letters in like vein were read from others who could not be present. The latter included L. L. Polk, who wrote: "Be assured of my earnest interest in this undertaking. How shall our youth be taught and prepared to make an honest living? This, in my judgment, is the great and paramount question of the hour. Practical training—practical education, is the only solution."[5] William J. Peele presented resolutions looking to the establishment of the school in Raleigh.

At a meeting of the Board of Agriculture in January, 1886, representatives of the capital city offered $5,000 in cash, a one-acre lot in the city, and the Exposition buildings west of the city with twenty acres of land adjoining. They confidently considered their proposal attractive enough to win acceptance. The Board, however, declaring that the funds were not sufficient, decided to postpone the whole matter.[6]

Those who had fought for the industrial school were indeed exasperated. Their feelings were well expressed by Walter H. Page in the first of a famous series that soon came to be known as the "mummy letters." Page's Raleigh *State Chronicle* had failed financially some months before, and he had left the state. From New York City he sent the letters to his friend and successor, Josephus Daniels, who printed them. It was soon after the decision of the Board of Agriculture that Page wrote:

> It is an awfully discouraging business to undertake to prove to a mummy that it is a mummy. . . . The old thing grins that grin which death set on its solemn features when the

[4] Raleigh *News and Observer*, Nov. 12, 1885, *passim*.
[5] Raleigh *State Chronicle*, Nov. 19, 1885, *passim*.
[6] *News and Observer*, Jan. 22, 23, 1886.

world was young; and your task is so pitiful that even the humor of it is gone.

Give it up. It can't be done. We all think when we are young that we can do something with the mummies. But the mummy is a solemn fact, and it differs from all other things (except stones) in this—it lasts forever. They don't want an Industrial School. That means a new idea, and a new idea is death to the supremacy of the mummies. . . .

. . . Old Governor Swain didn't want the railroad to go by Chapel Hill. We laugh at that now. Yet President Battle doesn't want an Industrial School; and who will say that President Battle is a greater man than old Governor Swain? . . .

. . . In God's name, with such a state, filled with such people, with such opportunities, are we to sit down quietly forever and allow every enterprise that means growth, every idea that means intellectual freedom to perish, and the State to lag behind always, because a few amiable mummies will be offended? It would be cheaper to pension them all, than longer listen to them. . . .

A week later, writing of the industrial school, Page said: "You see and know and feel the great burden of silent opposition to it. It is that opposition that kills. To be candid, I never expect to see it." [7]

Those still on the battleground, however, did not give up. Their unceasing fire slowly forced the Board to yield. In April, Raleigh's increased cash donation of $8,000 was deemed sufficient, but establishment of the school was postponed by a vote of seven to five. By July, not only did Raleigh offer additional land for a site, but pressure on the Board was becoming intense, and that body finally voted, eight to four, for the establishment of the school in Raleigh.

[7] *State Chronicle,* Feb. 4, 11, 1886. The disparaging reference in the first letter to Kemp P. Battle, president of the University of North Carolina, and the pessimistic allusion to the industrial school in the second letter are not included in the "mummy letters" as edited by Page's biographer, Burton J. Hendrick, *The Training of an American: the Earlier Life and Letters of Walter H. Page, 1855-1913,* pp. 177, 181-83.

Yet the movement for an industrial school went no further; in the summer of 1886 it was absorbed into a much greater and more powerful movement—the struggle for a land-grant agricultural and mechanical college.

Opposition to the industrial school was led by Kemp P. Battle, president of the University of North Carolina, and Alfred M. Scales, governor of the state, both of them members of the Board of Agriculture. Those two in particular were in Page's mind when he railed against the "mummies."

More than ingrained conservatism, though, accounted for Battle's resistance. The University, with a proud past dating back to 1795, had been forced to close its doors for several years after the Civil War because of political and financial difficulties. But with the invaluable assistance of the annual $7,500 interest on the land scrip fund provided by the Federal Government under the Morrill Act, the Chapel Hill school in 1875 had reopened, and with Battle as its new president was pushing bravely forward. From time to time someone would suggest that the land scrip fund should not go to the University, a "literary" institution, but should be applied to the creation of a "practical" school of agriculture and the mechanic arts. In the legislature of 1885 Representative E. F. Lovill, of Watauga County (fitting coincidence!), proposed that the $7,500 a year be diverted from the University to the new industrial school. Even though his proposal was defeated, the University president regarded it as a serious threat and determined, naturally enough, to keep the fund at all hazards.

The Morrill Land-Grant Act of 1862 was "an act donating public lands to the several States and Territories which may provide colleges for the benefit of agriculture and the mechanic arts." By its terms any state that accepted the Government's offer was granted from within its own borders 30,000 acres of public land for each senator and representative in Congress to which it was entitled under the 1860 apportionment. States that did not have the requisite amount of public land, like North Carolina, were issued land scrip. An accepting state was required to sell its land or scrip and invest the proceeds in securities yielding at least five per cent interest. The capital fund was to remain "forever undiminished," although up to ten per cent of it could be used for the purchase of college sites and experimental farms. It was the annual interest that was to be appropriated for "the endowment, support, and maintenance of at least one college, where the leading object shall be . . . to teach such branches of learning as are related to agriculture and the mechanic arts . . . in order to promote the liberal and practical education of the industrial classes. . . ." [8]

With this federal aid some states established new agricultural and mechanical colleges, while others expanded institutions already in existence. The General Assembly accepted North Carolina's quota in February, 1866, and a year later transferred the scrip to the trustees of the State University. In those troubled times the trustees made such a poor investment of the fund that it was completely lost. A few years later, however, the legislature restored the fund, and the University began to receive the interest.

When the General Assembly first designated the University of North Carolina as the recipient of the land-grant donation, the *Carolina Farmer,* of Wilmington, sounded a warning note:

> According to both the spirit and the letter of the law, the institution which receives this munificent endowment must become by the very terms of the grant, if not already such, an agricultural and mechanical college. . . . Classical and scientific studies not directly connected with the leading object are not excluded, but their pursuit must be *subordinated* to the great object of the donation. We hope that this requirement will be fairly met. The trustees of the University are general[l]y professional men and politicians, and are in some

[8] Benjamin F. Andrews, "The Land Grant of 1862 and the Land-Grant Colleges," United States Bureau of Education, *Bulletin, 1918,* No. 13, pp. 7-11, 36-38.

danger of placing an underestimate on the importance of agricultural education. They cannot however ignore the fact (we do not charge on them any disposition to do so) that the great interest of our State is agricultural. The University in accepting this donation, has assumed the responsibilities attached to it, and the agriculturists of the State are fairly entitled to expect that the income arising from this source shall be applied faithfully to the objects set forth in the Act of Congress.[9]

This friendly caution was wholly justified, for by 1886 it was clear to fair-minded people that the University's service to agriculture and the mechanic arts was definitely unsatisfactory.

As a part of a nation-wide trend toward more democratic and more practical education, the idea of a real agricultural college in North Carolina engaged the attention of many men over a period of many years. Before the Civil War such a school was occasionally advocated by newspapers, recommended by governors, and proposed by legislators. Some private citizens showed interest, too. In 1856 "several gentlemen of the State" published at Fayetteville a pamphlet entitled *Suggestions for the Establishment of a Polytechnic School in North Carolina.* Indicating the state's need for home-trained "agriculturists, geologists, engineers, miners, &c. &c.," they outlined a course of study which emphasized practical agriculture and applied science. "Some," said the Fayetteville *Carolinian,* "may think the Chair of Agricultural Chemistry at our University sufficient, but it is not; we want a school where the practice as well as the theory of Agriculture may be taught, where theory can be verified by practice, and where the results of that practice may be scattered among the farming community throughout our State."[10]

Further suggestions were forthcoming after the war. In 1870 J. S. Woodard, of Wilson, urged the creation of an agricultural college in connection with an eastern North Carolina agricul-

[9] Wilmington *Carolina Farmer,* I, 120-21 (Feb., 1869).
[10] Quoted in Raleigh *North-Carolina Planter,* I, 340 (Nov., 1858).

tural society, "the fair grounds to include the college buildings, and a farm to be cultivated by the students." [11] During the 'seventies, as might have been expected, members of the forward-looking Grange sometimes discussed the subject at their meetings. And there were doubtless others who gave thought to the matter.

Ideas, then, were plentiful enough, even if money and leadership apparently were not. In the significant year 1886 the land scrip fund, the possibility of still more federal aid, and the surplus revenue of the state Department of Agriculture combined to give promise of solving the financial problem, while the entry of L. L. Polk, his *Progressive Farmer,* and his organized farmers into the arena seemed to supply the needed leadership.

Polk had been a life-long believer in practical education. "It will be a glorious day for North Carolina, and for the South," he once said, "when our young men shall not be ashamed to hang their diplomas in their work shops, their machine shops, their art galleries, their laboratories, their school rooms, their counting rooms and their farm houses." [12] Though he was in sympathy with the Watauga Club's industrial school, he considered it inadequate. Weak, poor, and circumscribed as it must surely become, it should be supplanted by a whole system of such schools to be truly effective.

The early issues of the *Progressive Farmer* made plain Polk's central thought: there should be a new college or system of colleges in North Carolina devoted to agriculture and the mechanic arts, and the cornerstone of its financial structure should be the land scrip fund.

After reciting the history of the fund in North Carolina and pointing out what neighboring Georgia and Virginia had done, Polk turned his attention to the University. He argued that the Act of 1862 intended the establishment of agricultural colleges, and that the University by no stretch of the imagination could

---

[11] Tarboro *Reconstructed Farmer,* II, 20-21 (May, 1870).
[12] Henderson *Gold Leaf,* June 8, 1882.

be called one. Neither its curriculum nor its practice had been in accord with the meaning of the Act. For that reason "we are forced to say in all kindness, after a trial of a number of years, *it is a most lamentable failure."* The University authorities should therefore "surrender gracefully to the demand of the masses of the people. . . ." He referred to the Agricultural and Mechanical College of Mississippi, under General Stephen D. Lee, as an ideal that North Carolina should strive to match.[13]

When the new University *Catalogue* announced a "College of Agriculture and the Mechanic Arts" for the first time since the institution had begun to receive the annual $7,500 interest in 1875, Polk was satiric. "A long, very long hatching period for such a little chicken," he wrote. "It is a model of architectural beauty and admirably equipped in all its various departments. *It is located on the 49th page of the Catalogue of our University.* The Catalogue says that 'two courses are offered' in this elegant *paper* college. 'Offered' is a good word! These 'courses' we presume have been 'offered' to our farmer boys for these eleven years, but we search the catalogue in vain to find *one* who has availed himself of the 'offer.'" Not only did Polk fail to discover any agricultural students at Chapel Hill, but he found no evidence of an experimental farm or agricultural equipment there. If a "farmer boy" should ever enroll he would have to be content with "an occasional lecture on agricultural chemistry, botany, bugology, or something of that sort."[14]

Polk took care to emphasize that he was not attacking the University of North Carolina as such, or its officers. On the contrary, he said, its work and influence should be praised, and it should be strongly supported by both the people and the legislature. He merely wanted "simple justice and fair play" for the farmers. For too long they had been taxed to support the University without enjoying any practical returns. The total interest on the land

[13] *Progressive Farmer,* Feb. 10, 17, 1886, *passim.*
[14] *Progressive Farmer,* May 19, June 23, Aug. 25, 1886.

scrip fund had now come to $90,000, a sum that had not been used for the benefit of the "industrial classes" as the Morrill Act contemplated, but for the benefit of the University alone. To the charge that "the farmers of North Carolina are being organized to make war on the State University," Polk replied:

> This is a very great mistake. The farmers are not organizing to make war on anything. They are perfectly docile, and, considering how they have to scuffle to get along, in remarkably good humor. They have no hostile designs on the University. They wish it well, but they want it to stand, so to speak, on its own feet. They don't see why the University should have and, through its managers, continue to claim the land scrip fund which belongs to the farmers. That's all. They think the University (whose President pronounces [it] in a very healthy and prosperous condition) should, after eleven years of the use of this money, be able to get along without it—and they mean what they say. Thousands of people in North Carolina, who are not farmers, believe that they are right and their demand reasonable. . . .[15]

The editor of the *Progressive Farmer* and organizer of farmers' clubs put the essence of his thought into these words: "We need an Agricultural College for the practical training of the children of our farmers and other industrial classes, and there is but one way to get it—*build it with the money given to us by the Government for that purpose*. How are we to get it? BY ELECTING A LEGISLATURE THAT WILL GIVE IT TO US."[16]

President Battle recognized his chief antagonist from the beginning. The first number of the *Progressive Farmer* had hardly come from the press when he wrote Polk: "Of course I know that you are in favor of, and will advocate, the use of the Land Grant money in a different way from what exists at present. Equally of course I expect to advocate that the Univ^y is doing its duty. But this difference of opinion—honest on both sides—

---

[15] *Progressive Farmer*, Jan. 26, 1887.
[16] *Progressive Farmer*, Aug. 25, 1886.

should not make either of us careless about representing the other's views. I write frankly because I believe you are disposed to do right. . . . All I wish is *the truth*."[17] Polk could not ascertain whether the University president privately regarded his crusade as *"the truth"* or not. At any rate, after three or four of his "land scrip editorials" had appeared, he received this note from Battle: "I find that my newspaper list is so large I cannot read half I have paid for. Please discontinue yours & let me have bill."[18] It was promptly sent.

In his public defense Battle contended that the Morrill Act did not command the formation of agricultural and mechanical colleges, nor did it prescribe shops, experimental farms, and the like. "The preamble may seem to do so," he said, "but any lawyer knows that the preamble cannot be interpreted to violate the plain words of the statute." He pointed out that most states accepted the land grant for schools already in existence; a minority set up separate institutions, but only after the individual states had appropriated goodly sums for their support. In 1876 he had personally inspected various land-grant colleges in the Northeast and was satisfied that the University of North Carolina was fulfilling the terms of the Act as well as any of them.

The Act stated that the "leading object" of a land-grant college should be "to teach such branches of learning as are related to agriculture and the mechanic arts." Battle in his argument laid great stress on the phrase "branches of learning." His assertion was that the Act of Congress enjoined teaching "the scientific principles leading to the trades, not the trades themselves." The University's regular courses, therefore—in chemistry, botany, zoology, mineralogy, mathematics, and certain other subjects—made up the required "branches of learning." It was, moreover, of "inestimable advantage" to the "agricultural students of the

[17] Battle to Polk, Feb. 11, 1886.
[18] Battle to Polk, April 24, 1886.

University" to be "educated side by side with those in other pursuits. . . ." [19]

Times had changed, and public opinion seemed to favor a "new departure." In his construction of the Morrill Act Battle stood practically alone. Still, the Bourbon leaders of North Carolina were to all appearances as impervious to change as ever.

During the spring, summer, and fall of 1886 Polk, between editorials, was busy organizing farmers' clubs all over the state. So deeply did the farmers feel their grievances that by winter they were eager to follow the suggestion of holding a state convention—while the General Assembly was in session. The convention would not "dabble in politics" but would discuss vital issues. The voices of the farmers should be heard.

The meeting was originally scheduled for January 19, 1887, at Greensboro. Then Governor Scales, in what the farmers regarded as an attempt to split their forces, called for a meeting of farmers with the Board of Agriculture on the evening of the eighteenth in Raleigh. The "mass convention" was now postponed a week, while as many farmers as could do so went to the meeting with the Board of Agriculture.

Held in the hall of the House of Representatives, the meeting opened with a "neat and patriotic" speech by Governor Scales. Various members of the Board followed him. According to Polk, "It was painfully evident to every listener that . . . the speakers seemed to feel that they were on trial and that their hearers had been empanelled as a jury to try them." When the farmers' turn came, S. Otho Wilson, representing the Swift Creek Farmers' Club of Wake County, immediately presented these resolutions:

> *Resolved,* That the necessities of the farmers of North Carolina require the establishment of an agricultural college and

[19] Battle, in *N. C. Pub. Docs., 1881,* No. 26, pp. 9-11, and *Reports . . . to the Board of Trustees of the University of North Carolina, January 20th, 1887,* pp. 19-30.

that the proceeds of the land-scrip fund donated by the Federal Congress of 1862 and which has been applied to the State University should be transferred to the support of said college.

Resolved 2nd, That the State department of agriculture should be reorganized on such a basis as shall give the control and management of the same into the hands of practical farmers and thus bring it into closer union with the farming interests of the State.

A lively discussion ensued. Polk's friends were a determined majority, and the resolutions were adopted overwhelmingly, notwithstanding the objections of Battle. The farmers thus "mutinied and captured the ship." Polk himself, the recognized leader of the farmers' movement, kept in the background, busily taking notes, and did not speak until called upon by the chairman. [20]

On Wednesday, January 26, 1887, eight days later, some three hundred earnest farmers assembled in the state capital. [21] They preferred Raleigh to Greensboro because they intended to bring pressure to bear on the legislature. Though "formidable influences were brought against the movement," the farmers came and made ready to effect a permanent organization and lay their case before the public. Polk called the convention to order in Metropolitan Hall. The delegates first heard an address by former Governor Jarvis. Governor Scales was also invited, but "pressing engagements had called him from the city. . . ." Fraternal greetings were exchanged with the Knights of Labor, who were meeting in Raleigh at the same time. Then the delegates, representing clubs in forty counties, organized the "North Carolina Farmers' Association," electing as their president Elias Carr, of Edgecombe County.

The principal business of the convention was embodied in the two closely related topics, reform of the Department of Agri-

[20] *Progressive Farmer,* Jan. 19, 26, 1887; *State Chronicle,* Jan. 20, 1887; *News and Observer,* Jan. 19, 20, 1887.

[21] MS. proceedings, Polk Papers; *Progressive Farmer,* Feb. 2, 9, 1887.

culture and establishment of an agricultural college. Largely at the instance of Dr. Charles W. Dabney, State Chemist, the farmers asked the General Assembly to relieve the Department of all non-agricultural activities such as fish propagation, oyster surveys, mining explorations, analysis of stomachs, and encouragement of immigration. If this were done, $20,000 could be saved and applied to the college. Farmers should not be taxed for the benefit of other classes of citizens. Further, the Board of Agriculture should be reconstituted to include mainly practical farmers, and it should exercise control over both the Department and the college.

The convention petitioned the General Assembly to establish an agricultural and mechanical college and to transfer the land scrip fund to it from the University. The college should receive annually $7,500 from the land scrip fund, $20,000 from the Department of Agriculture, and $25,000 from the State Treasury. If the legislature could not "afford it," then let it impose a tax of $1.00 on every dog in the state. The University of North Carolina should be strongly supported by state appropriations.

Again Polk chose to remain in the background. His careful planning, however, was fully evident in every move that was made during the two-day session.[22] The delegates elected him to the executive committee, declared his paper the official organ of their new association, and thanked him for his devotion to their interests and for his successful efforts in organizing them.

In the legislature, of course, there was powerful opposition to the farmers' wishes. Yet the unusual and impressive spectacle of a mass meeting of farmers in the state capital had a marked, if not quite instantaneous, effect. Two other factors were also of immediate importance. Some sixty acres of excellent land, a tract well situated just west of Raleigh, were donated for the college by R. Stanhope Pullen. And on the verge of passage in Congress was the Hatch Bill, which would appropriate to those states es-

[22] Francis Joyner, Littleton, N. C., to author, April 21, 1938.

tablishing colleges under the Morrill Act $15,000 per year for agricultural experiment stations.

A bill incorporating the ideas of both the Watauga Club and the organized farmers was prepared by Dabney and Augustus Leazer and introduced in the House by the latter. Heated debate followed in both branches. A House amendment to locate the proposed college at the University of North Carolina lost by only seven votes. Finally, on March 1, the House approved the bill sixty-one to thirty-seven, and two days later the Senate concurred twenty-nine to thirteen. Leazer, Alexander, and Williams supported this bill as they had the industrial school bill in the preceding legislature, and on this occasion were joined particularly by Representative Henry E. Fries and Senators James H. Pou, Kope Elias, and J. B. Eaves. Both Democrats and Republicans worked for the school.

The institution was named the "North Carolina College of Agriculture and Mechanic Arts." In a wise effort to keep the school out of politics, it was required that the board of managers include an equal representation from each political party. Building material and convict labor were to be furnished by the State Penitentiary.[23] The cornerstone was laid in August, 1888, and the College was officially opened on October 3, 1889.

In the fight to reorganize the state Department of Agriculture and to establish a real agricultural college, a striking similarity—in time, problems, and events—existed between North Carolina and South Carolina. The respective leaders of the fight, Polk and Benjamin R. Tillman, were in contact. Tillman, who read the *Progressive Farmer,* sent Polk the published proceedings of a large farmers' meeting called by him and held at Columbia. Later he wrote: "I note in your paper the progress you are making & the similarity of our fighting. 'Hew to the line let the chips fall where they may' & you are bound to win." When the Raleigh Farmers' Convention had forcefully indicated to the General Assembly

---

[23] *N. C. Pub. Laws, 1887,* pp. 718-22 (ch. 410).

THE FARMER BUILDS A COLLEGE   179

the necessity of building a new agricultural and mechanical college, Tillman congratulated Polk on the success of the North Carolina farmers' movement and ordered "20 or more copies" of the proceedings.[24] The South Carolina legislature passed the act creating Clemson College in 1889. At the laying of the cornerstone in 1891 Polk was present by invitation and followed Tillman, then governor, in the speech-making.

Privately President Battle of the University agreed with Polk and "many, if not most, judicious persons" that the land-grant college should be separate. But, he stated, he felt compelled to carry out the wishes of his trustees in the matter. He was "fully persuaded" that the farmers' campaign would be successful after witnessing Polk and his friends capture the January 18 meeting with the Board of Agriculture. When the North Carolina College of Agriculture and Mechanic Arts had become an accomplished fact, Battle professed considerable relief. The loss of $7,500 a year was serious, to be sure. Yet no longer would the University be charged with "defrauding the farmers and mechanics" or be "embarrassed by the constant demand to build stables and work shops, buy prize cattle and modern machinery."[25]

Everyone felt certain, nevertheless, that the real reason for his constant opposition during the struggle was his determination to keep the land scrip money for the University. As Battle himself, with saving humor, once said in a speech: "Mr. Chairman, this giving up $125,000 which you have had for nearly twenty years is not an agreeable process. No one who has never tried it can imagine how unconstitutional and against nature it feels."[26] Prior possession of the fund had made it seem indispensable. Whatever the merits of Battle's devotion to the University, he did none the less strive to block a democratic movement that sought to bring justice and opportunity to the industrial classes of the people.

[24] Tillman to Polk, May 17, June 1, 1886, Feb. 28, 1887.
[25] Battle, *History of the University of North Carolina*, II, 374-78.
[26] Battle, *Memories of an Old-Time Tar Heel*, p. 253.

To Polk the victory taste was doubly sweet, for Battle had been instrumental in causing his resignation as Commissioner of Agriculture in 1880. But he did not pause to gloat. According to the University president, when the new college was assured Polk "was overheard saying to a friend in the lobby, 'Now we will let Battle alone.'" And, adds Battle, "He kept his promise." [27]

Unlike Athena, this institution did not spring forth fully armed from the head of Zeus. It was the product of many minds and many forces. Once it was in successful operation, however, its friends began to single out the men and movements they believed to be chiefly responsible for bringing it into life.

For about thirty-five years the Watauga Club received most of the credit. Men who had been associated with it could tell their story from the vantage point of the state capital. People found it easy to connect the thriving Raleigh college with the bright young men who had labored so constructively in Raleigh during the middle 'eighties. The later eminence of some of the Wataugans, notably Walter H. Page, lent further weight to the idea. [28]

Page greatly stimulated several young men who became important educational leaders, but his influence on the public life of North Carolina in the middle 'eighties was slight. The thirty-year-old editor left the state in 1885, and in February, 1886, despaired of seeing even the industrial school. Yet his biographer, who seems totally unaware of the farmers' movement, goes so far as to say that the North Carolina College of Agriculture and Mechanic Arts was "a direct outcome of Page's brief sojourn in his native state." [29] The cultivated Page scorned the "damned farmers," referring to their major movement as a "small agitation" and to their leaders as "the long beards." [30] This attitude makes

[27] Battle, *History*, II, 376. Battle's judgment of Polk, mild enough in the *History*, is quite harsh in the *Memories*, p. 248.
[28] *State Chronicle*, March 20, 1892; Hendrick, *Training of an American*, pp. 169, 173.
[29] Hendrick, *Life and Letters of Walter H. Page*, I, 47.
[30] Walter H. Page, "Address at the Inauguration of President Winston," *N. C. University Magazine*, XXII (1891-92), 65.

all the more absurd the statement in his autobiographical novel, "We of the Club, whose ideas were now beginning to become clear, welcomed the rising tide of rural discontent, and it gave us courage to prepare a plan to direct it." [31]

The less articulate farmers were scattered over the state. Polk, their leader, died in 1892, and a year or so before his death offended most of the molders of public opinion by renouncing the Democrats for the Populists. Many of the farmers did likewise. All this had the effect of minimizing their part, and especially his part, in the founding of the College.

In 1925 and 1926, after the political passions of the 'nineties had subsided, the pendulum swung back. The College "Catalog," which in the customary historical sketch had reflected the Watauga Club view, was revised to say:

> The North Carolina State College of Agriculture and Engineering is the outgrowth of an idea fostered by two distinct movements, each somewhat different in its original aims. One movement, represented by a group of progressive young North Carolinians, banded together in Raleigh as the Watauga Club, sought to bring about the organization of an industrial school for the teaching of "woodwork, mining, metallurgy, and practical agriculture." The other movement, originating among the farmers in North Carolina, and actively sponsored by Colonel L. L. Polk, then editor of the *Progressive Farmer,* had as its object the establishment of an agricultural college supported by State appropriations and by the Land Scrip Fund of the Federal Government.[32]

A new animal husbandry building was completed and named "Polk Hall." The address of dedication by Clarence Poe [33]—a successor of Polk as editor of the *Progressive Farmer* and also a close friend of Page and Peele and head of the revived Watauga Club—presented "compelling facts" that "made a deep impres-

---
[31] Page, *The Southerner,* p. 208.
[32] N. C. State Coll. of Agr. and Eng., *Record,* XXV, No. 1, p. 24 (July, 1925).
[33] Clarence Poe, *Col. Leonidas Lafayette Polk: His Services in Starting the N. C. State Coll. of Agr. and Eng.,* pp. 3-5.

sion" upon the audience. In the same issue of his *News and Observer* that reported the dedication, Josephus Daniels, who had fought shoulder-to-shoulder with Polk in his early battles, contributed a long editorial article on Polk's career. The paper could now proclaim in a two-column, page-one headline: "POLK GIVEN PLACE BY STATE COLLEGE AS CHIEF FOUNDER." [34]

William J. Peele, himself of prime importance in the struggle of the 'eighties, stated unequivocally that Polk was "the most powerful factor" in the establishment of the College;[35] and Kemp P. Battle ascribed to Polk's eloquence the success of that "formidable crusade."[36] Polk made no public claims but was content to say: "THE PROGRESSIVE FARMER will never have a prouder chapter in its record than the one which will tell of its battle for the farmer boys' college."[37]

Under his leadership North Carolina's laboring classes won a great victory.

[34] *News and Observer*, July 29, 1926.
[35] Peele, "Col. L. L. Polk: a Brief Sketch of His Life and Work," *N. C. Baptist Almanac for the Year 1893*, p. 47.
[36] Battle, *History of the Univ. of N. C.*, II, 374.
[37] *Progressive Farmer*, Oct. 27, 1887.

Chapter XI

ON THE EDUCATION OF WOMEN

LATE IN JULY, 1880, a reporter from the Raleigh *News* visited the "Dixie Floral Fair" at Wadesboro. During the day he inspected the various exhibits of colorful, fragrant summer flowers and made a thirty-minute speech on "Our Want of State Pride." That evening he attended the "hop" given by the young people. There he met the Queen of the Fair and commented with enthusiasm upon her beauty. He seemed to enjoy the sound of the music and laughter and the sight of the happy couples. At forty-three the father of six daughters himself, the reporter felt moved to write: "The truth is, that while I, as a chronicler of events, am no advocate of dancing, I could but feel a pardonable pride in the young men who demeaned themselves with such gentlemanly propriety and deferential respect, and of the young ladies who showed, by their dignified and true womanly bearing, that they fully appreciated the important truth, *that genuine modesty is the crowning glory of woman.*"[1]

L. L. Polk was an orthodox Southern Baptist whose code of conduct and morality a later generation would term "Victorian." From youth he had always been active in church work and sincerely religious. After becoming Commissioner of Agriculture and citizen of the state capital, Polk soon rose to be one of the pillars of the First Baptist Church of Raleigh. Between 1880 and 1890 his church usually sent him as one of its delegates to the annual Baptist State Convention, and in the latter year he jour-

[1] Raleigh *News*, July 31, 1880.

neyed to Fort Worth, Texas, as a state delegate to the Southern Baptist Convention. In connection with the North Carolina body he served on the Sunday School Board and the consolidated Board of Missions and Sunday Schools. At different times, he found himself on a committee "to nominate preachers for next session," a committee to consider plans for "superannuated ministers, their widows and orphans," a committee on periodicals, and several others. He was elected a vice-president of the State Convention in 1885.

The church-led prohibition campaign that demonstrated strength in North Carolina during the early 'eighties enlisted Polk's ardent support. He attended two state prohibition conventions and was a member of a committee which petitioned the General Assembly to enact prohibition legislation. With Elder J. B. Boone he agreed that, for both the material and the moral good of the commonwealth, the great quantity of grain consumed in whiskey-making should be used in stock-raising, and that the many men engaged in handling liquor would be far better employed in farming, manufacturing, mining, or some other worthy occupation.[2]

In the middle 'seventies, when the Polks were still living in Polkton, the two older daughters were sent to the Baptist Female Seminary of Raleigh. With obvious satisfaction, their father regarded it as a "first class City school." He highly recommended it to other Baptist parents for its strong program of mental, moral, and physical training—and for its economical rates. Twelve dollars per month, he told them, paid for board and furnished room, including fuel, lights, washing, and attendance of a servant! "Unnecessary extravagance in dress" was discouraged, he added, by the adoption of a "neat and cheap uniform" for all the young ladies.[3]

Yet the privately-owned Raleigh Seminary, like many such

---

[2] North Carolina Baptist State Convention, *Minutes, 1880*, pp. 40-41.
[3] Polkton *Ansonian*, Aug. 2, 1876; Raleigh *Biblical Recorder*, Aug. 1, 1879.

institutions, found the going difficult and soon expired. What the Baptists of the state needed was a girls' school of college grade adequately supported. Already the denomination had made provision for its young men by founding and maintaining Wake Forest College, which began its career as Wake Forest Institute in 1834.

At the Baptist State Convention the next year a committee of three had been appointed to consider "the expediency of establishing a female seminary." Sentiment seemed definitely favorable, but the pressing demands of Wake Forest came first. Then in 1838 Thomas Meredith, great Baptist leader who belonged to the original committee, declared in an important report that "it is expedient to institute a Female Seminary adapted to the existing wants of the denomination," and that it should be located "in the city of Raleigh or at some eligible point in the adjoining country." Meredith called upon the State Convention for quick action, yet a full fifty years passed by before that body took the decisive step.[4] During that half-century the short-lived Raleigh Seminary stood as the closest approach to Meredith's ideal.

By 1888 Baptist leaders had convinced themselves that the need was compelling and that circumstances were at last favorable. They took their decisive step through L. L. Polk. At the afternoon session of Saturday, November 16, Polk offered the following resolutions to the State Convention meeting in Greensboro:

Resolved, That a committee of nine, to wit: W. R. Gwaltney, R. R. Overby, T. H. Pritchard, J. D. Hufham, R. T. Vann, N. B. Broughton, R. H. Marsh, A. G. McManaway, H. W. Battle, be and is hereby appointed to consider the expediency and feasibility of establishing a Baptist Female University in this State.

Resolved, That said committee be, and it is hereby authorized and empowered to ascertain the best available locality,

[4] Richard T. Vann, "Historical Sketch of Meredith College," *Meredith College Quarterly Bulletin,* Ser. 4, No. 2, pp. 3-15 (Jan., 1911).

and to make estimates as to the approximate cost of inaugurating such institution, and report the same to the next annual session of this Convention.

The delegates added Polk to the committee as chairman and immediately adopted the resolutions.[5]

Polk's success in the fight to establish an agricultural and mechanical college made a deep impression upon the Baptists of North Carolina, who constituted the state's largest religious group. That great achievement, plus his past work in the denomination, caused many of them to look to him for leadership. They felt that his ability, energy, and prestige would be needed in the campaign ahead. Perhaps the fact that he had fathered and educated six young women of his own also had its effect!

For ten years Polk had served as an active trustee of Wake Forest College and had thus been able to gain an insight into the problems of higher education. Wake Forest, on a sound footing now, was prepared to yield the field, at least temporarily, to the girls' school.

Accordingly, Polk was elected president of the State Convention of 1889—elected mainly for the purpose of engineering action on the "Female University." That subject loomed as the most important one before the Convention, and the delegates awaited with keen interest the report of Polk's committee of ten. The committee, which had studied the matter during the past year, reported that "the great *need* for such an institution renders the enterprise *expedient,* and most encouraging assurances of moral and financial support convince us that it is now *feasible."* The members therefore recommended that the Convention "resolutely and joyfully assume the duty" which "the desires of the people and the demands of the times have laid upon us."[6]

During the discussion of the report, Polk stated: "I am not only proud that I am a Baptist, but I am proud of my brother Baptists.

---

[5] Bapt. State Conv., *Minutes, 1888,* p. 23.
[6] Bapt. State Conv., *Minutes, 1889,* pp. 20-22, 30.

Everywhere I go I stumble on boys fresh from Wake Forest College, which has become the object of the prayers and labors of this Convention." Then, with a twinkle in his eye and a smile on his face, he said: "I feel deeply for the women of my State, and I give you due notice that if you do not take some steps to help these girls . . . I will appeal to the power behind all our homes." [7]

The delegates voiced enthusiastic approval. Without dissent they voted to continue the committee and to increase its membership from ten to twenty-five, the enlarged committee to act with full authority as a Board of Trustees. While the Convention, held in Henderson this time, was still in session the group met to organize. The Board chose Polk as its president and appointed three subcommittees. The whole body, one of its leading members has written, "took its appointment seriously, and promptly entered upon the work committed to it." [8] That work was the building of a college for women which would give training equal to that which Wake Forest gave its men. As Polk put it, "The Baptist[s] have done well for their young men—they must now do equally as well for their daughters." [9]

The original committee of ten proved unable, "from the nature of the case," to come to any decision regarding the locality or estimated cost of the school. The new Board, however, fixed February 11, 1890, as the date when it would hear all propositions and render a decision. Durham, Raleigh, Greensboro, and Oxford had all wanted the college from the beginning. General Julian S. Carr of Durham attracted attention when he declared that he would put up one dollar for each dollar raised by members of the three Baptist churches there. Not to be outdone, interested Raleigh citizens held a couple of mass meetings; "Raleigh Determined To Secure It . . . Everybody Favors It," headlined the

---

[7] *Biblical Recorder,* Nov. 20, 1889.
[8] Vann, *op. cit.,* p. 8.
[9] *Progressive Farmer,* Nov. 26, 1889.

State Chronicle, which stressed the rivalry between Raleigh and Durham.[10]

On the appointed day eighteen of the twenty-five Board members, together with representatives from the towns, assembled in the First Baptist Church of Raleigh. Polk presided. Each of the towns offered a suitable site, and in cash Durham offered $50,000, Oxford $30,000, Raleigh $25,000, and Greensboro $10,000. Also, the Chowan Baptist Female Institute of Murfreesboro and the High Point Female College let it be known that they would donate their lands and buildings, with the former making 450,-000 bricks available as well. Though the competition was keen, fairness and moderation prevailed during the discussions. At length the Board, impressed by the offers made and the interest shown, went into secret session. After "careful and prayerful deliberation" the members chose Raleigh, believing Raleigh to be best suited for the future growth of the school.[11]

The Board made its official report to the State Convention at Shelby the following November. There the delegates again honored Polk by re-electing him president of the Convention. "Col. Polk is not only one of the most prominent men of this, his native State, but he is now one of the most distinguished citizens on the continent," commented the *Biblical Recorder,* the Baptists' state organ.[12] Polk's connection with the college project ended here, for his activities as president of the National Farmers' Alliance and Industrial Union kept him away from North Carolina except for brief visits. Still, his work was done. As in the case of the agricultural and mechanical college, he had provided the impetus that made the movement successful.

The executive committee of the Board and its financial agents now carried on. The charter of the college was granted by the legislature on February 27, 1891; a large square in Raleigh,

[10] Raleigh *State Chronicle,* Jan. 10, 24, 1890.
[11] *Progressive Farmer,* Feb. 18, 1890; *Biblical Recorder,* Feb. 19, 1890.
[12] *Biblical Recorder,* Nov. 19, 1890.

bounded by Edenton, Person, Jones, and Blount streets, was paid for by 1894; and, after various difficulties had been overcome, the school opened on September 27, 1899. Called first the "Baptist Female University," and then the "Baptist University for Women," the institution soon dropped these inappropriate names and in 1909 took the one it has borne since, "Meredith College."

This time, under L. L. Polk, North Carolina's Baptists won a victory.

CHAPTER XII

THE WRONG

WHEN IN THE 'SIXTIES the planter aristocracy of the South and the small farmers allied with it were overthrown by the new combination of manufacturers, laborers, and free farmers of the North, a revolution of the first magnitude occurred. The principles of Hamilton and the Whigs emerged triumphant over those of Jefferson and Jackson. The tariff was raised; a national banking system, characterized by conservative finance, was restored; and internal improvements on a grand scale, like the Pacific Railroad and the Homestead Act, were undertaken. The capitalist-industrialist, his "person" protected by the "due process of law" of the Fourteenth Amendment, now dominated the scene. In many ways it was truly the "Second American Revolution."

During the Gilded Age that followed, the Whiggish federal government favored business interests at the expense of agriculture. Farmers both North and South tried manfully to check this "silent drift toward plutocracy," but they were ill-equipped intellectually to cope with Hamiltonian lawyers. The farmer, moreover, came to be an unwitting instrument in his own undoing, for he "took pride in the county-seat towns that lived off his earnings; he sent city lawyers to represent him in legislatures and in Congress; he read middle-class newspapers and listened to bankers and politicians. . . ." As the prestige of the new business class rose, the prestige of the farmer declined. Soon his plight was distressing. Then he revolted. In his effort to right the wrongs of the times the farmer turned to politics. Thus the agrarianism of the closing decades of the nineteenth century was born of necessity and was homespun and hard-headed. As it was not supported by the "high authority of the schools," it was derided by the spokesmen of the prosperous middle class.

The editors, lawyers, bankers, and scholars all asserted that American farmers were simply producing too much, and that this accounted for the serious drop in farm prices. Agrarian leaders, however, repudiated the widely-circulated overproduction theory. Were not the makers of clothes underfed, and the makers of food underclad? Influenced to a degree by the "greenbackers" and the "silverites," the farmers charged that the volume of money was inadequate, inelastic, and "controlled by a powerful and heartless money trust." The remedy, they thought, was "free coinage," which the Government should immediately provide. Professor Woodrow Wilson of Princeton and Professor Frederick J. Turner of Harvard both noted in their histories the growing tendency of the nation's farmers during these years to look to Washington for assistance.[1]

As a matter of fact, the "plight of the farmer" in the 'seventies, 'eighties, and 'nineties was world-wide. Technological changes, the disproportionate increase of urban wealth, the falling prices of staple products, the burden of mortgages and taxes, and the scarcity of money plagued the farmers of many countries.

The pervasive importance of the "money problem" in the United States found illustration in a contemporary jingle:

> What will this country be noted for hence?
> Dollars and cents. Dollars and cents.
> What are men striving for hot and intense?
> Dollars and cents. Dollars and cents.
> What makes our politics reek with offence?
> Dollars and cents. Dollars and cents.
> What makes J. Gould, tho' a small man, immense?
> Dollars and cents. Dollars and cents.

[1] Woodrow Wilson, *History of the American People,* V, 128-31; Frederick J. Turner, *The Frontier in American History,* p. 148.

What makes our cashiers jump over the fence?
Dollars and cents. Dollars and cents.
What causes crime on the slightest pretense?
Dollars and cents. Dollars and cents.
Why is it stern justice often relents?
Dollars and cents. Dollars and cents.
What more than all shadows tell coming events?
Dollars and cents. Dollars and cents.
What makes you polite to a man of no sense?
Dollars and cents. Dollars and cents.[2]

In the Western states the grievances centered, understandably, about the railroads. The farmer welcomed the railroads as a means of getting his product to market, but he resented their selfish and unregulated practices—the high rates and discriminations, the disproportionate charges on long and short hauls, the secret agreements and monopolies, the corruption in management, the stock-watering and land-grabbing, and the control of editors and public officials through the use of passes. Advertised by promoters and financed by speculators, the New West developed with amazing rapidity along its new rail lines. But the result was a tremendous boom that could end only in collapse. In addition, the Western farmer had to contend with such difficulties as drought, low prices for wheat and corn, elevator monopolies and price-fixing, the rise of trusts, the effects of the tariff, and high interest rates. In the past a beleaguered farmer could pull up stakes, move still farther west, and start all over; now the frontier was gone, and he had to stay where he was. The complaint of Benjamin H. Clover, of Cowley County, Kansas, was perhaps typical:

> At the age of 52 years, after a long life of toil, economy and self-denial, I find myself and family virtually paupers. With hundreds of cattle, hundreds of hogs, scores of good horses, and a farm that rewarded the toil of our hands with 16,000 bushels of golden corn, we are poorer by many dollars than we were years ago. What once seemed a neat little fortune

[2] *Progressive Farmer*, Feb. 17, 1886.

and a house of refuge for our declining years, by a few turns of the monopolistic crank, has been rendered valueless.[3]

The farmer of the South had a sad story to tell, too. Up to 1860 the agricultural class stood as the most powerful in the section—politically, economically, and socially. Professional men were drawn from this class, hence represented its views. That meant the dominance of "all the cotton farmers," large and small. By 1890, however, dominance had passed from agriculturists to the rising business class, with which the professional groups were now allied. The farmers' political influence seemed slight, their economic distress great, and their social standing inferior to that of "city people"—even small tradesmen. The Civil War, Reconstruction, and the Negro problem had combined to accomplish this complex revolution.

Lack of capital after the ruin of war paved the way for the notorious lien system of the South. Introduced originally to help planters solve their credit and labor problems, it soon involved between eighty and ninety per cent of all the farmers. Whether owner or tenant, white or black, the farmer was compelled by circumstances to accept the economic dictation of the new "country merchant," who furnished him with all supplies in return for a mortgage on his cotton crop. Justifying the action by what he considered the great risk he was taking, the merchant raised his credit prices twenty to fifty per cent above his cash prices. His customer the farmer, securely bound to a single crop and without ready cash, was helpless and sank deeper and deeper into debt. Often he had to settle "this year's debt" by pledging "next year's crop." In short, he was in a state of peonage to the merchant.

The country merchant quickly took advantage of the Southern lien laws, and mortgage foreclosures occurred frequently. Yet the small merchant, too, was caught in the system. He depended upon a local banker, who in turn found himself at the mercy of a New

---

[3] Washington, D. C., *National Economist*, V, 329 (Aug. 8, 1891).

York banker. Interest rates were excessive, and special loan companies did more harm than good. Meanwhile, the price of cotton steadily declined.

The Southern farmer blamed his predicament on the middleman and the manufacturer, whose profits in the long run he paid, and eventually on the government and the Democratic Party, both of which placed the interests of other groups above his own. Still, it was partly the fault of the farmer himself that the South clung so persistently to the one-crop system. There could be no health in an economy that made it necessary for North Carolina, Virginia, Texas, and Georgia to import commercial fertilizers, household supplies, flour, bacon, lard, and butter.

None of this was lost upon agrarian leaders. At a mass meeting of farmers at Sandy Springs, South Carolina, L. L. Polk said:

> The siren voice that led the Southern farmer astray after the war was, "Twenty-five cents cotton." In the face of the devastation, destruction and despair brought about by the war, King Cotton promised to shower his blessings on our country, and our farmers listened to his seductive utterances. We told the North we would forget the past, just go ahead and make our clothes, our hats, our shoes, our plows, our axehandles, our fertilizers, raise our mules and our hogs, even grind our flour and meal, and we would raise one crop to pay for all, and the North could put its price on that one crop. We forsook the good old and only safe rule of making a living at home, and went to buying everything—bread, meat, clothing, tools, horses, mules, corn, hay—think of it—hay! *hay!* HAy! HAY! A Southern farmer buying hay to feed a mule to work all summer killing better grass than the North ever knew! Our farmers buy everything to raise cotton, and raise cotton to buy everything, and after going through this treadmill business for years, they lie down and die, and leave their families penniless.[4]

[4] Anderson, S. C., *Journal,* Aug. 25, 1887, quoted in Greenville, S. C., *Cotton Plant,* Sept., 1887. This item was kindly called to my attention by Miss Marjorie Mendenhall.

"Leonidas and Sallie were married on September 23, 1857, when he was twenty and she seventeen."

"Polk [upper right], chairman of the committee, reported a bill.... Ratified on September 20, 1861, the bill provided that the State Militia be organized."

Colonel and Mrs. Polk with their children, about 1883. Left to right: Lonnie, Juanita, Mary, Ina, Carrie. Deceased: Lula, the eldest daughter, and Lucius LaFayette, infant son.

THE ANSONIAN.

L. L. POLK. Editor.

POLKTON, N. C., APRIL 16th, 1874.

TO CORRESPONDENTS.

Communications, to receive any notice must have a responsible name accompanying them; in other words, if you do the writing you must do the fighting. The publication of an article, by no means, commits us to its endorsement.

SALUTATORY.

My course, as Editor of the ANSONIAN, towards my cotemporaries of the Press, shall be characterized by that courtesy, regard, and spirit of frankness which can but strengthen that co operation so essential to the accomplishment of the great mission of a Free Press, viz: the political, intellectual, social, and moral improvement and elevation of mankind.

I am by birth, education, habit, thought, feeling, and interest—a Conservative; and a North Carolinian—and shall guard, promote, and defend her interests with whatever ability and zeal I may command.

I claim, that under the organic law of the country, I have some of the prerogatives of an American freeman, yet left me, and as one of the Representatives of a Free Press, I shall exercise the right to combat error, in whatever form it may present itself, and from whatever source it may emanate.

In short, it will be my honest endeavor to observe faithfully, the spirit embodied in the motto of the ANSONIAN:

Fearlessly, the RIGHT defend,
Impartially, the WRONG condemn.

L. L. POLK.

GOV. VANCE—MR. ASHE—JUDGE BUXTON.

It has been modestly suggested to the good people of our District, to run

---

THE PROGRESSIVE FARMER.

L. L. POLK, . . **EDITOR.**
WINSTON, N. C.

—SUBSCRIPTION:—
$2.00 FOR ONE YEAR. $1.00 FOR 6 MONTHS.
POST-PAID.
Invariably in Advance

Subscribers will be notified two weeks before their time expires and if they do not renew the paper will be stopped promptly.
Liberal inducements to clubs.
Active agents wanted in every county, city town and village in the State. Write for terms.
Money at our risk, if sent by registered letter or money order.
Advertising Rates quoted on application.
On all matters relating to the paper,
Address
THE PROGRESSIVE FARMER,
Winston, N. C.

To Correspondents.

Write all communications, designed for publication, on one side of the paper.
Rejected communications will be numbered and filed, and the author will be notified. If not applied for in 30 days they will be destroyed. To secure their return postage must be sent with the application. Answers to enquiries will be made through our "Correspondents Column" when it can be done with propriety. We want intelligent correspondents in every county in the State. We want *facts* of value, results accomplished of value, experiences of value, plainly and briefly told. One solid, demonstrated *fact* is worth a thousand theories.
Address all communications to
THE PROGRESSIVE FARMER,
Winston, N. C.

Winston, N. C., Feb. 10, 1886.

Salutatory.

A properly conducted weekly Journal devoted to the agricultural and other industrial interests of our people, is a public necessity. Encouraged by the opportunity presented, and by gratifying indications of a generous support in the undertaking from all sections of our State, I assume the task and will devote to this, my chosen life-work, all the energy and fidelity of which

"Traces of printer's ink remained on his fingers, too."

THE REVIEW OF REVIEWS.

VOL. V.   NEW YORK, MAY, 1892.   No. 28.

THE PROGRESS OF THE WORLD.

Silver and Parties. The interest of the political situation does not flag as the convention month approaches; but it is chiefly the party out of power here, as in England, that focuses popular attention. When our monthly chronicle was written for the last number of THE REVIEW, the passage of the Bland free silver bill by the Democratic House seemed inevitable. But before the printed pages were distributed to their readers, the opponents of the measure had succeeded, by filibustering, in defeating the will of the majority and in postponing a direct vote on the question to an unnamed future— that is, until after the autumn elections. Unlimited silver coinage at the present ratio is not a cause with which we are in sympathy; but it must be confessed that its discomfiture was won by inglorious means. Obstruction in a legislative body is the denial to the people of free and open rule. The silver question ought to have come to a vote at the appointed time. No good end was served by the zealous and strenuous tactics of the handful of anti-silver Democrats whose whole energy was given to the task of preventing the House from voting upon a question that was fairly before it for a vote. It will be seen in the sequel, probably, that the subject was managed in the worst possible way for the fortunes of the party. It is usually well either to let so ticklish a business severely alone, or else to face it squarely and make a responsible record. As matters stand, the Democratic attitude on silver is frightening away the conservative "gold bugs" of the East, and it is disgusting the "silver fanatics" of the South and West. The Bland bill went far enough to show the East how strongly in favor of it the great majority of the Democratic Congressmen really are; while it failed to go far enough to please the constituents of Southern and Western Congressmen who had been elected upon definite and solemn pledges to vote for free coinage.

The Chance of the People's Party. It had been thought that the tremendous "Farmers' Alliance" wave of 1890 was subsiding, and that the People's party, which has grown out of that movement, would make very little trouble for the old parties in the Presidential, Congressional and State elections of this year. But the fate of the Bland bill has given the third party move just the fresh impetus that it could most have desired. The principal part of the platform of the People's party is the monetary

PRESIDENT L. L. POLK, OF THE FARMERS' ALLIANCE.

and financial creed it contains, and the cardinal article of that creed reads as follows: " We demand free and unlimited coinage of silver." The new party that swept several Southern and Western States in 1890 is not going to lose the opportunity that Mr. Bland's defeat gives it to enter the field this summer with a radical and unequivocal platform, and to attempt to capture the electoral vote of several States.

"In the spring of 1892 Polk looked upon himself, with reason, as the chosen leader of a great popular movement."

The editor of the Washington, D. C., *National Economist* observed: "Does it not look like rather a one-sided affair when the farmer, in buying a merchant's goods, must ask, What is your price? and when he desires to sell his goods to that same merchant he asks, What will you give? In fixing prices, the farmer's time never comes." [5]

Ordinary country folk found the situation puzzling. With heavy heart a farmer's wife could sing:

> My husband came from town last night
>   As sad as man could be,
> His wagon empty, cotton gone,
>   And not a dime had he.
>
> Huzzah—Huzzah
>   'Tis queer I do declare:
> We make the clothes for all the world,
>   But few we have to wear.[6]

And her husband, especially if he had a little "Alliance education," could add:

> ... All my life I've worked and slaved,
> Raised good crops and always saved;
> Trusts and combines make prices fall,
> Taxes and interest gobble it all. ...[7]

North Carolina of course suffered the ills of the South as a whole, and a few others of its own besides. After the war the state was "naked and without credit." Borrowed capital became an absolute necessity, and the only security that a small farmer could offer for a short-term loan was a mortgage on his crop. Therefore, to protect the landlord who advanced money or supplies, the legislature passed lien laws. At first they were beneficial as well as necessary. Within a few years, however, the crop lien became, in the hands of the landlord-merchant class, an instru-

---

[5] *National Economist*, I, 280 (July 20, 1889).
[6] Ida M. Tarbell, *The Nationalizing of Business*, p. 134.
[7] Florence H. Olmstead, *Alliance Nightingale*, song No. 26.

ment of oppression. In 1887 the newly-established North Carolina Bureau of Labor Statistics reported that the system had brought more misery to the farmers of the state than all other evils combined, including droughts, floods, cyclones, storms, rust, and caterpillars! Wherever the farmers depended upon the lien system for supplies, they were in debt; wherever they raised their own supplies, they were free from debt. But, stated the report, "It is useless to talk about diversified crops to a man who pays 40 per cent. for supplies."

Inevitably, the North Carolina farmer fell victim to the one-crop evil. Devoted entirely to cotton or tobacco, he was ignorant of most other crops and afraid to try the few he knew. He bought costly fertilizers for his worn-out soil, and, hoping to increase his purchasing power, often planted a larger crop than he could adequately care for. Above all, the merchant who "ran" him demanded the cotton or the tobacco because he could handle it easily. So, a North Carolina farmer would go to a North Carolina store for "a bale of Indiana prairie hay, a bag of Richmond meal, a sack of Milwaukee flour, . . . a side of Chicago bacon," and sometimes even "cabbages shipped from Germany and Irish potatoes from Scotland."

That North Carolina largely depended upon other parts of the country for some of its most elementary needs could be specifically illustrated. During the year 1885 the Wilmington and Weldon Railroad, which ran through the cotton belt, transported six basic articles as follows:

	From and to points in North Carolina	Received from adjoining states
Bacon, pounds	765,860	16,465,900
Livestock, head	235	2,172
Flour, barrels	9,496	56,589
Cotton ties and bagging, pounds	514,560	2,001,600
Grain, bushels	92,375	198,273
Lime, stone, etc., pounds	1,994,460	2,254,420 [8]

[8] Calvin H. Wiley, "North Carolina," in [Ser. No. 2476] 49 Cong., 2 Sess. (1886-87), *House Exec. Docs.*, XVII, 242.

From 1870 to 1887 agricultural conditions in the state had shown steady relative improvement, but the next several years were years of acute depression. The price of cotton hovered around eight and nine cents a pound; wheat fell from its average of $1.07 a bushel during the 1880's to eighty-six cents and less; corn dropped all the way from forty-six to twenty-eight cents a bushel. Nearly eighteen per cent of the state's taxed acres were mortgaged, with every acre averaging a mortgage burden of fifty-three cents. Land, of course, lay wholly in the open, while the property of merchants and bankers stayed largely hidden. Much official encouragement was given to the private building and expansion of railroads, but no efforts were being made to tax and regulate them for the protection of the farmers.

Here and there, it is true, one could find reasons for optimism. North Carolina was the only Southern state in 1890 to show an increase in the value of its farm lands over 1860. More efficient farming methods, improved agricultural implements, wider application of steam power, better housing, the rapid extension of transportation facilities, increased fruit production, and the development of truck farming were all in evidence.

Nevertheless, the general aspect remained dismal. Outside observers were struck by the strange paradox of poverty in the midst of plenty. Natural resources appeared to be both marvelous and abundant, yet the people suffered. William D. Kelley, after a trip through the state in 1887, remarked: "As I travelled through this native wealth and beauty I saw how sin had driven man out of Paradise, for never had I seen such poverty as I found in North Carolina, save in South Carolina, Alabama, and Mississippi, where people are starving in the midst of nature's richest bounties."[9]

Polk, in the *Progressive Farmer,* addressed himself seriously to the problem. In North Carolina men had always said: "As agriculture flourishes, everything else flourishes; as agriculture languishes, everything else languishes." Yet in 1887 the old saying no

[9] William D. Kelley, *The Old South and the New,* pp. 117-18.

longer held true. Towns and cities, banks, insurance companies, railroads, factories, speculators, and corporations were flourishing; yet agriculture languished. "Almost every week for the past year," Polk wrote, "we have seen beautiful and rose tinted pictures of the prosperity of the 'New South' in all its departments of industry but we have been careful not to transfer them to the pages of this paper, for we know that so far as they portrayed the condition of our farmers they were lamentably untrue and deceptive." Not since 1865 had the farmers of the state been "so depressed, so gloomy, so despondent, so hopeless." Hard times were causing many to leave their farms and move to the towns. "WHAT IS THE MATTER?" inquired one editorial. "WHERE IS THE WRONG AND WHAT IS THE REMEDY?" queried another. Polk asked rhetorically: Was the trouble the lien system? the one-crop system? the "buy-all" system?[10]

Fine crops and higher prices made 1887 a fairly good year, but 1888 and 1889 were disastrous. A committee representing the Farmers' Alliances of Chatham County wrote:

> The failure of the crops in this county last year necessitates the buying of almost our entire supplies to make another crop, and there is very little money in the hands of the farmers. Almost every farmer is depressed; many are disheartened; labor is unremunerative; the value of land is depreciating, and there is a growing disposition to abandon the farm and seek other employment. Unless something is done to bring relief, many will be compelled to give up their farms. The boasted progress and increase of wealth in North Carolina is not shared by the farmers. They are gradually but steadily becoming poorer and poorer every year.[11]

The general effect was much like that felt by the farmer after his annual experience with the "crap lien," as all honest-to-goodness Tar Heels called it:

[10] *Progressive Farmer,* Jan. 12, April 28, 1887.
[11] *N. C. Pub. Docs., 1889,* No. 25.

At the winding up of the year the crap lien began to draw, and it kept on drawing. It drew all the cotton and the corn, the wheat and the oats, the shucks, the hay and the fodder, the horses and the mules, the cows, the hogs and the poultry, the farm utensils and the wagons, the carriage and the buggy; and, not being satisfied with its drawing outside, it drew the household and kitchen furniture, and . . . it didn't quit drawing until it got the table, the plates and the dishes, the cups and the saucers, the knives and the forks, and, when it had gotten everything else, it reached for the dish rag, and wiped up the whole concern, not leaving even a grease spot.[12]

When things go wrong, go West—that was an old American tradition; and North Carolinians were among its most faithful adherents. North Carolina had always contributed generously to the population of the West. The census of 1890, reflecting of course a trend of many years, disclosed that almost 300,000 natives of the state were living elsewhere. Aside from neighboring Tennessee, Georgia, Virginia, and South Carolina, to which North Carolinians would most naturally migrate, the states that attracted most of the white emigrants were Texas, Arkansas, Missouri, and Indiana, while those that received the bulk of the colored emigrants were Mississippi, Arkansas, Louisiana, Texas, and Alabama. Both before and during the 1880's thousands of people seemingly considered North Carolina "a good place to leave."

The "Negro exodus" is of special interest. Since the end of the war many white people had expressed the wish that all the Negroes would leave the state and be replaced by white settlers. Polk, for instance, had "naught but feelings of kindness" for the Negro, whose bearing he thought had been "commendable." Yet he felt the Negro was "an incubus—a solid, dead barrier to our progress" who kept the white man away. Polk would, therefore, "hail with delight and rejoicing his peaceful departure, and would pray God's blessing to attend him."[13] When Negroes actually did

---

[12] Richard H. Whitaker, *Reminiscences, Incidents and Anecdotes*, pp. 101-2.
[13] *Progressive Farmer*, April 30, May 21, 1889.

emigrate, however, there was widespread alarm and angry opposition, for North Carolina depended heavily upon Negro labor. Dissatisfied with their economic and social status, and lured by "labor agents" and railroads, nearly 50,000 Negroes in 1889 alone left the state to seek fairer chances in the Southwest. Tenants and farm laborers in particular hoped to buy, settle, and improve land of their own. The leaders of the movement, chiefly preachers, protested the disqualification of Negro voters in North Carolina, the curtailment of educational opportunities, and the prejudice and discrimination invoked by the whites. Significantly, the "exodusters" also condemned the Farmers' Alliance, declaring it "an oppressive institution to the colored laborer."

Complementary to the economic ills suffered by the state were the social ills, of which perhaps the most striking was the illiteracy of the people. The 1880 census revealed that no less than 31.7 per cent of the native whites were "returned as unable to write" —the highest percentage in the nation. Only the fact that the Negro percentage of 77.4 was exceeded in four other Southern states kept North Carolina from ranking at the bottom of the list for the combined groups. Ten years later the percentage of white illiteracy stood at 25, and North Carolina had crept ahead of Kentucky. No doubt emigration played a large part in the change.

During the 'eighties little more than half the children of each race were on the school rolls, and but a fourth of them constituted the average daily attendance. School terms were reckoned in weeks rather than months, teachers' salaries were pitifully low, and public support was conspicuously apathetic. Few public libraries existed, and those were small. The average literate citizen did not have the means to buy books; the daily or weekly newspaper was about as far as he could get. The day of the apostles of education was yet to come.

In North Carolina, the South, and the nation all these factors created "the wrong." What, then, was "the remedy"?

CHAPTER XIII

THE REMEDY

THE FARMERS of the country turned again to organization as "the remedy" for their troubles. In the 'seventies the chief vehicle for their discontent had been the Grange; in the 'eighties it became the Farmers' Alliance.

The "Northern Alliance" developed from modest beginnings in New York and Kansas. It was molded into an effective agency for reform by the editor of the Chicago *Western Rural,* Milton George, who specialized in criticizing the railroad evils. This order reached its greatest strength in the Midwest and the Northwest during the deflationary years of the late 1880's.

The "Southern Alliance" originated in Texas. Curiously enough, it began as a secret society of farmers organized to assist civil officers in the apprehension of horse thieves. From this it turned into a social and fraternal order concerned mainly with co-operative buying and selling. The man behind the movement was the intelligent and versatile Charles W. Macune. Born in Wisconsin, he had roved in California, Kansas, and Texas, had studied law and practiced medicine, and had become deeply interested in agricultural conditions. He spoke and wrote with almost effortless ease and possessed a magnetic personality. In Dallas Macune founded the ambitious Farmers' Alliance Exchange, through which Texas farmers could sell their cotton and purchase all kinds of supplies. Like most other agricultural co-operatives of the time, it failed—because of overexpansion, cut-throat competition, the opposition of long-established business, and poor management. But the cash saving to the farmers and the lesson in co-operation were not easily forgotten. Macune succeeded in unifying the various elements of the Texas Alliance and quickly caught the enthusiasm of the members with talk of expanding the Alliance eastward. Realizing that certain fundamental differences existed between the agriculture of the South and that of the Midwest and Northwest, Macune believed that his organization should concentrate upon the cotton states only.

An "Inter-State Convention of Farmers," held in Atlanta in August, 1887, was a useful starting point. "Strong, brawny looking men, mostly bearded, with sun-tanned faces and necks, with a hardy color of good health," came by the score from ten Southern states to tackle the problem of agricultural depression in their region. Among the leaders were Macune and E. B. Warren from Texas; General W. R. Miles from Mississippi; J. S. Newman, president of the convention, and Reuben F. Kolb from Alabama; W. J. Northen, W. H. Felton, and L. F. Livingston from Georgia; and L. L. Polk, W. H. S. Burgwyn, and Dr. D. Reid Parker from North Carolina. The North Carolinians, riding the crest of the strong farmers' movement in their own state, headed the largest of the out-of-state delegations and took prominent parts in the sessions. A refreshing breeze stirred DeGive's Opera House just as the convention opened and put the delegates in a good mood as they listened to the welcoming speeches of Governor John B. Gordon, Henry W. Grady, and other notables.

Polk had been requested to prepare a paper on "Defects in the Agricultural System of the Cotton States."[1] In his presentation he listed the five principal defects as follows: first, the "one crop" or "all cotton" system, which forced Southern farmers to pay high prices to the North for supplies that they should be producing cheaply at home; second, the Negro tenant system, which should be replaced by white immigration; third, the "broad acre" system, a heritage of slavery days, under which the Southern

---

[1] L. L. Polk, *Address* . . . *Delivered before the Inter-State Convention of Farmers* . . . *Atlanta* . . . *1887*.

farmer was cultivating much land poorly rather than a little land well; fourth, "want of unity of action or co-operation among our farmers," which made them prey to all those groups already organized; and fifth, "a want of practical training and agricultural education for the masses."

Polk pointed out that fifty-one per cent of the American people were engaged in agriculture, that they paid eighty per cent of the taxes, and that they supplied over seventy per cent of the country's exports. In the ten cotton states represented at the convention, seventy-one per cent of the people were in agriculture and these constituted thirty-eight per cent of the agricultural population of the nation. Since this was so, it seemed hardly right that Southern agriculture should be so terribly depressed and that other industries should prosper at the farmers' expense. The Atlanta *Constitution* termed the paper "admirably read . . . one of the ablest essays ever delivered in Georgia"; and remarked that "Mr. Polk . . . is exerting a strong influence in the convention."[2]

For his part, Polk felt sure that the solution to the problem of agricultural depression lay in the immediate organization of the farmers. Early in the sessions he introduced a resolution looking to "closer union and co-operation of the farmers of the South, and . . . if practicable the co-operation of the farmers of the whole country." Macune, too, was ready. He spoke to the gathering on the subject of organization and took occasion to mention briefly the Farmers' Alliance.

Southern farmers in 1887 were obviously eager to organize. Some even favored independent political action, though this did not apply to the great majority. The pungent words of Alson J. Streeter, guest of the convention from Illinois, evoked sharp response from both groups:

> Here is the remedy for you. Now I tell you, if you are not a coward you can get it; I tell you, gentlemen, you can get it through political organization. That may not sound happy to

[2] Atlanta *Constitution,* Aug. 17-19, 1887.

many of you, gentlemen, who are politicians in the South. It may not suit you that there should be a third party in the land [applause] but let me tell you it exists and you can not help it.... I know that the aristocracy of wealth exists in this country to an alarming extent; and if you organize they will not like it. They will send the old bell wethers among you and the whippers in, and they will say: "Lambs, you make a mistake, you must stick to the old reliable party." They will say further, "lambs, I see that your fleece is gone, and that you are cold this October morning, [laughter and applause] but it is not our party that has got your fleece. It is the other old political party." [Applause.] Stick to the old reliable party, and when the November election comes the bell wether will ring the bell, and they will call the lambs to the polls and they will stick. [Applause.] ... Mr. President, I don't know whether I am diverging too much from the question. [Cries of "go on! go on!"]....[3]

Polk probably expressed the sentiments of the majority when he said next day: "Political parties in this country can and will take care of themselves. [Applause.] We want the farmers to take care of themselves. [Applause.]"

By acclamation the delegates elected Polk president of the Inter-State Farmers' Association and voted to hold their next meeting in Raleigh. The Association convened in Raleigh as scheduled in 1888, and in Montgomery, Alabama, in 1889. On each occasion Polk was unanimously re-elected president.

Farmers' Alliance organizers, under the skillful direction of Macune, entered the various Southern states beginning in 1887. One of the first of the states was North Carolina, where, for a year past, Polk had already prepared the ground with his independent organization of farmers' clubs. Polk had followed the career of the Texas Alliance with keen interest, and quickly convinced himself that it, more than any other organization, promised the greatest hope for the large-scale co-operation of the farmers. From the beginning he had hoped that all the agricultural organizations

[3] Inter-State Convention of Farmers, *Proceedings, 1887,* pp. 32-33.

of the country would eventually merge. Therefore he welcomed the Alliance and promptly joined it himself. He became a member of Oak Ridge Alliance, No. 24, in Wake County, on July 8.[4]

In Atlanta Polk conferred at length with Macune, who was president of the order, and met E. B. Warren, the secretary, and several other members. Upon his return to North Carolina Polk reported that the Farmers' Alliance "numbers already three-fourths of a million in the Southern States," and he predicted that within a year "the farmers of this State will be counted on its rolls by tens of thousands." Not long after the Atlanta meeting, on October 4, the North Carolina State Alliance was organized at Rockingham.[5]

Growth from now on was rapid. One of the visiting organizers, who began his itinerary at Raleigh, stated: "In spite of all opposing influences that could be brought to bear in Wake County, I met the farmers in public meetings twenty-seven times, and twenty-seven times they organized. . . . The farmers seem like unto ripe fruit—you can gather them by a gentle shake of the bush."[6] In Edgecombe County the Alliance soon came to be so strongly organized that there was "hardly an interval of five miles . . . that did not have an organization."[7] Polk wrote in December that twenty-one Alliance organizers were at work in the state, but that "it would employ over five times that number to meet the demand!"[8]

At Greensboro in January, 1888, the State Alliance absorbed the North Carolina Farmers' Association, which had been organized at the famous mass meeting of farmers in Raleigh exactly one

[4] Sydenham B. Alexander to Polk, June 9, 1886; *Progressive Farmer*, June 23, 1886, May 12, 1887, Jan. 5, 1888; William J. Peele, "Col. L. L. Polk: a Brief Sketch of His Life and Work," *North Carolina Baptist Almanac for the Year 1893*, p. 47.
[5] *Progressive Farmer*, Sept. 8, 22, Oct. 13, 1887.
[6] J. B. Barry, in William L. Garvin and S. O. Daws, *History of the National Farmers' Alliance and Co-operative Union of America*, pp. 49-50.
[7] J. Kelly Turner and John L. Bridgers, *History of Edgecombe County, North Carolina*, p. 292.
[8] *Progressive Farmer*, Dec. 8, 1887.

year before. When the North Carolina Farmers' State Alliance met jointly with the Inter-State Association in Raleigh in August, 1888, it reported a total of 1,018 local Alliances and 53 county Alliances with a membership of 42,000. At Fayetteville the next year the figures were 1,816 local units, 89 county units, and 72,000 members. By the time of the Asheville meeting in 1890 the number of subordinate Alliances had increased to 2,147, county Alliances to 95, and members to 90,000. The organization in North Carolina reached its peak in 1891, when at the annual convention in Morehead City, 2,221 subordinate Alliances, 96 county Alliances, and 100,000 members were officially reported. Even allowing for possible inflation, these figures are impressive. The growth of the Farmers' Alliance in the rest of the South appeared just as remarkable.

The Alliance was by no means the only farmers' order in the region. It was, however, the most powerful and the most appealing, and possessed excellent leadership. In a series of notable meetings the Farmers' Alliance now absorbed practically all of the other farm organizations in the South, together with two in the Northwest.

At Shreveport in October, 1887, the Farmers' Union of Louisiana united with Macune's group to form the National Farmers' Alliance and Co-operative Union of America. The following year at Meridian, Mississippi, the Agricultural Wheel was added. The Wheel was strongest in Arkansas but claimed many members in surrounding states as well. The consolidated organization was styled the Farmers' and Laborers' Union of America. At St. Louis in December, 1889, the Farmers' Mutual Benefit Association and the "Northwestern Alliance" joined the movement. The latter represented the grain states of North Dakota, South Dakota, and Kansas. Yet consolidation with the "Northern Alliance" as a whole, which was strongest in the Midwest, failed. Much sectional feeling still prevailed, and there were important differences of economic interest. The Northerners, moreover, feared the

THE REMEDY

greater numbers and influence of the "Southern Alliance," while the Southerners disliked the third-party bent of the "Northern Alliance." Even so, organizations representing over 2,000,000 farmers of the South and West united at St. Louis to form the National Farmers' Alliance and Industrial Union and arranged at the same time to secure the close co-operation of the Colored Alliance and the Knights of Labor.

As the Alliance gathered more and more farmers into the fold, more and more non-farmers asked the questions, What sort of organization is it? Why does it appeal so strongly to the farmers? What are its aims and objectives?

A contemporary publicist of the Farmers' Alliance wrote that it was "born of necessity, nurtured amid want and distress, and stands to-day as the champion of the down-trodden of earth." He added: "It is not properly an organization—it is a growth...."[9] The logical antecedent of the Alliance movement was the Granger movement, which also demanded the regulation of the railroads, advised the establishment of business co-operatives, and agitated for the improvement of agriculture. Although the Grange had sadly declined, farmers who once had enjoyed its benefits were quite ready to join another organization that, by more aggressive tactics, promised better results. Viewed broadly, the Alliance-Populist movement, like the Granger movement before it and the Progressive, New Freedom, and New Deal movements after it, was a struggle for industrial and agricultural democracy as opposed to corporate dictation.

The leaders, Macune above all, insisted that the Farmers' Alliance was primarily a business organization. "Let the Alliance be a business organization for business purposes, and as such necessarily secret, and as secret necessarily strictly non-political," he said.[10] The Alliance first attempted local co-operatives, then the

---
[9] Nelson A. Dunning, *Farmers' Alliance History and Agricultural Digest*, p. 180.
[10] National Farmers' Alliance and Co-operative Union, *Proceedings, 1887*, p. 4.

more important state business agencies. In some states individual agents were appointed—and in others joint stock companies were organized—for the purpose of making purchases advantageous to the farmers. For a time these flourished. As an instance, the capital stock of the North Carolina business agency eventually amounted to $30,000, and in the year 1890 $325,000 worth of business was done—in fertilizers, groceries, farm implements, seeds, fruit trees, and "notions." The state business agent reported:

> I found that the commercial world did not know the Farmers' Alliance, and it seems that they did not want to know them. Things have changed now. There is no trouble to get any article we want, if we only have the money to get it with. . . . To-day we can buy most any article at from 10 to 60 per cent. off. . . .[11]

It is interesting to note that the success of the North Carolina plan inspired the farmers of Indiana to adopt it. Nevertheless, such agricultural co-operatives, with their small capital and credit, met a hard life and after a little time disappeared. They seemed unable to solve the tremendous problem presented by farmers who had to depend upon credit for their supplies.

From its beginning the "Southern Alliance," unlike the "Northern Alliance," had been "secret." Together with the rigid membership qualifications, this policy of secrecy proved largely responsible for developing the unity and strength of the organization. Experience had shown that the secrecy of a fraternal order carried great appeal in the South. Also, as Polk pointed out, meetings of the Farmers' Alliance were secret for the same reason that meetings of bank directors or railroad executives were secret: so that the organization could *"manage its own business in its own way."* At the St. Louis convention a local reporter considered it noteworthy that "for one solid hour a row of delegates and members filed up the steps and in the corridor before the hall,

[11] North Carolina Farmers' State Alliance, *Proceedings, 1890,* pp. 13-15.

THE REMEDY

and each . . . farmer stepped up and gripped the doorkeeper's hand, . . . at the same time placing his mouth close to his ear and whispering the password." [12]

By the terms of the Alliance constitution only farmers, farm laborers, mechanics, country preachers, country school teachers, country doctors, and editors of strictly agricultural papers could join the organization. These had to be over sixteen years of age, and white persons. Lawyers, even "country lawyers," were pointedly excluded. One agricultural paper expressed a very common point of view when it asseverated: "One lawyer in a Farmers' order will raise more disorder than a hundred Farmers. . . ." [13]

Naturally the political possibilities of the great popular movement became a burning question in the land. "The farmer in politics" came to be a topic of animated discussion both outside and inside the Alliance. Aware that politics could easily disrupt the order, the leaders determined at the start that the order should be non-partisan and that its members would be at perfect liberty with respect to party affiliation.

"We don't want a farmers' party," Polk declared, "but we do want to see the farmers of this country take sufficient interest in political matters and political action to keep a strict eye on all that their party does." [14] Farmers who had faithfully served a political party for many years were certainly entitled now to ask their party to serve them a little. "Plainly," said Macune, "we will not consent to give indefinite support to men who are. . . unfriendly to our interests. . . . If this be party treason, make the most of it." Alliance policy should be to work for reform within the major party lines; only if that failed should a third party be considered. As for the leaders of the movement, "they are prepared to be misunderstood; they are prepared to be traduced

[12] St. Louis *Globe-Democrat*, Dec. 4, 1889.
[13] *Farm, Field and Stock*, Nov. 1, 1890.
[14] *Progressive Farmer*, Feb. 23, 1888.

and denounced; they are prepared for malice and scorn and hate...."[15]

In the four years between the conception of the *Progressive Farmer* and the St. Louis convention Polk's stature as an agrarian leader increased enormously. Without patronage, with only "faith, nerve and energy," he launched his paper at a time when the farmers of North Carolina were "in debt and discouraged." Still, the first year witnessed the creation of hundreds of farmers' clubs, the reorganization of the state Department of Agriculture, and the establishment of the College of Agriculture and Mechanic Arts. Polk then decided to move the paper from Winston to Raleigh, believing that in the state capital he would be able to exercise even more influence. When Polk became secretary of the North Carolina Alliance, the *Progressive Farmer* became the state organ, and thenceforth its circulation swelled rapidly. From about 1,200 subscribers in July, 1887, the number by January, 1890, had grown to 11,760—the largest circulation that had ever been attained by a North Carolina newspaper. The paper went to over 1,200 post offices within the state, and to two-thirds of the states of the union. The office at 13 West Hargett Street usually stayed busy from early morning until ten o'clock at night.

Influential as Polk the editor was, Polk the orator was even more so. "It was the day of personal equation," Josephus Daniels has written, "and when farmers were thrilled by Colonel Polk's eloquence they wished to read his paper. The spoken word was more effective then than the printed page."[16] Many a subscription the editor of the *Progressive Farmer* brought back to Raleigh after a speaking trip.

As secretary, Polk was the working head of the Alliance in North Carolina between 1887 and 1890. His arduous routine duties included the keeping of records and rolls, correspondence

[15] *National Economist*, I, 145 (May 25, 1889), II, 221 (Dec. 21, 1889), 281 (Jan. 18, 1890).
[16] Josephus Daniels, in *News and Observer*, July 29, 1926.

with county and subordinate Alliances, and the preparation of reports and proceedings. The salary for the position amounted to $1,200 a year. In 1888 farm leaders of Virginia and South Carolina called upon Polk to assist them in organizing their state Alliances.

Polk was unanimously elected president of the Inter-State Farmers' Association three successive times, as has already been noted. His rise in the Farmers' Alliance proved almost as spectacular. At the Shreveport meeting in 1887 he was elected first vice-president of the national organization, and a year later became chairman of its executive committee.

In 1888 and 1889 he and other Southern agrarians distinguished themselves by waging a winning fight against the obnoxious "bagging trust." A few millionaires, they charged, combined resources and arbitrarily raised the price of jute bagging 4¾ cents per yard, further impoverishing the cotton farmers while netting a cool $2,000,000 themselves. Led by the Alliance, the farmers began a boycott of jute bagging, at the same time attempting to produce some other material with which to cover their cotton. Polk suggested: "We can make bagging of the straw of our long leaf pine . . . of jute grown in our own fields . . . of our poor grades of cotton. We can substitute wire for ties. . . . It can be done. It ought to be done." An "indignation meeting" of Alliance men from all Southern states was held in Birmingham, and out of it came the unanimous recommendation that only cotton be used for bagging. This procedure, they believed, would save the South the $4,000,000 annually paid for jute and would establish another Southern textile industry. The fight soon brought results: by 1890 the price of jute bagging had been cut fifty per cent.[17] Looking ahead, Polk said:

> The bagging trust is simply an outpost on the picket line. We may capture it, but behind it we will find line upon line of formidable breastworks which, if successfully stormed and

[17] *Progressive Farmer*, July 31–Sept. 4, 1888, *passim*, May 21, 28, Sept. 3–Oct. 22, 1889, *passim*.

captured, will but reveal to us a mighty fortress planted on Wall Street, over whose frowning battlements float[s] defiantly the flag of arrogant monopoly.[18]

In October, 1889, Henry W. Grady, high priest of the New South, invited Polk to come to Atlanta and be the main speaker on the "Alliance Day" program of the Piedmont Exposition. Polk accepted, and, accompanied by two of his daughters and Mr. and Mrs. Josephus Daniels, journeyed to Atlanta in the special Pullman car that Grady provided. The weather on October 24 was ideal. A recent rain had settled the dust, the atmosphere was clear and bright, and a cool north breeze was blowing. Between forty and fifty thousand people crowded the grounds—signal proof of the popularity of the Alliance in Georgia. Grady told Daniels that "Alliance Day" was even greater than "President Cleveland Day" two years before. Polk delivered a vigorous address, and when he concluded, the immense throng gave him a tremendous ovation.[19]

Six weeks later Polk reached the pinnacle. At St. Louis during the first week of December, 1889, delegates from agricultural organizations in seventeen states and Indian Territory elected him president of the National Farmers' Alliance and Industrial Union. Thus, less than two and a half years after he joined Oak Ridge Alliance in Wake County, North Carolina, he became head of the national organization, which numbered over 2,000,000 members. When Evan Jones of Texas, president of the order, declined to run again, Polk's opponents were Macune, former president, and Isaac McCracken of Arkansas, current vice-president. Macune withdrew on the fourth ballot, and on the fifth Polk won by a margin of eight votes. The delegates then made his election unanimous. Chosen with him were Benjamin H.

[18] Atlanta *Constitution,* Aug. 23, 1889.
[19] *Progressive Farmer,* Oct. 15, 1889; Atlanta *Journal,* Oct. 24, 1889; Raleigh *State Chronicle,* Oct. 25, Nov. 1, 1889.

Clover of Kansas, vice-president, J. H. Turner of Georgia, secretary, and various other officers and committees.[20]

The constitution adopted at St. Louis provided that the president should receive an annual salary of $3,000, office expenses, travel expenses, and $900 for a stenographer. It also required that the chief national officers establish their headquarters in Washington, D. C. The St. Louis meeting gave the president and the executive committee large powers and greatly strengthened the leadership of the Farmers' Alliance. Macune, who was chairman of the executive committee, and Polk remained the most important men in the order. "With some justification," Professor Hicks has written, "the southern leaders now assumed the right to direct the whole farmers' movement."[21]

When Polk returned home to Raleigh, he was given a royal reception. Friday, December 13, became what Henry Grady would have designated "L. L. Polk Day." In the morning a large number of Alliance men, state officials, and prominent citizens in carriages met Polk at his home. Headed by the Oak City brass band, and flanked by twenty-five members of Oak Ridge Alliance on horseback, the party escorted Polk to Metropolitan Hall, where he spoke of the work of the great organization that he represented as president. In the evening a banquet for the honored guest was given at the Yarborough House. Lieutenant-Governor Thomas M. Holt, President Alexander Q. Holladay of the A. and M. College, William J. Peele, Kemp P. Battle, and many other distinguished persons were present. Josephus Daniels served as chairman. Fourteen toasts were given and thirteen responses made before the address of the evening by Polk. He chose as his title "The New Revolution."[22]

Early in January, 1890, Polk went to Washington. He resigned

---

[20] St. Louis *Globe-Democrat,* Dec. 7, 1889; *Progressive Farmer,* Dec. 10, 1889.
[21] John D. Hicks, *The Populist Revolt,* p. 126.
[22] Raleigh *News and Observer,* Dec. 14, 1889; banquet program, Polk Papers.

as secretary of the State Alliance but retained his membership in Oak Ridge Alliance, his editorship of the *Progressive Farmer,* and his citizenship as a North Carolinian. Henceforth his work would be done mainly on the national scene.

"It is beginning to dawn upon the people of North Carolina," remarked the Raleigh *Standard,* "that Col. 'Double L' Polk, of the Progressive Farmer, is a great man."[23]

[23] Raleigh *Standard,* Dec., 1889.

Chapter XIV

THE NATIONAL SCENE

AT ITS SHREVEPORT MEETING in 1887, the "Southern Alliance" enounced eighteen demands upon Congress. Almost a third of them dealt with the land question. The farmers urged that the Government provide for small holdings of public lands and easy payments, that large holdings be taxed, that public lands forfeitable by railroads be thrown open for private purchase, that fences set on public lands by monopolistic corporations or cattle companies be removed, and that ownership of land by aliens be prohibited. They demanded the abolition of the national banking system and an increase in the supply of money. They called for revision of the tariff and reduction of the import duty on cotton goods. Of their remaining demands, the most specific and the most interesting were more stringent immigration laws, government operation of the telephone and telegraph systems, establishment of a federal Department of Agriculture, a graduated income tax, and the direct election of United States senators.[1]

It did not take the Alliance leaders long to learn that eighteen demands were too many. Important though each might be, the fire was scattered. At St. Louis, therefore, the number of demands was reduced to seven. It might almost be said that the number was reduced to one: the famous "sub-treasury plan." The battling Alliance laid aside its shotgun to take up what it hoped was a high-powered rifle.

The first suggestion of the sub-treasury plan seems to have

[1] National Farmers' Alliance and Co-operative Union, *Proceedings, 1887*, pp. 11-14.

come from Harry Skinner, a rising young lawyer and politician of eastern North Carolina. In *Frank Leslie's Illustrated Newspaper* for November 30, 1889, appeared an article by Skinner entitled "The Hope of the South," which grew out of a much earlier essay of his called "A Landed Basis for Our National Bank Issue." [2]

In the article he pointed out that the United States produced three-fourths of the world's cotton, of which one-fourth was consumed at home and three-fourths abroad. Since the demand was always equal to the supply, there was no overproduction. The producers of this great wealth, however, lacked the protection that cotton manufacturers enjoyed. In all justice to the planters, then, a plan should be devised that would make it unnecessary for them to have to sell their product at a price dictated by the Liverpool Cotton Exchange.

Skinner suggested that the Government use part of its Treasury surplus to build warehouses in the South. Then let it increase the price of cotton to, say, thirteen cents a pound—forty-seven per cent over the prevailing market price. If the manufacturers refused to pay thirteen cents, the producers would store their cotton in the warehouses and wait for a price rise. On depositing his cotton an individual planter would receive "cotton certificates" based upon a rate of fourteen cents, the extra cent, paid by the planter, for handling charges. The certificates would be negotiable, and could be used as legal tender. Undoubtedly the manufacturers would rather pay thirteen cents for cotton than fourteen cents for certificates. In all likelihood the plan would destroy the Liverpool and New York exchanges, and with them "the cotton speculation of the world." The American monopoly of cotton, moreover, would prevent retaliation by other countries. Skinner went on to say that Western farmers, too, might wish to adopt the same general plan. In any case, an increase in the purchasing power

---

[2] "Sketch of Harry Skinner," in N. C. Bar Assn., *Proceedings, 1915,* pp. 238-41.

of the South would result in a greater demand for the foodstuffs of the West.

Precisely one week after the publication date of Skinner's article the sub-treasury plan of the Farmers' Alliance was officially announced at St. Louis.[3] On December 7, 1889, at the final session of the convention, it was presented to the delegates by a "committee on the monetary system" consisting of Charles W. Macune and H. S. P. Ashby of Texas, L. L. Polk of North Carolina, Leonidas F. Livingston of Georgia, and W. Scott Morgan of Arkansas. The committee report seemed to indicate clearly the influence of Skinner's ideas, but to just as great an extent it bore the unmistakable stamp of Macune. Out of the Texan's fertile mind and long experience came a greatly broadened version of the plan that was designed to appeal to the West as well as the South.

The report charged that the financial policy of the Government, under both political parties, favored the speculating class. Under law this class could fix prices, contract the currency, and speculate upon the products raised by impoverished farmers. Such "power of money to oppress" was evil. The report demanded as remedies the free and unlimited coinage of silver and the enactment of the new sub-treasury system.

As Macune and his fellow committee members conceived it, the plan first called for the abolition of "the system of using certain banks as United States depositories." In place of the national banks, the Government should establish a sub-treasury office in each of the nation's counties that annually offered for sale at least $500,000 worth of non-perishable farm products—wheat, corn, oats, barley, rye, rice, tobacco, cotton, wool, and sugar. Connected with the sub-treasury office would be a government warehouse or elevator, to which a farmer could bring his produce for storage. At the time he made his deposit there the

---

[3] Farmers' and Laborers' Union, *Proceedings, 1889*, pp. 57-65.

farmer would receive a negotiable certificate of deposit, and on it would be able to obtain, at a low rate of interest, a loan equal to four-fifths the value of his stored produce. He would be charged a nominal sum for handling and insurance and would have to redeem his produce within twelve months—otherwise it would be sold at auction. As an instance:

> A farmer has 10,000 bushels of corn, which at current rates is worth 25 cents per bushel, or $2,500. He wishes to hold the corn for a higher market, but he must have some ready cash. He puts the corn in a Government warehouse and receives a certificate of deposit which itself is negotiable, and also a loan of eighty per cent. of the value of the grain, or $2,000 in cash. He can redeem the corn at his pleasure on payment of the principal and interest at the rate of one per cent. per annum.[4]

The report of the "committee on the monetary system," sponsored as it was by five of the best-known figures in the Alliance, was adopted by the delegates as expected. Polk hailed this as "the most important action taken by any body of men in this country, since the adoption of the Federal Constitution."[5] With equal unrestraint, Macune's sobersided *National Economist* presented the committee report to the world under the first exclamatory headline of its career: "EUREKA! *Key to the Solution of the Industrial Problem of the Age.*"[6]

The proponents of the sub-treasury plan were fully convinced that it would prove ideal for the relief of the mortgage-burdened farmers of the West and the merchant-burdened farmers of the South. No longer would farmers be forced to sell their crops in the fall, when the sudden expansion of trade made money dear and prices low, and then buy their supplies in the spring, when money was cheap and prices were high. Short-term credit would

---

[4] Henry R. Chamberlain, *The Farmers' Alliance: What It Aims to Accomplish*, p. 21.
[5] *Progressive Farmer*, Dec. 24, 1889.
[6] *National Economist*, II, 225 (Dec. 28, 1889).

be provided. The rate of interest would be lowered from the ten per cent that borrowers paid the national banks to the one or two per cent required by the sub-treasury. The currency would be made more elastic—a condition that would favor debtors. Yet because of the sound and tangible security upon which it was based—the agricultural products of the country—the currency would be safe and stable. Also, gambling in crop futures would be effectually prevented.

Led by Polk and Macune, Alliance editors and lecturers attempted in 1890 to rally the members of the organization solidly behind the plan. The sub-treasury was to be the prime issue, and support of it a yardstick by which political candidates would be measured. Hundreds of petitions were showered upon Congress. Such legal and historical precedents as could be found were cited, and propaganda was freely issued to counter the inevitable opposition that so radical a scheme naturally aroused.

The non-agricultural world opposed the sub-treasury plan for several reasons. There would be the dangerous possibility of unlimited currency expansion, together with violent fluctuations of the currency at different seasons of the year. High prices for the farmer might seriously injure the urban consumer—and, in the case of a commodity like cotton, might eventually injure the farmer himself by stimulating cheap competitive production abroad. By the $500,000 provision the measure favored the more prosperous counties, whose farmers needed help least of all. There were also cries of "paternalism," "class legislation," and "unconstitutionality." Owing to its different economic interests and problems, the "Northern Alliance" never showed sympathy. Even a large segment of the "Southern Alliance" was outspoken in its opposition.[7]

Sub-treasury bills were introduced in Congress by Representative John A. Pickler, of South Dakota, and Senator Zebulon B. Vance, of North Carolina. On April 22 Polk, president of the National Farmers' Alliance and Industrial Union, and Macune,

[7] John D. Hicks, *The Populist Revolt*, ch. vii.

chairman of the executive committee and editor of the national organ, appeared before the Senate Committee on Agriculture and Forestry to state the case of the farmers. "I intend to make things *rattle*," Polk had written his son-in-law. His speech, however, dealt with the general subject of agricultural depression. Macune followed with a detailed explanation of the sub-treasury idea. The members of the Committee "evinced a deep interest in both addresses, and asked many questions." Of the Senate bill, Polk said: "We do not claim that it is the best, or the only measure through which relief may be brought to our oppressed, suffering and distressed people, but we submit it as the best we have been able to devise. We would be only too happy to receive at your hands a wiser and a better measure."[8]

Eighteen-ninety, of course, was an election year. With the sub-treasury plan now in the hands of Congress, the Alliance turned its main attention to politics. Officially the organization was non-partisan. It encouraged its members to support only those candidates who favored the reform program of the farmers. As a North Carolina paper expressed it, the farmer's duty was "to see that every man elected to legislate for the people is an alliance man in principle if not by membership."[9] Political activity dearly appealed to human nature, and to Alliance men it promised highly significant results. The New York *Sun* predicted that if "these Hayseed Socialists" are able to work together, "there may be, in the next year or two, some of the liveliest and most surprising politics ever known in these United States."[10]

Every Alliance leader knew full well the first requirement for national political success: the co-operation of the South and the West. A community of interest based upon agriculture would seem to draw the two sections close together. At times in the past they *had* stood together in opposition to the commercial and industrial

[8] L. L. Polk, *Agricultural Depression. . . . Speech . . . before the Senate Committee on Agriculture and Forestry, April 22, 1890.*
[9] Clinton *Caucasian*, May 29, 1890.
[10] Quoted in *Public Opinion*, VIII, 532 (March 15, 1890).

Northeast. Yet, even in 1890, the practice of party politicians in reviving old war passions for the purpose of winning votes threatened to keep the sections apart.

The elimination of sectionalism early came to be an Alliance policy. Obviously, political expediency was an important consideration. Many Alliance leaders, however, had more idealistic motives as well. This certainly applies to Polk, whose crusade against sectionalism undoubtedly became the most dramatic and the most fervent of his career. He had declared many times in earlier years that the tragic past should be forgotten.[11] Just before the St. Louis convention he told Scott Morgan: "It is my heart's desire that the North and South shall be united. Neither section can make this fight alone. Our interests are the same."[12] As president of the great farmers' organization Polk found himself in a position to make his influence felt. He wrote:

> As a rule, the soldiers of the North and the South were willing and anxious to accept and abide by the result, in good faith. They knew they had fought like men, and they were willing to accept the result like men. . . .
> But the selfish, sectional agitator again appeared upon the scene, and, with unholy purpose, spared not even the sacred dust of the heroic dead that he might inflame and keep alive the bitter recollections and animosities of the past. . . . Ordinarily he was the man, North and South, who was "invisible in war, and had become invincible in peace." . . .
> The evils under which the great laboring millions of America are suffering are national in their character, and can never be corrected by sectional effort or sectional remedies. . . . Failing in all else we may undertake as an organization, if we shall accomplish only a restoration of fraternity and unity . . . the Alliance will have won for itself immortal glory and honor.[13]

---

[11] Raleigh *Evening Visitor*, April 16, 1880; Raleigh *News and Observer*, Oct. 13, 1883; Raleigh *Farmer and Mechanic*, June 11, 1884.
[12] W. Scott Morgan, in St. Louis *New Forum*, June 16, 1892.
[13] L. L. Polk, "Sectionalism and the Alliance," in Nelson A. Dunning and others, *Farmers' Alliance History and Agricultural Digest*, pp. 249-53.

Against odds that seemed formidable, much progress toward reconciliation had been made between 1875 and 1890. A new generation grew up. The various centennial celebrations of the period commemorated a common past. Northern and Southern veterans held numerous joint reunions. Business became more and more nationalized. Literature portraying the essential harmony of the sections appeared. Former Confederate leaders, like Jefferson Davis, expressed the sincere hope that the nation would remain forever united.

The Farmers' Alliance now plunged into the political campaign with the three-fold object of unifying the farmers of the country, electing legislators sympathetic to agricultural interests, and securing financial reform through the passage of a sub-treasury bill.

The campaign proved to be most spectacular in the Northwest, particularly in Kansas. There, in the happy words of one of its historians, "it was a religious revival, a crusade, a pentecost of politics in which a tongue of flame sat upon every man, and each spake as the spirit gave him utterance." [14] Alarmed by continuing hard times and incensed by the failure of their legislators to relieve their distress, many farmers supported new political groups —first the Union Labor Party and then the People's Party. With oratory, songs, and parades they rallied their cohorts. The Alliance, under the leadership of men like Jerry Simpson, Ignatius Donnelly, James B. Weaver, and William A. Peffer, and women like Mary E. Lease and Annie L. Diggs, anticipated a revolution.

John J. Ingalls of Kansas was perhaps the leading symbol of what these farmers were fighting against. In eighteen years in the United States Senate, they charged, he had done nothing for the farmer or the laborer, and he was a preacher of sectional hate. Early in 1890 the Kansas Alliance called upon Ingalls to state his views with respect to the farmers' various demands. He did not answer. The Alliance thereupon campaigned to defeat him,

[14] Elizabeth N. Barr, "The Populist Uprising," in William E. Connelley, *Standard History of Kansas and Kansans*, II, 1148.

refusing to support any candidate for the state legislature who favored his re-election. A contemporary poet was moved to write:

> Yet, 'mid all this calamity, there's Ingalls—
> What hath he done for Kansas? He doth flaunt
>   His brains around, and with the nation mingles,—
> But it is cash, not brains, the people want.
>   Down, down with Ingalls! brains don't represent
> The people *now* in Kansas worth a cent.[15]

In the summer and again in the fall Polk toured practically every state of the Midwest and the Northwest. The organized farmers and their friends gave him a hearty welcome and displayed tremendous zeal for the Alliance cause. "The people are terribly in earnest," Polk wrote, "and the politicians are correspondingly depressed. One thing I note with great pleasure, any and all expressions from me against sectionalism are hailed with genuine and enthusiastic approval."[16] At Columbus, Ohio, it was reported, his "noble sentiments for fraternity and brotherhood between the North and South, especially among the farmers, created the warmest response from the audience." At Coldwater, Michigan, "the meeting closed with three rousing cheers for the speaker and the Alliance"; and the paper noting that fact declared, "When a Southern orator can address a Michigan meeting, and receive three rousing cheers, it begins to look like the 'bloody shirt' war was about at an end."[17] Upon being told by Polk of this feeling in the Midwest and Northwest, Alliance men in North Carolina at once passed resolutions expressing their friendship and appreciation.

The celebration at Emporia, Kansas, in July was typical. The headlines in the local paper told the story: "The Largest and Grandest Demonstration Ever Witnessed in the City of Emporia. The Farmers Out in Force With Bands of Music, Flags Flying

---

[15] Eugene F. Ware, in Connelley, *Ingalls of Kansas: a Character Study*, p. 206.
[16] *National Economist*, III, 285, 316 (July 19, Aug. 2, 1890).
[17] *Progressive Farmer*, Aug. 26, Nov. 4, 1890.

and Banners Waving. . . . The Procession about Four Miles Long —20,000 People Assembled on the Grounds. When the Head of the Procession was Under the Equator the Tail was Coming Around the North Pole." [18] After Polk's speech scores of farmers surged forward to shake hands. As a result of their hearty greetings his right hand became so badly swollen that he could not use it for hours afterward.

On a return visit to Kansas in October, Polk was accompanied by a delegation from the Georgia Alliance headed by Leonidas F. Livingston. Amid much cheering, an escort of eighty-two Union veterans met the party at Topeka. The speakers that evening included Mrs. Lease, who "spoke the first hour in her strong and matchless style," fourteen-year-old Charlie Richardson, who delivered "a most remarkable speech," Livingston, and Polk. When Polk mounted the platform he was welcomed by the Negro chairman, who was candidate for state auditor on the People's Party ticket. As the former slave owner and the former slave shook hands warmly, "the enthusiasm knew no bounds." [19]

Polk's reception by the agrarian element of Kansas seemed uniformly cordial. Through the Topeka *Capital,* however, Republican leaders attacked him without stint. He was a Southerner, a Democrat, and an ex-Confederate, and that gave them their issues. Senator Ingalls "caused inquiries to be made concerning the history of Polk," and passed on the "mass of facts at his disposal." [20] A "North Carolina democratic paper" gladly furnished additional data.[21] The *Capital* itself, managed by J. K. Hudson as majority stockholder and editor-in-chief, was a $250,000 corporation.[22]

Three times during the campaign the *Capital* ran a long letter on Polk, signed by former Governor Samuel J. Crawford but probably written by Ingalls. The letter accused Polk of cowardice

[18] Emporia *Daily Republican,* July 5, 1890.
[19] *Progressive Farmer,* Oct. 28, 1890.
[20] Des Moines *Iowa State Register,* Sept. 18, 1891.
[21] Topeka *Weekly Capital,* July 24, 1890.
[22] North Topeka, Kansas, *Topeka Mail,* June 13, 1890.

in the Civil War, of being an "ultra-secession" Democrat, of embezzling public funds while Commissioner of Agriculture, of letting his partners "hold the bag" after the failure of his business ventures, and of making himself president of the Alliance by a *coup d'état* so that he might cheat the farmers out of their money. It also referred to his "small paper at Winston," which "soon collapsed." The author described Polk and Ralph Beaumont, who appeared with him in Kansas, as "worthless schemers," "tramps," "regular renegades," "designing demagogues and disreputable scoundrels," "disturbers of the peace," "pests to communities," "enemies of God and man," "co-conspirators," "political and visionary schemers," "wolves in sheep's clothing," "designing, wicked mo[u]ntebanks," and "would-be revolutionists," who gave "pernicious advice" and wielded "hellish influence." [23]

Behind this invective lay the dread that Polk's advice and influence would be powerful enough to turn Ingalls and his friends out of office. As election day approached, it was charged that Lieutenant Polk had shot down Federal prisoners in cold blood at Gettysburg. When he made still another tour of Kansas a year later he had sunk even lower. No less a one than the Republican candidate for coroner of Sedgwick County "recognized in the person of Polk the governor of Salisbury prison." To make sure, he looked up an old sick-parole, "and, behold, the signature was L. L. Polk, brigadier general." Another Kansan's memories were even more vivid:

> My recollection of Polk is that he had charge of a prison near Morganton ... little if any better that [*sic*] the prison at Salisbury ... cattle ... known to be diseased were knocked in the head, their hides pulled off and their carcas[s]es thrown in to our prisoners at Salisbury. You could take hold of a rib, twist it out, and it was as green as poison ... not one word of sympathy did we ever hear from L. L. Polk at that time. ... When one would reach across the dead line at Salisbury prison

[23] *Weekly Capital*, July 24, Sept. 18, Oct. 16, 1890.

for a cup of water, he was shot down like a dog. . . . Polk must have known it. . . . Twenty-seven years is a long time. Some of you may have forgotten; I have not. The truth has never half been told, and never will be . . . may write you more startling facts soon.

The story was invented that, for these cruelties, the "old soldiers" of Wichita had threatened to tar and feather *"The Escaped Prison-Hell Keeper."* [24]

The Hudson paper seemed especially angry that Polk should come "calamity howling" from North Carolina, "where your illiteracy is the biggest thing you have," to prosperous Kansas. That ranked as "one of the most sublime exhibitions of gall of which there is any record in ancient or modern history." A few issues afterward, however, the editor remarked that within the last two years the *Capital* had "suffered from the general depression." He continued by saying that his aim was to publish "a complete newspaper, honorable and clean in character." [25]

Alliance men in Kansas enthusiastically supported the People's Party in 1890. There the "Populists," as they came to be called, combined effectively with the Democratic minority against the dominant Republicans. In the South it was different. Owing to the general fear of "Negro rule" in connection with a return of the Republicans to power, Alliance leaders took great pains to quiet third-party nervousness. The strategy of the Farmers' Alliance in the South was simply to control the Democratic Party. Under Polk's leadership the organization took an aggressive stand during the campaign.

The popularity of the Alliance caused the managers of the major parties considerable anxiety. They knew the organized farmers would influence the elections, but they didn't know how much. In some quarters their concern amounted almost to panic. In the West the managers accused the Alliance of plotting to oust

[24] *Weekly Capital,* Oct. 30, 1890, Sept. 24, Oct. 29, 1891.
[25] *Weekly Capital,* Nov. 20, 1890, Jan. 8, Sept. 17, 1891.

the Republicans and put Democrats in office, while in the South they charged the order with attempting to defeat the Democrats and elevate Republicans to power.

The balloting of November 4, 1890, was indeed highly significant. Alliance-backed candidates by the hundred were swept into office in both West and South. For the first time, the country at large became conscious of the political power of the Farmers' Alliance. "Hayseed socialists" sang:

> You can no longer keep us in serfdom,
>   For the people have opened their eyes;
> In the next Presidential election
>   We will give you another surprise.[26]

While "On Train" Polk scribbled to his wife: "The election news is exciting & everybody is stirred, except me." [27] He could not be surprised; he had seen the revolution in the making.

In various interviews after the elections Polk asserted:

> Up to the present time it is a certainty that ... Congress will contain thirty-eight straight out Alliance men, and there are twelve or fifteen more who are pledged to us.... We are here to stay. This great reform movement will not cease until it has impressed itself indelibly in the nation's history. Financial reform is the necessity of the hour and it must come.[28]
>
> People who believe that the issue was won on tariff lines are mistaken. It was financial reform that caused the sweep.[29]
>
> Congress [failed] to meet the demands of the people. We went before Congress armed with petitions representing the will of over 3,000,000 voters, and Congress said: "We are your masters; you are not ours." [30]
>
> The people of this country are desperately in earnest. They will no longer put up with nonsense. Old party fossils have lost their grip. The people want men; they want live issues;

---

[26] Leopold Vincent, comp., *Alliance and Labor Songster,* p. 26.
[27] Polk to Mrs. Polk, Nov. 6, [1890].
[28] *Maryland Farmer,* Nov. 21, 1890.
[29] Chicago *Inter-Ocean,* Nov. 22, 1890, quoted in Frank M. Drew, "The Present Farmers' Movement," *Political Science Quarterly,* VI, 309 (June, 1891).
[30] Philadelphia *Inquirer,* quoted in *Public Opinion,* X, 169 (Nov. 29, 1890).

they are going to have them.... The result of this election is only a beginning. Who can foretell the end? [31]

Alliance leaders believed that the election had dealt a telling blow against sectionalism. Though bitter partisans raised the issue as usual, the organized farmers showed scant interest, and the reform press predicted that the days of the "old war horses" were numbered. A fervent Floridian proclaimed: "We shall knock sectionalism in the head, wrap the bloody shirt about it for a winding-sheet, and bury it so deep that it will never hear the call on resurrection day." [32]

Both his friends and his enemies recognized Polk's part in the fight. The *National Economist* declared that he deserved "great credit" for the "able war" he was waging in that "grand cause." [33] Even the savagely hostile *Iowa State Register* of Des Moines admitted that it was "only fair to say ... that his denunciation of sectionalism met the approval of all good people." [34] As for himself, the Farmers' Alliance president exclaimed: "Why, if my own father were a candidate for office to-day, and upon the stump he should abuse Yankees, I would refuse to vote for him if it was the last act of my life. I'm sick of that rot and rubbish—heartily sick and tired of it." [35]

As if to supply the exclamation point to the political verdict of the Alliance, word soon came that the newly-elected Kansas legislature had relegated John J. Ingalls to what the farmers felt was well-deserved oblivion. William Alfred Peffer, editor of the *Kansas Farmer,* was chosen Senator in his stead.

"I regard the result of the Senatorial fight in Kansas," said Polk, "as the greatest blow at sectionalism that has been struck for twenty-five years." [36]

---

[31] *Progressive Farmer*, Nov. 11, 1890.
[32] Jacksonville *Florida Times-Union*, Nov. 30, 1890.
[33] *National Economist*, V, 241 (July 4, 1891).
[34] *Iowa State Register*, Sept. 19, 1891.
[35] Chamberlain, *Farmers' Alliance*, pp. 31-32.
[36] St. Louis *Globe-Democrat*, Jan. 29, quoted in *Progressive Farmer*, Feb. 10, 1891.

Chapter XV

THE ALLIANCE IN NORTH CAROLINA

IN NORTH CAROLINA, as in the rest of the South and West in 1890, the Farmers' Alliance showed amazing strength. Nowhere was the strategy of controlling a major party demonstrated more effectively. Quite within the Democratic Party, the organized farmers were able to overthrow the conservative Bourbons, who had ruled the state for thirteen years. This notable accomplishment did not result from a sudden, violent upheaval, but was rather the culmination of a movement that had gradually been gathering momentum. First came Polk's organization of farmers' clubs, the formation of the North Carolina Farmers' State Association, and the establishment of the Agricultural and Mechanical College. Then followed the entry of the Alliance and its extremely rapid development.

The choice of Polk and the farmers for governor of North Carolina in 1888 was Syd Alexander, president of the State Alliance. At the state Democratic convention in the spring, Alexander contested the nomination with Daniel G. Fowle, generally considered the Richmond and Danville Railroad candidate, and Lieutenant-Governor Charles M. Stedman. The old-line politicians were in control, and Fowle was nominated, although twenty-three ballots were necessary before he received his majority. As a sop to the farmers, the convention offered Alexander the nomination for lieutenant-governor. He quickly declined it, however, as did Augustus Leazer also, and it went then to Thomas M. Holt, the manufacturer. Ironically, Fowle died in office, and Holt, rather than Alexander or Leazer, succeeded to the governorship in 1891.

After Alexander's defeat, the farmers concentrated upon the election of a friendly legislature, which Polk regarded "as of greater importance than even the National ticket." Here they seemed to be successful. The General Assembly of 1889 contained a majority of farmers, and Leazer became speaker of the House. As the farmers' leader, Polk presumed to offer the new legislators some advice: "Make no pledges, involving your free action as a representative. . . . Do not accept a free pass or a free ticket on a railroad under any circumstances. . . . Make no swaps or trades. . . . Don't fall into traps. . . ."[1] The Alliance men in the legislature, however, lacked experienced leadership, and the "old regulars" outmaneuvered them.

The most important measure agitated by the State Alliance at this time was the creation of a railroad commission. The nation-wide demand for government regulation of the railroads was fully shared by the farmers of North Carolina. Even in the 'seventies they had condemned some railroad evils, particularly high rates. Yet the significant "Granger laws" of the West in those years had practically no influence upon the state. During the 'eighties the power of the railroads in North Carolina increased greatly, a development that the farmers regarded as sinister. By means of constant lobbying—and outright bribery when necessary—the railroads were able to block all serious attempts at regulation.[2]

The granting of passes to legislators, judges, and editors came to be an especially notorious evil. Inveighing against the corrupt nature of the practice, Polk wrote in his *Progressive Farmer:* "There are thousands of free passes issued on our railroads. The roads are not so generous as to ride all these favorites for nothing. Somebody pays these bills. Who is it? They are those who pay

---
[1] *Progressive Farmer*, Nov. 13, 1888.
[2] Robert W. Winston, *It's a Far Cry,* p. 179.

their fares and who pay their freights. And who are *they?* ..." ³

Four successive legislatures defeated railroad commission bills. The last of these was the session of 1889. The House, dominated by Alliance men, passed the bill sixty-five to forty-three; but the Senate, amid charges of venality, rejected it twenty-eight to twenty-two. The circumstances may have led Polk to recall part of the unusual prayer once uttered by the Reverend Francis Marsten, a Presbyterian minister, before the Ohio House of Representatives:

> Remember, O Lord, the welfare of these, Thy servants, gathering here in this maelstrom of iniquity, fraud and corruption. Thou knowest with what suspicion this legislature is looked upon by the people of this great State. Lord, deliver us from the bribes, the bribers and the bribe-takers in our midst, and keep them from the ways of temptation which surround them on every hand, and may their acts be righteous and not corrupt. ⁴

As 1890 opened, battle lines were drawn for what all expected to be a fierce struggle. Deployed on the left were the organized farmers and their friends. The membership of the State Alliance had now passed 80,000. Arrayed on the right were the business and professional classes of the towns, led by corporation executives and lawyer-politicians. With them stood some conservative farmers who disapproved of the Alliance.

The press leaders of the respective forces were the *Progressive Farmer* and the *News and Observer,* published not far from one another in the city of Raleigh. In their pages the ideas and tactics of each side were vividly mirrored. When Polk became president of the National Alliance with headquarters at Washington, he employed J. L. Ramsey, of Statesville, as editorial manager of the *Progressive Farmer*. Later the Reverend Baylus Cade, of Louisburg, occupied this position, but soon resigned because he could not support the sub-treasury plan. Following a brief arrange-

---
³ *Progressive Farmer,* Nov. 26, 1889.
⁴ Clipping, no place, no date, Polk Papers.

ment with P. F. Duffy, of Wilmington, Ramsey again took charge and remained as the actual editor for several years. The *News and Observer* in the early 'eighties was edited by Samuel A. Ashe, formerly a lawyer. When he was appointed postmaster of Raleigh during President Cleveland's first term, J. I. McRee became editor. Then, shortly after Cleveland gave way to Harrison, Ashe returned to the paper.

For a few months in 1880 and 1881 Polk and Ashe, both Democratic "regulars," worked together on the *News and Observer*. Their relations were friendly. When Polk left the paper, Ashe expressed appreciation for "his many excellencies of character" and wished him success that would be "commensurate with his industry and merit." "During the close intercourse which we have enjoyed with him," the editor wrote, "we have found him admirable in all those traits of character which commend a gentleman to the friendship and esteem of his associates."[5] Ten years later Ashe was still an "old regular," but not Polk. The acid controversy that developed between them reflected in a sense the larger fight between Bourbonism and the Alliance.

The rise of the Farmers' Alliance and the popularity of its leaders deeply disturbed Ashe. Following the magnificent reception accorded Polk at Henry Grady's Atlanta Exposition, and the eager hearing in North Carolina given Ben Terrell, Alliance lecturer from Texas, Ashe wrote that their purpose apparently was "to convert the 'Farmers' Alliance' into a political organization" that would disrupt the White Man's party. Polk in reply charged that the *News and Observer* acquiesced in Bourbon dictation, but that when the farmers attempted to dictate it howled. Instead of being sympathetic with agricultural interests as it professed, the paper highly favored the big corporations and the railroads.

As proof, Polk called attention to the paper's shift on the issue of a railroad commission. On February 1, 1889, when McRee

[5] *News and Observer*, Feb. 6, 1881.

was editor, the *News and Observer* stated that it had "always favored a commission and favors one now," and that "it would be an institution of great practical benefit to all classes of the people, and to the railways as well." But on January 29, 1890, with Ashe as editor, the newspaper declared: "We do not think that a railroad commission bill will accomplish any great result for the farmers in this State. We do not know of any great reason for passing a bill taking the control of railroad property out of the hands of the owners."

Polk's spectacular tour of Kansas in July, 1890, and the enthusiastic welcome extended him by People's Party elements there, persuaded Ashe that he was "seeking to array Alliancemen against the Democratic party" and thus pave the way for a third party in North Carolina. The same trip convinced Polk that Ashe's *News and Observer* had furnished the "facts" of his career to Senator Ingalls and the Topeka *Capital,* and he did not hesitate to say so. After Polk had made his charges, Ashe asserted:

> It is not the people. It is not the Alliance. It is not any number of Alliancemen. It is only Col. Polk. That's all. It matters not what Col. Polk's purpose and object is—it is very plain that he is bent on mischief and is intent on creating a new disturbance. He has set his head to stir up strife. . . .
> He proposes to accomplish his designs by sowing seeds of suspicion, by appealing to prejudice and by inflaming the passions of the people. That he can do harm goes without saying. He has already done harm in North Carolina. As a disturber of the peace, he has certainly achieved some success. We believe he has failed in former undertakings. He was a failure as a soldier. He was a failure as a farmer. He was a failure as Commissioner of Agriculture, and when the legislative examining committee came to examine into matters connected with his office, if we recollect aright, he locked up his desk, left his office and resigned. . . .
> He then went into journalism, and was a failure at that. His next venture was in connection with a medicine, Polk's Dyptheria [*sic*] Cure, and he failed at that. . . . The people

of North Carolina are a right thinking people. They are honest in their hearts, upright in their purposes, and follow no leader blindly as a flock of sheep. . . .

We believe the people will turn a deaf ear to Col. Polk's entreaties in this matter. It seems to us he must fail. As he has failed in all his other undertakings, he will fail in this. He was born to failure as his lot and inheritance in life, and it will be so to the end. The good people will not let him have his will in this matter.[6]

The Polk forces were certain that this attack was of a piece with the one made against him by the Kansas Republican paper. In an editorial entitled "ASHE, INGALLS & Co." the *Progressive Farmer* remarked: "This is a magnificent team! They trot beautifully, in double harness, along certain lines."[7]

Early in 1891 Ashe accused Polk of effecting a combination with Josephus Daniels to bargain for the state printing contract against the *News and Observer*. Ashe had held the contract in the early 'eighties. The last two legislatures, however, had, by large majorities, awarded it to Daniels on the merits of his superior *State Chronicle*. Polk accurately described Ashe's charge as "without the slightest foundation in truth." Even though Ashe offered to take the contract at fifteen per cent below the Daniels figure, he received no support at all in the Alliance-run legislature. His appeal, just before the voting, was characteristic: "The old soldiers —the wounded old veterans—have rendered service to the State and their condition appeals for aid. Mr. Daniels was too young to have rendered similar services. The two are in the scale! Will the donation be to the one or to the other?"[8]

Later in the year a Milwaukee newspaper quoted Polk as saying that every step in the progress of the Alliance in the South was made almost in the face of shotguns in the hands of Democratic leaders. On the basis of this report Ashe again flayed Polk. The

[6] *News and Observer*, Sept. 2, 4, 1890.
[7] *Progressive Farmer*, Sept. 9, 1890.
[8] *News and Observer*, Jan. 20, 22, 1891; *Progressive Farmer*, Feb. 3, 1891.

Alliance president then procured, from two Wisconsin reporters who had heard him, letters denying that he had ever seriously said such a thing. He requested Ashe to publish the letters, but Ashe refused to do so. For several issues thereafter the *Progressive Farmer* ran a standing inquiry, asking the *News and Observer* why it would not print those letters.

The *News and Observer* now contained an almost daily attack on the president of the Alliance. Ashe was writing:

> Doubtless Polk would like to pose as a martyr. . . . There is not enough sincerity in his nature to make any kind of a martyr. . . .
> We want peace and good feeling among all our people, and this is what we shall contend for. . . .
> Polk shall not use his responsible office to lead our people into the council chamber where Peffer and Mrs. Lease administer as high priest and priestess, at the altar of a third party. . . .
> [Does Polk approve of the action of the Georgia legislature] in extending a welcome to Mrs. Lease and Peffer, and rejecting the offer of a home for the disabled veterans of the Confederate army? . . .
> So far as Polk is concerned, we care nothing about what he says or writes in his paper. . . . [He is] a coward and a hypocrite. These are strong words, and we would not apply them to any good man . . . .[9]

"Tell Ramsey," Polk wrote James W. Denmark, his son-in-law and business manager of the *Progressive Farmer,* "to laugh at the rantings of the N. & O. & *ridicule* him . . . *ridicule* is the weapon to use on that sheet. He is mad because we demanded the publication of the Flannery letter. Keep calling for it."[10]

The Polk forces at this point took the initiative with marked effect. At the annual meeting of the State Alliance at Morehead

---
[9] *News and Observer,* Aug. 20, 26, Sept. 4, 30, 1891, *passim.*
[10] Polk to Denmark, Aug. 21, 1891.

City they urged Alliance men who subscribed to a single anti-Alliance paper to change to one favorable to their cause. This, of course, was interpreted as a slap at the *News and Observer*. About the same time, the *Progressive Farmer* published an advertising circular that its adversary had issued on behalf of its weekly edition. The anti-Alliance daily circulated mainly in the towns and along the railroads, but the weekly went largely to farmers. The circular read:

THE NEWS AND OBSERVER
The Old Reliable—Always True and Faithful

Advocates the Sub-Treasury bill. Advocates unlimited coinage of silver and the issue of $500,000,000 more paper money.

Advocates distributing $100,000,000 of the money now in the Treasury to the States on the basis of their agricultural products to relieve agricultural depression.

Advocates repealing the national bank law, and allowing State banks to issue notes. Advocates the repeal of the internal revenue system and a tariff for revenue only.

Favors the Farmers' Alliance; seeks to promote its objects, and advocates the protection of the freemen of North Carolina against imposition from any quarter.

Advocates that the white men of North Carolina shall all stand together and work for the prosperity of all classes and conditions of men.

We print a large eight-page paper. Price $1.25. In clubs at $1.

S. A. ASHE,
Raleigh, N. C.
Ed. *News and Observer,*

The action at Morehead City and the publication of the circular infuriated Ashe. Presently he trained on Polk what he considered his heaviest artillery: the War Record. Among Polk's enemies in the 'nineties were a few who had also been his enemies in the 'sixties, and these revived the dark stories of his conduct during the war. Ashe gave them immediate publicity, and they were widely circulated. Polk, however, quickly refuted these charges by producing the complete record of the court-martial before which he had been tried and honorably acquitted in 1864. Just as quickly, Ashe seemed ready to change the subject. "It is a far more pertinent inquiry as to what Col. Polk is now doing than what he did during the war," he said.[11]

The bitter quarrel between the Raleigh editor and the Alliance president gave rise to the sensational story that Ashe had challenged Polk to a duel. The story was pure invention, yet it appeared in newspapers all over the country. Alliance men in particular were greatly alarmed, and letters and telegrams poured in to Polk from all quarters. "Some of the letters," he remarked, "have come from Vermont." Ashe, too, received letters. The partisans of each entreated him to show his moral courage and Christian manhood by refusing to fight. The dead seriousness of the matter, relieved by just a hint of comic opera, is disclosed in these telegraphic messages:

> San Francisco, Cal.
> Aug. 26, 1891
>
> To L. L. Polk, President N. F. A. & I.U.
> Raleigh, N. C.
>
> My dear sir and brother: In the name of your family, of the Alliance, and of civilization, you cannot afford to accept that challenge. It is a Wall Street plot to ruin us. The world has its eye upon you. Your brethren expect better things. Let your moral courage predominate.
>
> Endorsed by J. S. Barbee,   J. L. Gilbert, Lecturer
> National Organizer   State F. A. & I. U. of Cal.

> Durham, N. C.
> Aug. 28, 1891
>
> To J. L. Gilbert, Alliance Lecturer
> San Francisco, Cal.
>
> Thanks for kind advice. No cause for anxiety. No challenge received and none would be accepted. Duty to home, country, and God shall be my guide of action.
>
> L. L. Polk[12]

---

[11] *News and Observer*, Oct. 7, 1891.
[12] Polk Papers.

Samuel A. Ashe was not important as a Bourbon leader so much as he was an editor who reflected Bourbon philosophy and methods. He and those he spoke for enjoyed their power and their privileges and for that reason "deprecated the dominancy of the Democratic party by the leaders of the Alliance." In his assault upon Polk, Ashe was of course egged on by his friends. When Polk was being accused of cowardice during the war, for example, a New Bern lawyer wrote Ashe: "The way you are dealing with 'Hon. L. L. Polk' is meeting with the admiration and approval of all the best people of this section."[13] To a man, no doubt, the conservatives would have agreed with the eulogist who declared of Ashe: "In his controversy with Colonel Polk he bore himself with a force, a vigor, a consecration to the right that gave him a great triumph."[14]

Polk's friends, both in and out of the Alliance, were shocked and angered by the character of the attacks upon him in the Topeka *Capital* and the *News and Observer*. Rising instantly to his defense, they condemned them as slanderous and unprincipled. First to pass resolutions were the Wake County and Anson County Alliances. The latter stated: "*Resolved,* That we have known Col. L. L. Polk from his birth (this being his native county), and that we know him to be an honest, worthy and Christian gentleman."[15] W. S. Lacy, Norfolk pastor and graduate of Davidson College, said: "I know Col. Polk well. We were fellow-students at college and in some of the same classes. . . . Whatever view may be taken of Colonel Polk's political affiliation he is a gentleman and a Christian."[16] And Josephus Daniels one day used three columns of his editorial page to censure the "Unparalleled Infamy" of the *Capital's* defamation of Polk.[17]

[13] Leonidas J. Moore to Ashe, Oct. 6, 1891, Samuel A. Ashe Papers, North Carolina Department of Archives and History, Raleigh.
[14] Theodore B. Kingsbury, "Samuel A'Court Ashe," *Biographical History of North Carolina* (Ashe, ed.), I, 73.
[15] *Progressive Farmer,* Oct. 21, 1890.
[16] Concord *Times,* Oct. 15, 1891.
[17] Raleigh *State Chronicle,* Oct. 22, 1890.

In 1890 the Farmers' Alliance in North Carolina seemed too powerful to be broken by a frontal assault. The strategy of the Bourbons, therefore, was to try to weaken the order by alienating the members from their leaders. The Alliance chiefs exercised great influence, and the masses of the farmers, new to co-operation, were peculiarly dependent upon them. This explained why Polk, especially, was singled out for abuse. Ex-Governor Jarvis, who recognized the strength of the Alliance in the state, sent friendly word to Ashe cautioning him to keep on the good side of that organization. Another of Ashe's correspondents suggested: "Let us handle the Alliance kindly and gently, always bearing in mind however that 2L Polk does not own the Alliance."[18]

The organized farmers, and Polk himself, were not slow in fathoming this strategy. Ben Clover of Kansas spoke early of the "collusion of the Democratic 'gang' of North Carolina and the Republican 'gang' of Kansas to rob L. L. Polk of his good name and destroy his influence."[19] Marion Butler, elected president of the State Alliance at Morehead City, devoted four successive issues of his paper to an analysis of the Bourbon scheme. Declaring that the misrepresentation of Polk was a cheap trick to create dissension in the Alliance, Butler concluded:

> It is the Alliance they must crush; they dare not fight it openly and squarely. It is too strong and their fight would make it stronger, and then too, they can not answer or deny the just demands of the Order. So they resort to the shrewd strategy of abusing the leaders and at the same time give taffy to the rank and file of the Order.[20]

Time for the nomination of party candidates now approached. For several years Polk had urged the adoption of primary elections for this purpose rather than the usual primary conventions. The conventions, he observed, were "too often manipulated by 'wire

---

[18] Thomas J. Jarvis to Ashe, Feb. 14, W. W. Carraway to Ashe, Oct. 30, 1890, Ashe Papers.
[19] *Progressive Farmer*, Aug. 12, 1890.
[20] Clinton *Caucasian*, Sept. 10–Oct. 8, 1891.

pulling' in the interest of the few, without regard to the wishes of the many." Yet in 1890 the farmers were in a position to control the conventions.

The cases of Furnifold M. Simmons and John S. Henderson well illustrated the potency of the Farmers' Alliance in North Carolina. Simmons, of New Bern in the east, had represented the Second Congressional District for one term and announced his candidacy for a second. Three weeks before the nominating convention, a committee from the Alliance visited him to ascertain his views on the Alliance demands. When he made it plain that he could not support them, the farmers of the District backed another candidate and Simmons withdrew from the race.[21] Henderson, of Salisbury in the west, was the incumbent Congressman of the Seventh District. Augustus Leazer appeared to be his probable rival. In letters to his wife Henderson revealed his concern:

> I am afraid I will not be renominated. The Alliance organization is so strong, that efforts will be made to have Alliance candidates everywhere. I cannot tell yet what the future will be. . . . the Alliance may do something any day which may compel me to decline to be a candidate.
> So far as I am concerned everything depends upon the Alliance. If that organization takes ground against me, as a body, I will not be a candidate. Otherwise, I will have a walk over. . . . There is no chance for him [Leazer], unless the Alliance takes him up.[22]

Henderson, although he did not favor the sub-treasury plan, acceded to the other Alliance demands and was re-elected.

Overshadowing all other contests in the state, however, was the one involving Senator Vance. In this Polk played a principal part. Vance was serving his twelfth year in the United States Senate

---

[21] Furnifold M. Simmons, *F. M. Simmons, Statesman of the New South: Memoirs and Addresses* (J. Fred Rippy, ed.), p. 18.

[22] John S. Henderson to Mrs. Henderson, March 7, April 16, May 2, 1890, John S. Henderson Papers, Southern Historical Collection, Chapel Hill. Permission for me to use these and similar items was graciously granted by Henderson's daughter, Mrs. Lyman A. Cotten of Chapel Hill.

and would come up for re-election at the next meeting of the state legislature. "Old Zeb" occupied a unique place in the life of North Carolina. For thirty years—beginning as war governor—his popularity with all groups and classes had been unequaled; his contemporaries regarded him as the state's greatest son.

The Alliance, none the less, measured Vance with the same yardstick that it applied to all other candidates: the seven demands. On May 16 Eugene C. Beddingfield, who had succeeded Polk as secretary of the State Alliance, asked the Senator how he stood. Vance replied at once. Three of the demands he favored: the free coinage of silver, the prohibition of alien ownership of public lands, and the issue of fractional paper currency for convenience. But he opposed the other four. He did not favor either the abolition of national banks or the prohibition of dealing in agricultural futures. As to government control of railroads and telegraph lines, his inclination was "decidedly against it." On the sub-treasury bill—most important of all to the Alliance—he said: "I am in favor not of this particular bill (for it is crude and imperfect) but of the principles of the bill, provided it be not established that it is unconstitutional. . . . Whether it be constitutional or not I am not now prepared to say. It is a great departure in our financial policy and will require careful and elaborate examination. . . ."[23]

As Vance himself had introduced the bill, a more detailed explanation appeared necessary. This the Senator made in a letter to Elias Carr, president of the State Alliance, on June 29. Vance wrote:

> On the 24th of February, 1890, at the request of Col. L. L. Polk, President of the N. F. Alliance and Industrial Union, I introduced in the Senate bill 2,806, popularly known as the sub-Treasury bill, and procured its reference to the Committee on Agriculture and Forestry, where it was supposed that it would receive more friendly consideration than from the

[23] Vance to Beddingfield, May 18, 1890, in Clement Dowd, *Life of Zebulon B. Vance*, pp. 282-83.

Committee on Finance, to which it would otherwise have gone according to the rules. On receiving it, I told both Col. Polk and Dr. Macune, the Chairman of the Legislative Committee of the Alliance, that I was not prepared to promise them to support the bill; that it was a great and radical departure from the accustomed policy of the legislation, and that there were questions both of practicability and constitutionality which I wished to reserve. I told them also that I hoped for good results from its introduction; and believed that its discussion would attract the attention of the country to the condition and wants of the agricultural classes, and if this bill was not deemed the proper one, that some other would be formulated in the direction of the needed relief.

I procured an early consideration of the bill by the committee, and a very able and most interesting discussion by Messrs. Polk and Macune was had. But so far without result. The committee has not yet made a report, though I am assured that a majority of its members are anxiously seeking to devise a method of relief which shall not be open to the objections of that bill.

My own position remains the same. I can not support this bill in its present shape. But I am not opposed to the principle and purposes of the measure. . . . I cannot gain my consent to vote for this sub-Treasury bill which provides for the loaning of money to the people by the government, and which, in my opinion, is without constitutional authority.

In the letter Vance asserted that the depression in agriculture had resulted from the bad finance and tariff legislation of the Republican Party. Observing that "bitter feeling is springing up between town and country," he advised the Alliance to work conservatively with business and professional groups under the banner of the Democracy. Not the sub-treasury plan, but a united fight by the Democrats against the Republicans, would bring relief to the farmers.[24]

An open letter, of course it was widely published in North Carolina. Vance so timed its release that the letter would be a prime

[24] Vance to Carr, June 29, 1890, in Dowd, *Life of Vance*, pp. 283-87.

topic of discussion on the Fourth of July, when many meetings were held. He told Ashe that he had introduced the sub-treasury bill only because "in courtesy" he "could not refuse to do so." He did not "propose to enter into any controversy" with Alliance leaders but to "let the storm expend itself." The Senator believed, nevertheless, that it would be "dangerous" to allow Congress to expire "without proposing something for the relief of the Farmers." [25]

For his position on the sub-treasury bill, Ramsey in the *Progressive Farmer* and Macune in the *National Economist* forthrightly criticized Vance. If he modified the Alliance bill to suit himself, why couldn't he support it? If he really thought it was unconstitutional, why did he wait so long to say so? "Senator Vance," declared Macune, "introduced the bill in all candor, and honestly stood by it as long as he could, but he did not possess the moral courage to stand the terrible onslaught of ridicule and abuse that was being prepared for those who cast their lot with the farmer all the way through." [26] Ramsey complained that those who called the measure unconstitutional never explained *why* it was unconstitutional. "The farmers of North Carolina pay Senator Vance," he said. "It is his business to work for them whether the measures are constitutional or not . . . if the bill is not in proper shape he should have gone to work and put it in shape." He concluded with an appeal to the farmers to support only those who supported them. [27]

Ramsey's unprecedented arraignment of Vance caused a furor among the Democratic papers. They defended their idol vehemently, and some of them, thinking that Polk had written the editorial, accused him of scheming for Vance's seat in the Senate. Ramsey hastened to explain that he alone was responsible for the editorial; that Polk was in Kansas at the time and knew nothing

---

[25] Vance to Ashe, June 29, July 10, 1890, Ashe Papers.
[26] *National Economist,* III, 259-62 (July 12, 1890).
[27] *Progressive Farmer,* July 8, 1890.

of it. The Bourbons, however, saw in all this an issue too good to drop. When Polk, after his tour of the West, came to North Carolina for a speech at Greensboro, they were ready for him. The Greensboro *Patriot* misrepresented the speech to indicate a personal attack on Vance, and the other organs did the rest. The facile mental process involved was well illustrated by that editor who penned: "We have not seen his oration(?) We have only seen a short editorial in a Greensboro paper and heard others speak of it. From these we are led to believe that it is his intention to drag the Alliance into politics with himself on top." [28]

At length Polk presented his side of the dispute. [29] The *Progressive Farmer,* he said, existed as the organ of the State Alliance, and as such it always sought to serve the masses. It reserved the democratic privilege of criticizing public acts or men. When Senator Vance declared himself against a majority of the Alliance demands—particularly when he announced his opposition to the sub-treasury bill—Ramsey believed him to be in the wrong and so stated. With this position Polk entirely agreed. "According to the dictum of the papers," he remarked, "a candidate must answer: 'How do you stand on Vance?' Let us, like men having rights, ask: 'How does Vance stand on our principles?'"

On Vance and the sub-treasury bill Polk wrote:

> The Sub-Treasury bill was prepared in compliance with the St. Louis meeting of the National Alliance. That body represented Democrats and Republicans from the North and South. It was the people's measure, and the Legislative Committee of the Alliance desired its introduction and consideration to be free from party bias or coloring. Hence, it asked Representative Pickler, of South Dakota, a Republican and an Alliance man, representing a strong Alliance constituency in the Northwest, to introduce it in the House. Mr. Pickler was asked to state that he introduced it by request. This was the original bill drawn by the committee, and is known as

---

[28] Undated clipping from Tarboro *Banner.*
[29] *Progressive Farmer,* Sept. 2, 1890.

House Bill No. 7162, entitled "A bill to establish a system of sub-treasuries, and for other purposes."

Senator Vance was selected to introduce it in the Senate, as he represented a strong Alliance constituency from the South. He was told that it was not the purpose or desire of the committee to commit him in any manner by the introduction of the bill, to its support, and hence he was asked to state that he introduced it by request. He very kindly suggested that after an examination of the bill, he might probably be able to make some improvements, and full liberty was given him to do so. He modified the bill and introduced it. It is known as Senate Bill No. 2806, and is entitled "A Bill to establish a system of agricultural depositories for the accommodation of farmers and planters, and for other purposes." Subsequently, and after a conference with Senator Casey, of North Dakota, who had manifested some interest in the matter, Senator Vance introduced a third bill, known as Senate Bill No. 2876, and entitled "A bill to establish a system of government store houses for agricultural products, and for other purposes." Neither of these two bills were submitted to the Alliance Committee. . . .

Senator Vance manifested a kindly, and we may say more than ordinary interest in the matter from the beginning, expressing always an earnest desire to secure the adoption of some measure for the relief of the farmers. We all agreed that if we could get the bill discussed before either House of Congress, and thus bring the public mind to bear on the subject, something would most likely grow out of it for the relief of the people, even though this measure should be defeated. Replying to the suggestion that possibly the bill would die in the committee room, the senator said that under the rules of the Senate, he could introduce a resolution requiring the committee to report, and whether the report was adverse or favorable, the matter could be discussed. We had frequent interviews on the subject, and from the day of the introduction of the bill by him, in February, down to the 24th of June—the day we left Washington [for the West] —we had no reason to apprehend for a moment that he was unfriendly to the measure, or would oppose it. Indeed, some months after the bill had been introduced we said to the Senator that we had purposely avoided all the while approaching him in such way as to elicit an expression of his conclusions as to the bill, but that if he had made up his mind, of course we and his friends were anxious to know how he stood. He replied: "I shall have to give you the answer I have made to Senators who have approached me with that question: 'We will have to stand by it until we get a better one.'"

Hearing, on the 19th of June, that the Senator had written a letter against the bill, and would publish it in THE PROGRESSIVE FARMER, we promptly sought an interview with him and told him if it were true, we had called to see it, or get a copy before it was published. He said "there is not a syllable of truth in it," and said the only letter he had written in regard to it was in response to a letter from Secretary Beddingfield. . . .

For three decades Polk, like most North Carolinians, had been a loyal and enthusiastic "Vance man." He had always enjoyed cordial relations with Vance, had admired him personally, and had approved of his record. But in 1890 Polk believed that the Senator had broken faith with the farmers and with him. Vance's opposition to most of the Alliance demands, his refusal to press for action on the sub-treasury bill or a substitute, and the public announcement of his position when the president of the Alliance was a thousand miles away from both Washington and Raleigh, convinced Polk that this was so. The *Progressive Farmer,* therefore, would not support for re-election to the Senate any man who opposed a measure that was "so near the heart" of the Alliance.

Probably two out of every three Tar Heel farmers favored the sub-treasury bill. Those who did not were doubtless impressed by the argument that, under the provisions of the bill, only twelve "cotton counties" and three "tobacco counties" would have sub-treasury offices; the other eighty-one counties would have none. An informal survey by the middle-of-the-road *State Chronicle* indicated that Alliance men in general regretted Vance's failure to support the sub-treasury bill yet endorsed him for re-election. [30]

The charge that Polk aspired to succeed Vance was so plausible and so oft-repeated that it came to be widely believed. Charles B. Aycock, Goldsboro lawyer, asserted that Polk was "courting abuse" for just that purpose and "ought not to be gratified" by the "Democratic Editors of the State." [31] Polk strongly denied all such rumors, declaring that he had "steadily declined political honors since the war" and that he was "not a candidate for Congress, for Governor, for the United States Senate, nor for any political or other office." He countercharged that Vance's defenders were not helping him for himself so much as they were trying to use the power of his name to wreck the Alliance. As Polk told Daniels, "if there ever was a time in all his grand life when the Senator should pray to be delivered from his so-called friends, that time is now." [32]

A few of Polk's friends wanted him to run for governor as early as 1880. Four years later, when Walter H. Page was editor of the *State Chronicle,* that paper issued a circular letter which named L. L. Polk as its choice for governor and said that he would appeal to North Carolina's farmers and young men more than anyone else except Vance. In 1887 Polk was boomed again. This time he felt it necessary to state his position formally in his paper:

> I am no aspirant for political honors. I am no candidate for political office.
> I have chosen what I hope is my life-work. With me it is "a labor of love.". . .
> I would rather be the Editor of THE PROGRESSIVE FARMER, sending it weekly to the homes of ten thousand of our people, than to be the honored recipient of one hundred and fifty

---

[30] *State Chronicle,* Aug. 9, 1890.

[31] Aycock to Theodore B. Kingsbury, Nov. 13, 1890, Kingsbury Letters, Southern Historical Collection, Chapel Hill.

[32] *Progressive Farmer,* Feb. 18, Sept. 2, 9, 1890; Josephus Daniels, *Tar Heel Editor,* p. 448.

thousand of their votes for any political office. In this capacity I can accomplish greatly more good.[33]

There was no substantial evidence to indicate that in 1890 he had altered his stand. As president of the Alliance he occupied a position of power, prestige, and promise, and the constituency of two million that he represented was nation-wide. He certainly desired Vance's defeat. But that he desired Vance's place—even to push the sub-treasury bill—seems doubtful. Syd Alexander, most probably, would have been his choice for Senator.

Both the Democratic state convention of August and the general election of November were dominated by the Farmers' Alliance. Of the nine Congressmen chosen, four were members of the Alliance and three others found themselves in accord with its principles. In the new North Carolina General Assembly members of the Alliance constituted an actual majority. Most of the state legislators were pledged to support the Alliance program but at the same time were pledged to support Vance for re-election.

The Durham *Globe,* a rarity because of its independence, made this racy observation of the situation:

> The *Globe* had hoped that after the November elections politics would be allowed a rest for at least a year. . . .
>
> But now comes a wild scream from the Vance organs; they . . . insist that Mr. Vance shall be returned to the United States Senate.
>
> And so this fight is on—on for days and weeks and months. Colonel Polk's paper, *The Progressive Farmer,* slyly intimates that it is camped on the trail of Mr. Vance with a desire for blood and a hanker for gore; and it gives all to understand that the Farmers' Alliance has still a finger in the pie. . . .
>
> Many of the State papers, those who wheedled the Alliance by making that body believe that the Democratic leaders were sincere, are now busily engaged in writing Colonel Polk down an ass, and they also swear by all the fabled gods of war that

[33] *Progressive Farmer,* July 14, 1887.

he, in the depths of his egotism, wants to inherit the brogans of the venerable Zeb.

Vance has evaded the Sub Treasury bill by declaring that it is unconstitutional. This is always a happy way over a political question. . . . Every one knows that Vance wants to go back, and unless something unheard of in politics transpires, he will go back, and he will do as he has always done, vote on measures to suit himself. . . .

The Democratic party has been successful [in the 1890 elections] because of the Farmers' Alliance. . . .

And so, if Mr. Vance is returned, his successor will have a hard time, and Mr. Ransom [the other Senator from North Carolina] will go down as sure as fate. . . .

A new party, purged of all the blotches of corruption, is forming . . . this Farmers' Alliance will eventually develop into something.

And if Mr. Vance does not see and read and heed the handwriting on the wall, he will always regret that he didn't. Colonel Polk may be a politician, but the army of men at his back is composed of sturdy sons of toil, and it is not for the partisan press to say that they are satisfied.[34]

During the interval between the fall election and the meeting of the General Assembly in January, Vance maintained his already close contact with Ashe. Late in November he wrote that editor:

I do not know that I have any plan to propose in the way of counter work to the machinations of Polk. It seems to me from the best information I can get that the situation is satisfactory. I do not believe it possible for the Alliance Leaders like Polk to force the members of the Legislature to prove false to their pledges. I think the proper course is to treat such an idea with contempt and incredulity. It would probably be a good idea to ask [the] Polk organ to say unequivocally if it counselled and advised their proving false to their solemn pledges, there being no change in the situation. If Polk does admit such a thing the monstrosity and dishonor of

[34] Durham *Globe*, Nov. 17, quoted in *Progressive Farmer*, Nov. 25, 1890.

it would shock the moral sense of every body. And if he refuses to say straight out that he does so admit it would be an admission that the members ought to stand by their pledges. I will of course advise you from time to time.

Ashe followed the Senator's suggestion, but Polk did not rise to the bait. Vance then wrote:

I hope you will commend the answer of the P. Farmer to your question about pledges of candidates—treating it as settling the question, producing harmony &c &c. We think here it was most important & if supported by the Alliance people is an end of wrangling.[35]

Vance's popular strength was demonstrably great, and it was manifest that the legislature would return him to the Senate. There remained to the Alliance the hope that the legislature could force him to support the sub-treasury bill. Through a letter from President Carr, Vance was accordingly asked: "If the Legislature instructs you to advocate and vote for the Sub Treasury plan of financial reform, will you carry out said instructions in good faith?" Vance replied: ". . . I recognize the old Democratic doctrine of the right of the people to instruct their representatives to the fullest extent to which it has ever been carried in North Carolina."[36]

With this reply Polk professed to be satisfied; he now looked to harmony between the factions. "We think the Senator's letter," he said, "is a full, fair, unequivocal answer to the question presented to him. . . . Our quarrel hitherto has been with the Senator's position, and not with the man." Polk added that the General Assembly's instructions should be as liberal as possible, so that Vance—and Ransom—would be helped rather than hindered in their action.[37]

The legislature first proposed, none the less, than Vance sup-

---

[35] Vance to Ashe, Nov. 28, Dec. 10, 1890, Ashe Papers.
[36] Dowd, *Life of Vance*, p. 289.
[37] *Progressive Farmer*, Dec. 23, 1890—Jan. 20, 1891.

port the sub-treasury bill. At this embarrassing request the Senator, in spite of his statement to Carr, balked. Delicate negotiation then resulted in a compromise acceptable to each side: North Carolina's Senators were instructed, and the Representatives requested, "to vote for and use all honorable means to secure the object of the financial reforms" advocated by the Farmers' Alliance. Vance agreed, the General Assembly passed the resolution, and Vance was re-elected by acclamation.

It was Zeb Vance's misfortune to be caught between two hide-scorching fires. Only the most adroit maneuvering of a seasoned politician enabled him to escape his unhappy predicament. During the first two decades after the Civil War his Democratic constituents were generally united—united in their memories, their poverty, and their hope. By 1891, however, the Bourbon-Alliance dichotomy became well marked. Vance could hardly hope to please both Ashe and Polk. His inclination was conservative, but he dared not offend the Farmers' Alliance. Happily for him, the people and their representatives esteemed and trusted him and regarded him as a symbol that should not be destroyed.

The "farmers' legislature" of 1891 established a record more constructive and more progressive than that of any North Carolina General Assembly since ante-bellum days. The emphasis was upon modernization and reform. To advance material interests the legislature provided for a new geological survey, authorized a World's Fair exhibit, chartered many new banks, and restricted the activities of emigration agents. In the field of education it increased the school tax, appropriated $10,000 to the College of Agriculture and Mechanic Arts, and created a Negro A. and M. College and an institution for the deaf and dumb. It prohibited gambling at agricultural fairs and the sale of cigarettes to minors. Most important of all was the establishment of a State Railroad Commission and a Normal and Industrial School for girls.

The Railroad Commission law "forbade rebates and unjust discriminations of any kind, established the 'long and short haul' principle, and gave the commission full rate-making authority, subject to the usual limitations of judicial review." Three commissioners were provided for. While the bill was still pending in the legislature, Polk was invited to address a Democratic caucus on the subject. Among other things, he advised that the commissioners be paid living salaries so that they would thus be encouraged to tend strictly to business.[38]

Establishment of the Normal and Industrial School for girls by the "farmers' legislature" brought to reality the dream of Charles D. McIver. Undoubtedly heartened by the creation of the College of Agriculture and Mechanic Arts, McIver and his colleague Edwin A. Alderman waged a fervent campaign all over North Carolina in behalf of popular education and teacher-training. As the whole Farmers' Alliance—like the Grange before it—was vitally interested in the practical education of the masses, no one doubted that the Legislature of 1891 would pave the way for the school. The idea of the educational evangelists was thus translated into concrete form by the farmer-legislators. Winthrop College in South Carolina, a similar institution and a product of the similar forces of the Tillman movement, was founded the same year.

Polk, on February 19, 1889, became one of the first to subscribe to the idea of a teacher-training school for girls. Three months previously he had introduced his resolution calling upon the Baptists of the state to establish and maintain a college for the young women of the denomination. On the above date he wrote:

> Say what we will of our chivalrous regard for woman (and this is the just and proudest boast of our manhood), the neglect and failure in our system of education to provide for their liberal education is a stigma on our civilization.... "The hand that rocks the cradle moves the world." The mother moulds the mind of the child. Give the noble girls of the

[38] Raleigh *North Carolina Intelligencer,* Jan. 28, 1891.

State—those who are not able to go to our expensive colleges, a chance to get an education. . . .

One of many *Progressive Farmer* editorials on public education, dated January 13, 1891, read:

It is no use to say the State is too poor to make ample provision for the education of her children. The State is not poor; and, if she were never so poor, she could not afford to retrench at the expense of the intellectual and moral development of her children. There ought to be a commodious, comfortable and well furnished public school house in every school district in the State. . . .

We want it understood that we embrace in this appeal to our General Assembly the negro children of the State. . . .

Such was the power of the Farmers' Alliance in North Carolina. What, now, could be done on the national scene?

Chapter XVI

MR. PRESIDENT

AT THE ST. LOUIS CONVENTION of December, 1889, the delegates from Florida invited the National Farmers' Alliance and Industrial Union to hold its next annual meeting in Jacksonville. Much to their surprise and delight, the organization accepted the invitation. But the citizens of Jacksonville, failing to realize the importance of the occasion, proved indifferent toward making the necessary arrangements. The alert promoters of Ocala in central Florida quickly took advantage of the situation to offer inducements so attractive that the Alliance executive committee changed the place of meeting.

During the great Ocala convention, held in December, 1890, the farmer-delegates and their families were truly regaled. An impressive Alliance Exposition was staged for them; all entertainment was free; their hotel bills and railroad fares were paid; carriages were provided for drives in and around the towns; and a thousand boxes of oranges were distributed among them. After the convention a party of three hundred enjoyed a week's free tour of the state! This wonderful hospitality was, of course, intended as persuasive advertising for Florida in general and Ocala in particular. L. L. Polk, president of the Alliance, shared the treat with Mrs. Polk and two of their daughters.

The delegates approached the serious side of the convention with mixed emotions. Because Congress had shown little disposition to relieve the distress of the farmers or even discuss their problems, a pronounced feeling of bitterness existed. Yet because the Alliance had made such a remarkable showing in the recent elections, an inevitable feeling of elation prevailed. A combination of the two developments had stimulated within the organization some strong third-party sentiment. Consequently, an air of expectancy hung over Ocala as the men and women of the Alliance assembled.

Twenty-five states and Indian Territory were represented. In his presidential address, which opened the sessions, Polk declared that "Congress must come nearer to the people or the people will get nearer to Congress." Referring to the "evident subserviency" of both Democratic and Republican parties "to the will of corporate and money power," he advised the delegates that the time had come for "bold and determined action." Though the Alliance was not partisan, it was political, and much would depend upon "the action of the present Congress in regard to the financial system of the country."[1]

The Ocala convention readopted, with slight modifications, the seven demands of the St. Louis platform; reaffirmed the faith of the Alliance in the sub-treasury plan; laid more emphasis upon the demands for a graduated income tax and the direct election of United States senators; recommended a pure food law; and condemned Senator Lodge's Force Bill. Macune pointed out that the seven demands would require of Congress only about thirteen laws, as follows:

First demand: 1. Law abolishing national banks. 2. Law establishing sub-treasury plan. 3. Law establishing system of 2 per cent land loans direct to the people. 4. Law increasing volume of money to $50 per capita.

Second demand: 5. Law prohibiting dealing in futures.

Third demand: 6. [Law establishing] free coinage of silver.

Fourth demand: 7. Law prohibiting alien ownership of land. 8. Law forfeiting unearned railway land grants and limiting their land holdings.

Fifth demand: 9. Law revising tariff in the interest of the

[1] National Farmers' Alliance and Industrial Union, *Proceedings, 1890*, pp. 3-12.

producer. 10. Law creating a graduated income tax. 11. Law reducing Government expenditures.

Sixth demand: 12. Law creating efficient control of railroads.

Seventh demand: 13. Law for the election of United States Senators by direct vote of the people.[2]

The revelation of two scandals involving prominent officers of the Alliance enlivened the Ocala proceedings and provided the newspapers with many rumors and much copy.

First came the exposure of D. H. Rittenhouse, Polk's secretary. Rittenhouse, who hailed from Panacea Springs, North Carolina, had been associated with Polk for about two years. Over the pseudonym "Old Fogy" he had written prolifically and well for the *Progressive Farmer* and other papers. Soon after Polk established headquarters in Washington, Rittenhouse joined him as secretary and demonstrated considerable ability. At the time of the Ocala meeting, however, serious charges were made against him, and he was relieved of his position. Rittenhouse, unknown to Polk, had taken advantage of that position to betray Polk and the Alliance by means of a "deal" with "the enemy." He seems to have contrived with James G. Blaine a scheme to throw Alliance support to the Republicans in 1892. Hal W. Ayer, of Raleigh, succeeded him as Polk's secretary.[3]

More important was the famous "Georgia senatorial affair." As in North Carolina, the Farmers' Alliance in Georgia proved to be exceedingly strong in 1890, electing a majority of the Congressmen and the state legislators. Yet Georgia's "Alliance Legislature," unlike that of North Carolina, made a poor record. Both the political campaign and the ensuing legislative session seemed notably conservative.

Three main candidates vied for the legislature's choice as United

---

[2] *National Economist*, IV, 261 (Jan. 10, 1891).

[3] W. A. Platt, in New York *Mail and Express*, Dec. 3, 1890; Atlanta *Constitution*, quoted in Raleigh *State Chronicle*, Dec. 10, 1890; *Progressive Farmer*, Jan. 5, 1892.

States Senator. General John B. Gordon, like Vance in North Carolina, stood as a popular symbol of the past who advocated free silver and low tariff but who opposed the sub-treasury plan. His opposite number, Thomas M. Norwood, supported the entire Alliance program. Most unusual of the three was Patrick Calhoun, a railroad lawyer who surprisingly came forth as a defender of the sub-treasury plan and the monetary demands of the St. Louis platform. Calhoun gained the backing of Leonidas F. Livingston, head of the Georgia State Alliance, and Charles W. Macune. In the *National Economist* the latter frequently noted and praised Calhoun's articles on finance and described him as a statesman of high order.

Conscientious Alliance men denounced Livingston and Macune for making a trade with the railroads for personal and political advantage. Polk, especially, was highly indignant at the bald attempt to push Calhoun forward as the "Alliance candidate." He himself preferred Norwood. In speeches to Georgia Alliance men he had indeed urged them to support someone who favored the sub-treasury, but never a railroad lawyer. Upon receiving an urgent telegram, Polk rushed to Atlanta to address a caucus of anti-Gordon legislators. Mentioning no names, he advised the members to adhere strictly to Alliance principles in making their choice. When to his surprise and chagrin the caucus nominated Calhoun, he immediately wrote Norwood: "I know nothing of it and absolutely repudiate the whole thing. With me the Alliance cause is first and above all things else. I cannot and will not grind any man's ax. I cannot and will not agree to any 'entangling alliances' with corporations."[4] The Gordon forces conveniently lumped Livingston, Macune, and Polk together and scolded them for their interference. "Find crooked work done in Georgia to involve me in the Senatorial matter & 'Rome will be made to howl,'" Polk wrote his wife.[5]

[4] Josephus Daniels to author, Nov. 23, 1937; *State Chronicle,* Nov. 21, 29, 1890.
[5] Polk to Mrs. Polk, Nov. 18, [1890].

On November 20, in a victory for sentiment and conservatism, Gordon won the election, with Norwood second and Calhoun third. During the twelve days between the election and the opening of the Ocala convention so many charges were hurled and so many rumors were circulated that the leaders of the Alliance decided to conduct a thorough investigation. At the meeting, therefore, a committee of one from each state was appointed for that purpose.

In the interests of unity and harmony the committee's report was very gentle. No one was found guilty of wrong-doing. The members could not endorse Livingston's course in the affair; they regretted Macune's official connection with it. As for the third principal in the case: "We have been unable to ascertain a single fact implicating in any way, shape or form, the high character and standing and personal and official reputation of our worthy President L. L. Polk, but we regret the writing of the Norwood letter."[6]

Unofficial information was more revealing and more interesting. Because the committee report whitewashed Macune and reproved Polk for writing his letter to Norwood, the Missouri member refused to sign it. The Tennessee member stated that the committee unanimously exonerated Polk and Livingston, but that the vote on Macune was only fifteen to ten. The actual evidence against Macune appeared damning: he admitted before the committee that he had lobbied sixteen days in Georgia for Calhoun, that he had borrowed $2,000 from him, and that he had traveled on free passes of the Terminal Company.[7] The Ocala delegates reelected Polk to the presidency by a unanimous vote. Significantly, Kansas nominated him, and each of the other twenty-four states seconded the nomination. The "wildest applause" greeted the decision. Polk's leadership of the Alliance during 1890 thus received complete endorsement.

[6] *Proceedings, 1890*, p. 27.
[7] *News and Observer*, Dec. 9, 1890; *State Chronicle*, Dec. 10, 1890.

Together, the November elections and the Ocala convention focused national attention upon the Farmers' Alliance for the first time. Not a little of the attention was devoted to the president of the organization. Under both the constitution and the unwritten law of the Alliance, its president possessed large powers, which he was expected to use. Inasmuch as the rank and file of Alliance men had unbounded confidence in Polk, his official position became one of great authority and influence. Much of what he did and said as president, therefore, stimulated wide general interest.

When Polk first went to Washington he shared the offices of Macune and the *National Economist* at 511 Ninth Street, Northwest. Later, however, for reasons that should now be clear, he moved to offices of his own, first at 344 D Street, and then in the Atlantic Building on F Street. Polk and his assistants usually worked from sixteen to eighteen hours a day—from six o'clock in the morning until well after midnight. "He is built for hard work and has a wonderful capacity for dispatching business," wrote Marion Butler.[8] "There is an air of 'we mean business' about the place," a *News and Observer* correspondent said of Polk's office, adding: "It is daily frequented by members of Congress."[9]

Polk and the other Alliance representatives in Washington lobbied for the farmers as best they could. They wrote letters and petitions, appeared before Congressional committees, and held private conferences with legislators. Yet in comparison with its affluent competitors, the farmers' lobby seemed negligible. Aside from the sub-treasury plan, the "Southern Alliance" during the early 1890's put forth its greatest efforts in behalf of free silver and the Paddock Pure Food Bill and expressed its greatest opposition to the Conger and Butterworth bills, which threatened the cottonseed oil interest.

Polk did his most effective work not at Washington, but "in

---

[8] Clinton *Caucasian,* Jan. 21, 1892.
[9] *News and Observer,* March 16, 1890.

the field." Of the twenty-five states represented at Ocala, he had in 1890 officially visited all save one—California. Between February and April, 1891, he actively assisted in organizing the state Alliances of Arkansas, Iowa, Ohio, New York, and Pennsylvania. It was with the blessing of General James B. Weaver that Polk established the "Southern Alliance" in Iowa. In that state he found the farmers "represented by an intelligent lot of men,—indeed the best informed as to our principles of any I have met." [10]

According to the constitution adopted at St. Louis, the president of the Alliance was to receive not only office and travel expenses but an annual salary of $3,000. All such expenditures came from the dollar-a-year dues and the fifty-cent initiation fees paid by individual members. Soon after his first election Polk received this good advice from Isaac McCracken, of Ozone, Arkansas: "I know there is always a great big estimate placed upon the willingness of the members to pay dues and if your wife and little ones are depending upon your personal exertion for their support don't make any large calculation on receiving the $3000^{00} ... I firmly believe that the mileage and per diem ... will very nearly absorb next years dues." [11]

McCracken was right; he had belonged to farm and labor organizations for twenty years and knew whereof he spoke. Polk experienced the greatest difficulty in collecting his salary. At the time of the annual conventions he received most of it, but never the full amount. Partly because the states were remiss in collecting dues, and partly because of "reckless expenditure," the Alliance treasury showed a deficit of about $6,000 as early as the Ocala meeting.

The salary difficulty made vitally important to Polk the financial condition of the *Progressive Farmer,* his only other source of income. Early in his journalistic career, during the Hayes-Tilden contest of 1877, he had learned that "Money in a printing office

[10] Polk to James W. Denmark, [March 15, 1891].
[11] McCracken to Polk, Dec. 24, 1889.

is like honesty in a Radical Returning Board." [12] Eleven years later he was writing: "Money is scarce and hard to get . . . if you can't spare a dollar for our paper, make up a club at 50 cents for 6 months. This will reach the next cotton crop." When crop-time came he remarked: "Many of our friends asked us to extend their subscriptions to the fall. We did not see how we could do it, but we did do it." And he begged them to pay up. [13]

The late 'eighties were lean years for the *Progressive Farmer*. The early 'nineties were somewhat better, yet not so prosperous as the large circulation of the paper seemed to indicate. During a fifteen-month period ending December 31, 1891, receipts amounted to approximately $15,000 and expenditures to $12,000. On that date the paper's liabilities came to some $2,000 and the assets to $8,500. Two-thirds of the assets, however, were of doubtful value, as they consisted of unpaid subscription accounts that would be hard to collect. Business Manager Denmark reported that, for 1891, Polk would receive $2,000 and he himself $1,000. They paid Ramsey, the editor, an average of $83.33 per month, promising him $100 if things picked up. The *Progressive Farmer* greatly desired offices that it would own rather than rent, and it badly needed a press. When Denmark asked the Colonel if he could collect his Alliance salary and lend it to the *Progressive Farmer,* Polk replied from Washington: "It is out of the question to count on my salary. We have no money & often I am greatly embarrassed to pay my board & rent bills." [14]

Fortunately, Polk's new house in Raleigh was paid for. Fortunately also, several of his friends advanced money for his most pressing needs. At about the time mentioned above Syd Alexander, Elias Carr, and four others held his notes for $700, of which $220 had been paid. "These notes must be met," Polk wrote Denmark, saying he would "pay them tomorrow if it were possible." [15]

[12] Polkton *Ansonian,* Feb. 21, 1877.
[13] *Progressive Farmer,* May 15, 1888, Sept. 3, 1889.
[14] Denmark to Polk, Jan. 12, Polk to Denmark, Jan. 15, 1892.
[15] Polk to Denmark, undated.

The year 1891, which followed the off-year elections and the Ocala meeting and preceded a Presidential election year, became largely a year of discussion and debate. Agricultural distress and revolt came to be a subject of national attention. Ever present, lending spice to the political situation, was the possibility that the Farmers' Alliance would turn itself into a third party.

Many writers of the day belittled the farmer's difficulties and felt contemptuous toward his efforts to overcome them. Their attitude was not far from that of the Kansan who wrote:

> A howler of calamity,
> He needs no brains, for damit 'e
> Can work on cheek and vanity
> Big whiskers and inanity.[16]

Others, however, showed more sympathy. The New York *Press,* a Republican newspaper, said:

> It is useless to deny that the Farmers' Alliance movement is one of great importance and significance. . . .There has been a general disposition on the part of the Eastern newspapers to treat the movement in a spirit of good natured badinage. But under all the chaffing about overalls, cowhides and sockless statesmen there has been a current of real respect for the honesty and sincerity of purpose that unquestionably characterizes not only the rank and file, but also most of the leaders of the Alliance.

The *Press* compared the sturdy Americanism of Alliance men with that of Lincoln and the early Republicans, and the current caricatures of farmers with the old caricatures of "Abe" and his associates.[17]

Thanks to their leaders, the organized farmers were experiencing an "intellectual ferment." The Alliance gospel came to them on the tongues of official lecturers. The Alliance papers they read belonged to the new Reform Press Association, all of whose

[16] Eugene F. Ware, in William E. Connelley, *Ingalls of Kansas,* p. 203.
[17] Quoted in *Public Opinion,* XI, 26 (April 18, 1891).

members were required to support the Ocala platform. In North Carolina, to take an example, the "reform press" was headed by the state organ, the *Progressive Farmer,* and included smaller papers in Asheville, Hickory, Salisbury, Trinity College, Whitakers, Tarboro, Wilson, Goldsboro, Whiteville, and Clinton. The farmers bought and read Nelson A. Dunning's *Farmers' Alliance History and Agricultural Digest,* W. Scott Morgan's *History of the Wheel and Alliance and the Impending Revolution,* N. B. Ashby's *Riddle of the Sphinx,* Senator William A. Peffer's *The Farmer's Side,* and other books that recited Alliance history and expounded Alliance doctrine. The famous *Looking Backward,* by Edward Bellamy, and *Caesar's Column,* a novel by Ignatius Donnelly, were widely read and talked about. Also considered "good Alliance literature" were many government documents, including speeches of Congressmen. A series of "Alliance lessons," complete with blackboard exercises and directions to the instructor, and specially composed "Alliance songs" came into use at meetings.

Alliance Lecturer Harry Tracy was one leader who strongly urged women to join the organization, declaring that the "moral element" contributed by them was absolutely necessary for success. As women had to pay no dues, thousands did join, and they exercised a notable influence. Their interest in all the great problems of agriculture was quite as unfeigned as that of their men-folk. Two letters that came to Polk from Nash County, North Carolina, are illuminating. Zenobia Wheeless, a farmer's wife of Castalia, wrote:

> We rode sixteen miles . . . to hear Bro. Tracy; started about sun-up and trotted all the way . . . Bro. Tracy's lecture was very interesting . . . it seemed that all eyes were riveted upon him; then it would seem as if there were as many on me. I could not help feeling like some of them thought I . . . was in the wrong place. . . . Bro. Polk, if you will come to some of our appointments in reach of us, I will ride the same dis-

tance again to hear a lecture from you, if I knew there would not be a single sister to accompany me. I have heard you once and am anxious to hear you again.

Nellie F. Dozier, of Nashville, wrote:

I am a girl 16 years of age . . . I joined the Alliance . . . with 11 members, and now we have 24. . . . My father and mother are both members. . . . [I heard] your grand speech. . . . Oh! I enjoyed it very much indeed, and especially the part for the ladies.

The *Progressive Farmer* "always did think that girls could do a great deal for reform." At Sartoria, Nebraska, it reported, "the girls won't dance with a young man unless he is a member of the Alliance, and the dancing has to be done on the Ocala platform." [18]

As president of the Alliance, Polk made scores of speeches all over the country. Many of them, in the best oratorical tradition of the time, consumed more than two hours in delivery. Yet his basic ideas, arguments, and appeals were few and simple.

He often began by contrasting the alarming decline and plight of agriculture with the remarkable growth and prosperity of other enterprises. In 1850, he would say, agriculturists owned seventy per cent of the nation's wealth and paid less than fifty per cent of its taxes, while in 1890 they owned but twenty-three per cent of the wealth yet paid eighty per cent of the taxes! Neither God nor the farmer was to blame for this, but the financial system of the Government. The system contracted the currency, caused the dollar to appreciate in value, and made money dear. The result was "high-priced money and low-priced products." True, a dollar would buy more now. "But where is the dollar? . . . Does not the dollar cost us from two to four times as much as ever before? . . . It is not so much in the *purchasing* power of the dollar that the farmer is interested, but . . . the *debt-paying* power of the dollar." To put the matter in practical terms:

[18] *Progressive Farmer*, Aug. 7, 1888, July 9, 1889, Dec. 15, 1891.

If you owed $100 then [1867-69], you could pay it with sixty bushels of wheat. Today, ninety bushels are required to pay the debt. Two bales of cotton now are only worth one of 1870. That is, WE PAY TWICE AS MUCH for a dollar as we did then, but the same dollar pays no more taxes. . . . [19]

If a farmer had given a mortgage for $1,000 in 1870, he could have paid it with 1,050 bushels of corn. Ten to seventeen years later, it would have taken, without interest, 2,702 bushels to have paid it, and so with his other crops. The farmer pays his debts with his labor. [20]

Obviously, federal legislation since the Civil War had favored big business—chiefly at the expense of agriculture. "Equal rights to all, special privileges to none" had become a mockery. "Thirty-one thousand people," Polk asserted on one occasion, "own over half the wealth of this country. They did not get it honestly and fairly; they can't do it." And a voice from his audience chimed in, "they got it by robbery." [21] Such centralization of wealth was ominous. It sapped the great middle class and tended to create only the very rich and the very poor, "the weakest defenders of liberty." "By its aggressive encroachment and arrogant assumptions," declared Polk, centralized wealth "overrides law, disregards private rights, controls conventions, corrupts the ballot box, invades our temples of justice, subsidizes the press, intimidates official authority, and dictates legislation, State and National." [22] To say that "the unjust and ruinous exactions of capital and corporate power are made in conformity to law" is no answer, for "there is no tyranny so degrading as legalized tyranny—there is no injustice so oppressive as that which stands entrenched behind the forms of law." [23]

The farmer saw "the rich growing rapidly richer, and the poor

---

[19] Chattanooga *Daily Times,* May 22, 1890.
[20] L. L. Polk, *The Protest of the Farmer: Address . . . Washington, D. C. . . . April 14, 1891,* pp. 5-6, 9-13.
[21] *Progressive Farmer,* March 17, 1891.
[22] Inter-State Farmers' Association, *Proceedings, 1889,* p. 6.
[23] Raleigh *Daily Call,* Dec. 14, 1889.

growing rapidly poorer." Yet each year he continued to "sow in faith, toil in hope, reap in despair." Well could he echo the thought expressed by an earnest Granger of North Carolina eighteen years before. From time immemorial, the Granger said, the farming interest of the country had been "the pack horse to bear the burdens of government; or rather the ass loaded with ingots of gold, driven through the city gates, relieved of his precious burden and turned out to graze upon the commons."[24] There ought to be, said Polk, a system of assessment that would unearth the hidden property of the capitalist and make it bear a just share of the tax burden. Notes, bonds, and money should be assessed and taxed as carefully as land, livestock, and machinery.

Though the politicians had conjured up as "the main issues" the tariff, the "bloody shirt," and "Negro supremacy," the farmers should not be deceived; most important was the money question. Congress, however, offered no relief to agriculture. While the lawmakers appropriated millions for pensions and public buildings, they allowed the sub-treasury bill and the free-silver bill to suffocate in committee. That Congress would do anything about the bills seemed unlikely.

The time had come, Polk declared, for direct, vigorous action. Farmers and laborers must unite against corporate corruption. The wealth-producing masses must contest for supremacy against the wealth-absorbing classes. A revolution was in the offing, and the ballots of the many would prevail over the money of the few. Like most farmers, Polk cared as little for the strikes of labor unions as he did for the "domineering assumptions of greedy capital." Still, he respected the power of such organizations as the Knights of Labor and believed that the fundamental interests of farmer and laborer were the same. He even made overtures

[24] H. T. Guion, in *Proceedings . . . of Atlantic Council, Patrons of Husbandry . . . . Kinston, N. C., Dec. 18th, 1873.*

to the merchant, saying "you are in our boat . . . we are neighbors and should be friends."

The Alliance president suffered no illusions regarding the nature of the struggle ahead. He said:

> We should not be discouraged if the relief, the justice we are demanding does not come at once, but should work with still greater determination. . . . We have the wrongdoings of a quarter of a century to right. . . . It is a fight not of a month or a year, but of a lifetime. . . . [25]
>
> I believe I am doing God's work in advocating the principles of this order, and I have consecrated all that I am, and all that I ever expect to be, to this great work. . . . [26]
>
> Let us stand by our principles till the last man falls in the fight, and then the volunteers will come up and take our places.[27]

At Wadesboro, North Carolina, to a crowd that included many kinsmen and old friends, Polk said:

> Let me make you a prediction; let me tell you what I believe. You may see a third party in this country, but it will not be for long. The masses of the Northwestern States, the Southern States and the Western States will be arrayed on one side, and on the other will stand the plutocrats and monopolists of the Northern and Eastern States. There will be but two parties—the people against the plutocrats. The contest is coming, and I say let it come. I believe we have God and right on our side.[28]

The time was February, 1891.

[25] Clinton *Caucasian*, Oct. 16, 1890.
[26] *Progressive Farmer*, March 17, 1891.
[27] *State Chronicle*, Aug. 14, 1891.
[28] *Progressive Farmer*, March 17, 1891.

Chapter XVII

THE PEOPLE'S PARTY

THIRD PARTY SENTIMENT in the United States during the early months of 1891 was widespread. The *National Economist* reported that, on the basis of letters and articles received by its office, three times as many people were thinking and writing about that subject as were thinking and writing about any other. "It is like an epidemic which suddenly spreads over the whole country," the paper said.[1]

Many reform organizations favored independent political action at once. The leaders of the Knights of Labor, to take an example, voted fifty-three to twelve for a new party and at Ocala tried to persuade Polk and his friends to do likewise. But the official attitude of the National Farmers' Alliance and Industrial Union, largest and strongest of the reform groups, was more conservative.

Everyone knew that the third party movement flourished among Alliance men. The elections of 1890 in particular gave the movement powerful impetus. In Kansas, South Dakota, and other states new political parties had appeared and had achieved some success. The "Northern Alliance" clearly leaned in that direction. Yet Polk, Macune, and other officers of the "Southern Alliance" had their reasons for holding back. Eighteen ninety-one, they believed, ought to be "the great educational year," when all the various organizations should strengthen themselves and consolidate. By so doing, they could win converts much more rapidly than through a political party in a year when no elections

---

[1] *National Economist*, IV, 309 (Jan. 31, 1891).

were held. To launch their new party the forces of reform should wait until February, 1892. Then, on the eve of a national campaign, they could harmonize their differences effectively and make a mighty, united effort. The Alliance as an organization, however, must remain officially non-partisan.

Most of the other bodies would not wait. Consequently a "National Union Conference," to which representatives of all reform groups were invited, was called for May, 1891, in Cincinnati. At the appointed time over fourteen hundred delegates swarmed into the city. Kansas alone contributed more than four hundred —almost as many as Ohio and Indiana combined. Present were Alliance men, Greenbackers, Nationalists, Single-Taxers, and numerous others. Terence Powderly and Samuel Gompers, the labor leaders, were on hand. From the two national Alliances came Macune, Livingston, Simpson, Weaver, and Donnelly. The delegates appeared to be a most determined group of men.

The Cincinnati meeting quickly developed into a struggle between those who wanted a third party at once and those who advised waiting until February. The former declared it useless to delay a day longer. The latter, aware that the success of the third party would depend upon support from the South, argued that more time was needed for the "education" of that section.

Polk thought it best not to attend the meeting. But of course the delegates wished to know his views. At one of the sessions, therefore, a letter from him was read. In the letter Polk suggested that the Conference "formulate nothing besides a conservative, but manly address to the country, setting forth the evils by which the people were oppressed, and ask them to come together, and name a time and place where a National Convention should be held." Not only would this refer the matter to the people, in whom all power was vested, but would give friends of reform time enough to prepare for the battle ahead.[2]

"The letter," said the Cincinnati *Enquirer*, "was received with

[2] Cincinnati *Enquirer*, May 21, 1891.

painful silence . . . ." An Arkansas delegate then moved that "we sit down on that communication as hard as we can," and was loudly applauded. Nevertheless a delegate from Kansas, explaining that if Polk were not ready to go with them "today" he might be "tomorrow," succeeded in getting the letter referred to the committee on resolutions. "Let 'em rage," Polk wrote Denmark. "I will come in on home stretch. . . . Tell Bro Worth & *all* of them to stand steady. *I* am not scared & feel cool & calm. The letter to Cincinnati—*all right* & will do *no harm* to *me* or *our Cause.*" [3]

In spite of the sharp division of opinion at Cincinnati, the meeting produced a compromise entirely acceptable to each side. The People's Party, with an executive committee and other machinery, was created immediately. The formal entry of the new organization into national politics, however, was postponed until February, 1892.

Before reaching the home stretch Polk had to negotiate the turns and the back stretch. Upon him rested much of the responsibility for education and exhortation in 1891. A visit to California in October, and the annual convention of the Alliance at Indianapolis in November, thus assumed particular significance.

Farmers' Alliances had sprouted on the Pacific Coast just as they had back East. Since California was a strong member of the "Southern Alliance," Polk naturally desired to pay the state a presidential call. After stopping over briefly in Des Moines for the "greatest Alliance meeting ever held in Iowa," he journeyed by way of Omaha, Cheyenne, and Sacramento to his destination at Los Angeles. There the State Alliance and other organizations had convened. Polk, it was reported, spoke "morning, noon and night to audiences spellbound with his eloquence." One evening he addressed a mass meeting of seven thousand men and women, holding the giant crowd with ease for over two hours. Another evening, in tribute to his campaign against sectionalism, some

[3] Polk to James W. Denmark, undated, and May 27, 1891. "Bro Worth" was W. H. Worth, state business agent of the North Carolina Alliance and close friend of Polk's.

three hundred Union and Confederate veterans jointly "serenaded" him at his hotel. Taking the southern route back to Washington, Polk returned after a round trip, according to his own calculations, of 7,234 miles. The day he left Los Angeles the reform groups assembled there united to organize the People's Party of California.[4]

By this time Polk was generally regarded as a "third party man." Yet, partly because he headed an organization that was "educational" and "non-partisan," and partly for reasons of strategy, he avoided making any pronouncement on the subject. At Indianapolis the Alliance again endorsed his leadership, electing him president for the third successive time. Convention gossip had named Livingston of Georgia, now in Congress, a possible rival for the post. When, however, the delegates learned that Livingston did not favor independent political action, his name dropped out of consideration immediately and Polk became president without opposition. The incident well revealed the temper of the Alliance.[5]

At the Indianapolis meeting the delegates reaffirmed their faith in the Ocala platform, including the sub-treasury plan. The Alliance now comprised thirty-three state organizations, and the leaders reported a large gain in membership during the year past. Facts none the less contradicted their assertions; actually the Alliance had lost strength. The results of certain state elections, notably in Kansas, seemed to prove this.[6] In North Carolina, confidential reports showed a consistently sharp decrease in membership all over the commonwealth.[7] Even the *Progressive Farmer* was moved to observe that the order had been "in a comatose state for some months" owing to financial conditions

---

[4] *Progressive Farmer*, Oct. 27, Nov. 17, 1891; Polk to Denmark, Oct. 27, 1891.
[5] Indianapolis *Journal*, Nov. 19, 1891; Atlanta *People's Party Paper*, Nov. 26, 1891, March 3, 10, 1892.
[6] *Public Opinion*, XII, 99-100, 124-26 (Nov. 7, 14, 1891).
[7] "Quarterly reports" of W. S. Barnes, secretary of the North Carolina Alliance, Dec. 31, 1891, Marion Butler Papers, Southern Historical Collection, Chapel Hill.

"and other causes." [8] Politics, the Georgia senatorial affair, internal dissension, failure of the agricultural co-operatives, third-party fright—each played its part.

Had the education and exhortation of 1891 failed? Or was this merely the off-year lull before the election-year storm? Only 1892 could tell.

If the leaders of the Farmers' Alliance felt discouraged as the new year opened, they gave no hint of it. On the contrary, they seemed to radiate optimism as the all-important "Industrial Conference"—set for February 22 at St. Louis—approached. Polk, for instance, was writing Denmark: "Every thing indicates that the great bulk of the delegates will be conservative but very determined.... I do not believe that any power on earth can prevent independent political action.... If the Conference acts prudently and wisely there will be such a revolution in this country as has never been witnessed." [9]

The Conference, Polk thought, would be "important as a declaration that the great industrial elements of the American people are dissatisfied with existing conditions ... a calm and deliberate expression on the part of the conservative laborers and taxpayers of the United States, that 'equality of rights before the law' must be respected and maintained." For that reason the convention's platform should be "bold, clear cut and unmistakable in its terms." [10] As for the imminent duty of Alliance men: "Plainly, it is to stand loyally and manfully by our principles, vote for no man nor party who oppose our principles, extend the hand of friendship and fellowship to any man or party who favor our principles. Place principles above parties. Place measures above men. Place country above section." [11]

Before the convention opened, Polk and other reform leaders

---

[8] *Progressive Farmer,* March 15, 1892.
[9] Polk to Denmark, Feb. 3, 8, 17, 1892.
[10] *National Economist,* VI, 261 (Jan. 9, 1892).
[11] *Progressive Farmer,* Jan. 12, 1892.

held several private meetings in St. Louis. One reporter read deep significance in the fact that the president of the Alliance and the executive committee of the People's Party were quartered in the same hotel.[12]

Twelve hundred heterogeneous delegates, and many visitors, filled Exposition Music Hall on the afternoon of February 22 as the Industrial Conference began. Two-thirds of these delegates represented agrarian organizations, and twenty-nine per cent labor groups. The remainder, for the most part, embraced "single issue" reformers such as prohibitionists and woman suffragists. The organizations with the largest representation were the National Farmers' Alliance and Industrial Union ("Southern Alliance"), 246; the Colored Farmers' Alliance and Co-operative Union, 97; the Knights of Labor, 82; the Patrons of Industry, 75; the Farmers' Mutual Benefit Association, 53; and the National Farmers' Alliance ("Northern Alliance"), 49. Ben Terrell of Texas, the temporary chairman, told his diverse hearers that the purpose of the convention was agreement upon a platform; and he advised that the platform be restricted to the subjects of land, money, and transportation.

When Polk came forward to respond to an address of welcome the crowd rose to its feet and gave him a prolonged ovation. The delegates had come to St. Louis to ratify the People's Party, and they had learned shortly before the convention that Polk now unequivocally favored independent political action. The Alliance president struck the keynote as he said:

> The time has arrived for the great West, the great South and the great Northwest, to link their hands and hearts together and march to the ballot box and take possession of the government, restore it to the principles of our fathers, and run it in the interest of the people....
> Sirs, we are not applying to Congress or elsewhere for sym-

[12] H. E. Taubeneck to Ignatius Donnelly, Feb. 5, 1892, Donnelly Papers, Minnesota Historical Society, St. Paul; *People's Party Paper*, Feb. 25, 1892.

pathy or charity, but in the dignity and power of American manhood, we are demanding justice, and under the favor of God, we intend to have it. We want relief from these unjust oppressions, and as I have said from New York to California, in my speeches, we intend to have it if we have to wipe the two old parties from the face of the earth! [13]

At this "the house went wild with enthusiasm." In the restrained language of a local reporter, "Some of the delegates rose to their feet, and at the top of their voice announced their intention of carrying out Mr. Polk's suggestion." [14]

The next session witnessed the election of Polk as permanent chairman of the convention. Terrell had also been nominated, but the Polk sentiment appeared to be so overwhelming that Terrell withdrew. As the North Carolinian advanced to receive the gavel "the applause was deafening and lasted some time." More than his recognized ability and experience as a presiding officer, it was his willingness to lead the Alliance into the new party that caught the imagination of the delegates.

The platform—most important business of the convention—emerged from committee on the third and final day. Containing the demands first crystallized by the Alliance at the St. Louis meeting of 1889, it was notable mainly for its classic preamble, written by Ignatius Donnelly of Minnesota. Following the reading of the document, the assembly became a pandemonium: "Yells of joy ... hats were thrown ... bannerets were waved ... men shook hands and embraced, the national flag was waved and the audience united in singing patriotic airs."

Immediately after adjournment of the Industrial Conference, a "political convention" of "individual citizens" opened under the chairmanship of General James B. Weaver of Iowa. A committee of fifteen, including Polk, Macune, and Mrs. Lease, was appointed to confer with the executive committee of the People's

---

[13] *Progressive Farmer*, March 15, 1892.
[14] St. Louis *Globe-Democrat*, Feb. 23, 1892.

Party as to the details of a national convention. The group decided that on July 4, at Omaha, 1,776 delegates would forgather to put a Presidential ticket in the field. St. Louis and Omaha would stand as a second Declaration of Independence; and November would see a second Revolution.

Turbulence, no less than enthusiasm and patriotism, marked the St. Louis meeting. As each of the many organizations represented there strove to advance its favorite reforms, scores of people had to be heard. Sometimes ten, twenty, or thirty delegates clamored for the floor at once. On one occasion a certain Fred Swaine attempted to introduce a resolution calling for an eight-hour working day but was forcibly ejected from the building when it was discovered that he was not a delegate. It should hardly be necessary to add that Polk's task as presiding officer was both difficult and exhausting.[15]

Led by Miss Frances E. Willard, the "suffragettes" and the prohibitionists were particularly active. At least one woman, however, failed to sympathize with them. The St. Louis *Globe-Democrat* quoted Mrs. Lease as saying: "Oh, this demand for woman's suffrage and prohibition planks is so absurd. Give us planks on money, land and transportation and the farmers are satisfied. Who cares if the people can get whisky, [just] so it is pure and they have plenty of money to pay for it with?"[16] Perhaps the true spirit of the gathering found expression in the lines of Ella Wheeler Wilcox:

> The time has come when men with hearts and brains
> Must rise and take the misdirected reins
> Of government, too long left in the hands
> Of aliens and of lackeys. He who stands
> And sees the mighty vehicle of State
> Hauled through the mire to some ignoble fate
> And makes not such bold protest as he can, is no American.[17]

[15] *People's Party Paper*, March 3, 1892.
[16] St. Louis *Globe-Democrat*, Feb. 25, 1892.
[17] *Arena*, V, 748 (May, 1892).

In the spring of 1892 the South seemed to hold the key to fulfillment of the reformers' hopes. "You of the South," a Californian wrote, "have it within your power to make this movement a complete success...." [18] And Polk, speaking of the Alliance, said: "We are the people and the party of the South." [19] Continued hard times, the certainty that Grover Cleveland would again be the Democratic nominee for President, and the persistent refusal of major-party leaders to heed the appeals of the farmers caused the People's movement to grow by leaps and bounds. Still, a large proportion of Alliance men shunned the third party for fear that a split in Democratic ranks would result in another Republican-Negro regime.

In North Carolina, Samuel A. Ashe was writing: "There should be no split among the good people of our State. Let us all abide in the ship which has proven an Ark of Safety for so many years." [20] Josephus Daniels could say: "The principles of the Democratic party are imperishable, its practice unimpeachable. It is good enough for the South." [21] Yet William J. Peele declared: "If I could hear less talk of the Democratic party and more talk of Democratic principles, I should have more hope of reform.... A Democrat from principle will see to it that his party, or some party, shall advocate what is right.... Much, if not most of what Col. Polk [has] said is the best Democracy I ever saw. If my party is hurt by it, then it needs reform." [22] Finally, on March 29, Polk himself answered the question "What is the duty of friends of reform in the South?" as follows:

> With me, this is the alternative presented: Should the South continue to lie supinely in the octopus arms of this great autocratic money power [of the Northeast] ... or should she accept the outstretched, fraternal hand of the great North-

[18] Marion Cannon to Denmark, in *Progressive Farmer*, June 6, 1891.
[19] Indianapolis *Journal*, Nov. 15, 1891.
[20] *News and Observer*, Feb. 28, 1892.
[21] *State Chronicle*, June 9, 1891.
[22] *Progressive Farmer*, Dec. 8, 1891.

west, whose interests are her interests . . . ? To me, this is the supreme question of the hour and dwarfs all questions of party expediency or policy into utter insignificance. . . .

To be consistent, to be fair and manly, what is my duty as a citizen? Plainly, it is to stand loyally and faithfully by [the pledges made at St. Louis, and by the Western farmers]. . . . Have they been true to our demands? Let the record of their representatives in Congress answer. Although born and raised as abolitionists or Republicans, they stood with Roman courage by the people on the silver bill, against the combined Democracy and Republicanism of Wall Street. Is it right, is it just, is it manly for so-called Southern Democrats to abuse these patriotic representatives of the People's party, or their friends, because they will not consent to abandon the cause of the people and lick the hand of Democratic and Republican Wall Street power? Would it not be more consistent and manly to turn the shafts of their wrath against the traitors in their own ranks? . . .

To my mind, my course is clear and my road of duty plain. I shall pursue it without regard to consequences to myself, personal, political or otherwise.[23]

This declaration, added to his words and acts at St. Louis, removed any trace of doubt as to where L. L. Polk stood. He believed that only federal legislation could relieve the distress of the farmers, and that only the People's Party—directly or indirectly—could bring such legislation to pass.

Polk's hold upon the farmers of his native state, his position as president of the Alliance, and the intriguing possibility that he would win a place on the "Populist" national ticket combined to lend tremendous vitality to the third party movement in North Carolina. As the regular Democrats began to lay plans for the coming campaign they could hardly conceal their anxiety. For two years Alliance Democrats had dominated the legislature and the party. That had been bad enough; would they now turn Populist? As in 1890, Furnifold M. Simmons and John S. Hender-

[23] *Progressive Farmer,* April 5, 1892, and many other papers.

son were in difficulties. Simmons accepted rather reluctantly the chairmanship of his party's executive committee, "for Democratic defeat seemed almost certain."[24] Congressman Henderson wrote his wife: "How to get elected is the rub. The people seem to be running wild into the third party. . . . I have never known such a doubtful condition of politics."[25] If ever a state belonged in the doubtful column, it was North Carolina in the spring of 1892.

Of course Polk's all-absorbing activities as head of the national Alliance prevented any close, constant leadership of the North Carolina organization. The active local leader was Marion Butler, who the previous summer had been elected president of the State Alliance at the age of twenty-eight. He was shrewd and capable. A native of Sampson County and a graduate of the University of North Carolina, Butler had been a farmer, school principal, Alliance organizer, newspaper editor, and state senator. His decisive election to the "farmers' legislature" on the issue of establishing a railroad commission was scored at the expense of an incumbent "railroad senator," Edwin W. Kerr. His Clinton *Caucasian* stood as a strong Alliance paper in a strong Alliance county. He had attended the Indianapolis meeting and at St. Louis had served on the important platform committee.

Early in 1892 young Butler quietly proposed fusion of the People's Party and the Democratic Party in state politics. Polk naturally disapproved of the idea. Convinced that a large number of Alliance men would never co-operate with the Democrats, Polk believed that the better course would be to make a completely independent fight. He feared, however, that he would be unable to convert Butler. Polk wrote Denmark:

> Give yourself no concern about my being complicated with the fusion matter. I cannot give such a policy my endorse-

[24] Furnifold M. Simmons, *F. M. Simmons, Statesman of the New South: Memoirs and Addresses* (J. Fred Rippy, ed.) p. 19.

[25] John S. Henderson to Mrs. Henderson, March 28, 1892, John S. Henderson Papers, Chapel Hill.

ment, for I can see in it elements of great weakness and I think, defeat. My honest opinion is, that any man who attempts to keep the people of North Carolina from an open and bold declaration for the People's Party will be run over. I verily believe, that if we would boldly unfurl the People's banner, throw down the gauntlet and make the issue squarely, we could carry the state by a tremendous majority. Unfortunately I am in such position that I cannot lead such a movement. It seems to me that trouble and embarrassment will hang heavily on the present plan. . . . You may look out for squalls in North Carolina. So far as I am concerned, I cannot in any manner, shape or form commit myself to any line of policy dictated by the Democratic Party. I am an out and out People's Party man, and shall conduct myself accordingly.[26]

He also wrote John D. Thorne: "I think it hazardous to our cause to enter into any fusion with the . . . Democratic Party . . . even in state politics. . . . I can never agree to attempt any fusion with them . . . we must make a clear-cut fight."[27]

All factions now maneuvered with the Democratic state convention of May 18 in mind. As that date drew near the political situation seemed unusually confused. Many local People's Party clubs had appeared, and much third-party sentiment undoubtedly existed, yet no state organization of the People's Party had been formed. The Bourbons therefore feared that the Populists might capture the Democratic state convention, nominate a governor, and send delegates to Omaha! The Populists on their part suspected that the Bourbons would make a deal with the Republicans, if necessary, to defeat the third party. The Alliance Democrats, who held the balance of power, were anxious both to keep the Bourbons in their place and to forestall any possibility of a Populist-Republican fusion. The Republicans, of course, sat by and enjoyed the fight; they had everything to gain and nothing to lose from either Democratic factionalism or a third party.

Late in March, Butler issued a call for Alliance men to meet

[26] Polk to Denmark, March 10, 12, 15, 1892.
[27] Polk to Thorne, March 29, 1892, Butler Papers.

in Raleigh on May 17, the day before the Democratic gathering opened. Apparently he did intend to capture the convention and send delegates to Omaha. In this Polk seems to have supported him. "I do sincerely hope that the Butler program may be carried out successfully," he wrote on April 29. J. L. Ramsey, in the *Progressive Farmer,* suggested the necessity of compromise with the Democrats to prevent "negro supremacy." On May 10, however, Polk wrote: "Things are really in a great muddle in our state, and I have serious doubt about any satisfactory compromise as matters are now going." [28]

The Alliance caucus, with both Butler and Polk present, met as scheduled. Details and results of the meeting remained an Alliance secret. Yet certainly the fundamental differences between the Democratic and Populist wings received a thorough airing. Events that soon followed clearly indicated the feeling of the two groups.

In the convention which opened the next day, most of the Alliance Democrats supported for the gubernatorial nomination Elias Carr, Butler's predecessor as head of the State Alliance. Elias Carr was a successful planter and conservative agrarian who had recently told Polk: "I am an Allianceman now and forever but not a Third Party man by any means." [29] The Bourbon element rallied around Thomas M. Holt, the incumbent, who had become Governor the previous year upon the death of Daniel G. Fowle. Holt also had agricultural interests but was more vitally concerned with textile manufacturing. Two other candidates before the convention—George W. Sanderlin and Julian S. Carr—also attracted more than a little support.

Without favoring any particular candidate, Polk's *Progressive Farmer* nevertheless opposed vigorously the nomination of Holt, asserting that the Governor was not really in sympathy with the farmers. This opposition brought on a violent clash with the leading Holt organ, the Raleigh *State Chronicle.* Formerly con-

[28] Polk to Denmark, April 29, May 10, 1892.
[29] Carr to Polk, March 28, 1892.

trolled by Josephus Daniels, this paper was now backed principally by Holt himself. The editor, Thomas R. Jernigan, for a time had been associated with Ashe on the *News and Observer,* another paper that now of course supported Holt. Polk's opposition, the *Chronicle* declared, was inspired by "an unhealthy ambition": his desire to defeat the "regular Democrat" in order to strengthen his own chances of getting the Presidential nomination at Omaha.[30]

The Alliance Democrats showed their power in the convention as Elias Carr received the nomination for governor on the sixth ballot. Five ballots gave no one a majority, yet revealed accurately enough the relative strength of the four candidates. The "regular Democrats" could but yield; no doubt they felt relieved that the Populists had not been able to seize control. In a letter to Polk two weeks later, Denmark mentioned that a "deathly stillness" had followed the convention.[31]

Polk, as well as Butler, approved Carr's nomination, hailing it as a victory for the Farmers' Alliance and a defeat for the Bourbon machine. Immediately afterward, however, the Populist forces created the People's Party of North Carolina, adopting the St. Louis platform, providing that delegates be sent to the national convention on July 4, and endorsing L. L. Polk for the Presidency or any other position.

County conventions, to select representatives to the congressional district meetings that would send North Carolina's delegates to Omaha, were set for the morning of Saturday, June 11.

[30] *Progressive Farmer,* May 10-24, 1892; *State Chronicle,* May 4-18, 1892.
[31] Denmark to Polk, June 2, 1892.

Chapter XVIII

"I AM STANDING NOW . . ."

In its issue of September 3, 1891, the *American Nonconformist,* a Populist paper of Winfield, Kansas, printed a cartoon that tickled all the third-party people who saw it. Benjamin Harrison ("Tweedle Dum") and Grover Cleveland ("Tweedle Dee") perched stiffly astride each end of a seesaw. Harrison held aloft a little flag marked "high tariff," while Cleveland waved one inscribed "low tariff." The seesaw rested upon the backs of two partisans—a Republican and a Democrat—who crouched side by side on the ground. With patently forced enthusiasm, the Republican cried " 'Rah for Harrison" and the Democrat " 'Rah for Cleveland." The caption read "Tariff is the issue for '92."

To Alliance and Populist leaders the cartoon seemed quite apropos. Perhaps they underestimated the importance of the tariff as a cause of agricultural depression. Nevertheless, they felt certain that the old parties used the tariff issue largely to obscure more vital matters, such as the sub-treasury plan and free silver. On the national scene, Republicans and Democrats looked alike to Populists; neither would do anything for the masses of the people. Harrison, the current President, and Cleveland, the chief contender, were indeed tweedledum and tweedledee. As the time for the national conventions of 1892 approached, it appeared almost inevitable that these two would again be the nominees of their respective parties.

Because of his conservative financial views, Grover Cleveland was widely unpopular in the South. Not only Populists, but many

Democrats—at least until his nomination—found him entirely unacceptable. The words of W. H. Kitchin, an old-fashioned Democrat of Scotland Neck, North Carolina, may be taken as an illustration of the feeling. On April 8 he wrote:

> The party in Congress has played hell & given great impetus to the third party move. At this time I am not able to perceive any very great difference between the two parties North. I have never discovered any difference in the Cleveland administration of the finances of the country and the republican administrations. I cannot & will not support Cleveland. . . . We have denounced the republican party since 1873 . . . for demonetising silver. . . . Not thirty days ago the democratic members of the House made a combine with the Republican members & defeated the silver bill. This can not be explained except upon the theory that the party is not true to its principles. I tell you the . . . Cleveland democracy is no better than the enemy.[1]

Back in 1887 Polk had favored the renomination and re-election of President Cleveland because he wanted to see "a higher type of moral manhood in public office." In 1891, however, he opposed him because he represented the "money power." Polk gave Cleveland credit for courage in declaring against free silver but stated that the "industrial classes" would never support him in 1892.[2]

Polk, of course, stood squarely on the Ocala platform. During the contest for Speaker of the House in the winter of 1891-92 he wrote: "The wrangle over the speakership is up to white heat. The railroad power of the country backs up one of the leading candidates and Wall Street and the Whiskey ring backs [sic] up the other, and the Southern Alliance Democrats walk blindly into the trap. I am 'hands off' and will remain so." He advised Alliance Congressmen not to enter any caucus to nominate a Speaker unless the Ocala platform were made the test of admis-

---

[1] W. H. Kitchin to Ed. Chambers Smith, April 8, 1892, Ed. Chambers Smith Papers, Duke University Library, Durham.
[2] *Progressive Farmer,* Feb. 24, 1891; Wilmington *Messenger,* Aug. 22, 1891.

sion. Alliance men should stand together and fight anyone who opposed their organization. "There will be a reckoning in 1892," Polk asserted, "and some people will hear music in the air."[3]

The Alliance president believed in the sub-treasury plan, the free coinage of silver, government issue of all notes intended for circulation as money, a graduated tax on all incomes over $10,000, and the election of United States senators by direct vote of the people. Unlike most of the other leaders in his organization, he also favored government ownership of railroads. He felt that this brief platform, and a Presidential candidate from the Northwest, would draw enough votes away from the old parties to enable the Populists to sweep the country.[4] Two months before the Omaha convention Polk was trying to get the platform down to the single issue of financial reform. "Nothing," he said, "would so demoralize the enemy."[5]

First as head of the Farmers' Alliance, and then as the apparently outstanding leader of the entire reform movement, Polk came to be regarded as Presidential timber himself. Some of his admirers began as early as the Ocala meeting to discuss his name in connection with a Presidential nomination. When at both Ocala and Indianapolis he was re-elected head of the powerful Alliance by unanimous vote, and when he made clear his unqualified endorsement of the People's Party, speculation about him increased greatly. On February 12, 1892, he wrote his son-in-law: "Don't know what to do. Every mail brings letters from some part of the Union, saying I *must* be on the Nat. ticket. Can't tell yet what to do. Will probably know after going to St. Louis."

Polk scored a personal triumph at the Industrial Conference ten days later and won additional support from reform elements all over the country. Certainly he could count on the South. At this time, however, most Westerners naturally wanted the candidate

[3] Polk to Denmark, Dec. 5, 1891; *Progressive Farmer*, Jan. 19, 1892.
[4] *News and Observer*, March 10, 1891.
[5] Polk to Denmark, April 29, 1892.

for President to come from their section, with the South getting the Vice-President. The West could offer General James B. Weaver, of Iowa, an able man and experienced campaigner who had many friends, or perhaps Ignatius Donnelly, of Minnesota, whose accomplishments at Cincinnati and St. Louis had attracted so much attention. Colonel Polk, of North Carolina, would be eminently acceptable for second place. In states like Iowa, Missouri, and Oklahoma early in 1892 strong sentiment for a Weaver-Polk ticket developed.

Yet during the spring the movement to give Polk the Presidential nomination gained great momentum. That the South would solidly support him at Omaha seemed a foregone conclusion. Conventions in North Carolina, Georgia, and Kentucky announced for him well in advance. The result of a preference vote at a People's Party meeting in Greenville, Texas, was Polk 74, Weaver 45.

More significant was the growing evidence that the West would favor him for first place. Paul Vandervoort, of Walla Walla, Washington, a leader of the Grand Army of the Republic, Union veterans' organization, declared for Polk largely because of the North Carolinian's efforts to reunite the North and the South. H. L. Loucks, of South Dakota, who had succeeded Ben Clover as national vice-president of the Alliance, came out for a Polk-Vandervoort ticket. Davis H. Waite, reform leader of Colorado, put up Polk's name immediately after the St. Louis Conference. The young Populist Congressman from Georgia, Tom Watson, wrote that he had received "letters from prominent leaders of the North and West" that "left little doubt of the result of the coming convention of July 4—little doubt of the readiness of the West to concede the head of the ticket to the South—to Col. Polk."[6] Peter M. Wilson, too, reported that Senator William A. Peffer of Kansas showed him correspondence that did not appear to leave

[6] Atlanta *People's Party Paper*, June 17, 1892.

the matter in doubt.[7] A month before the Omaha convention L. L. Polk's nomination for the Presidency of the United States on the People's Party ticket seemed as certain as anything in politics could be.

In many ways he appeared to be the logical choice. The reform movement of 1892 was primarily an agrarian movement. For two and a half years Polk had headed the National Farmers' Alliance and Industrial Union, largest and strongest of the reform organizations. St. Louis, moreover, had demonstrated his acceptability to all the reform groups. Of all possible candidates, unquestionably he would be the best vote-getter in the South, and hence a formidable opponent of Cleveland. At the same time, as much because of his war on sectionalism as anything else, he would prove quite satisfactory to the West. His character, personality, ability, popularity, and availability were all distinct assets.

When Polk first became president of the great agrarian order and set up headquarters in Washington, he may have dreamed of leading the plain people to a national victory. From its beginning he regarded the farmers' movement as a revolution that could not be stayed. It must have been at the Ocala meeting, however, that he first took seriously the possibility of running for President of the United States. Until 1890 he hoped for reform through the Democratic Party. But the defeat of free silver by Congress, the refusal of Congress even to discuss the sub-treasury plan, and the preoccupation of the Democrats with the Negro, the Republicans with the "bloody shirt," and both parties with the tariff, extinguished that hope. The elections of 1890 manifested the power of the farmers' movement; and his unanimous re-election at Ocala exhibited Polk's own power.

During the next year and a half, therefore, the thought that he might win a place on the national ticket of the third party undoubtedly influenced his acts and words to some degree. His

[7] Peter M. Wilson, *Southern Exposure*, p. 161, and letter (per Mary Badger Wilson) to author, June 16, 1937.

usual activities as president of the Alliance—particularly his speaking tours—kept him prominently before the public as a political possibility. His enemies accused him of a soaring ambition and of using the Alliance merely as a stepping-stone to high office. His friends, however, retorted that his unselfish leadership was based upon the open-eyed confidence of hundreds of thousands of farmers and laborers.

When interviewers questioned him in 1891 about his chances for the nomination, Polk always stated that he desired no political office and that he had consistently declined political honors since the war. He considered his work as head of the Farmers' Alliance the most important that he could be doing. Yet no one thought for a moment that he would turn down a Presidential nomination. In the spring of 1892 Polk looked upon himself, with reason, as the chosen leader of a great popular movement. It seems clear that he both expected and desired to be nominated for President at Omaha, and that most Populists stood ready to support him.

He felt supremely confident of the coming success of the People's fight. *"Red hot* all over the South—& getting hotter," he wrote in May, following a rally of Alliance and Populist leaders at Birmingham. As early as March he made the astonishing statement that his party expected to carry eight Southern states and at least fourteen Northern states.[8]

After the Birmingham conference came the critical North Carolina meetings discussed in the preceding chapter. Late in May Polk was back at work in Washington. All his energies were now devoted to the campaign. As always, he wrote almost daily letters to James Denmark, his son-in-law and confidant, and sent editorial matter to the *Progressive Farmer*. Mainly because of its position as organ of the North Carolina Alliance, the paper had expanded its circulation to approximately 25,000, an extraordinary figure for the state in those days. The *News and Observer,* no friend, declared: "The influence arising from that position has

[8] Polk to Denmark, March 16, May 6, 1892.

been beyond anything ever before known in North Carolina. . . . It has controlled at least fifty thousand people in this State."[9]

Widely read and quoted elsewhere, too, Polk's paper ranked with the best reform publications in the country. Copies now went probably to every state in the union. The *Progressive Farmer* also served as Polk's personal organ, and for this reason, as well as for the larger People's cause, he mailed it broadcast.[10]

Polk and his editor, J. L. Ramsey, found it difficult to keep the paper non-partisan, as the constitution of the State Alliance required. The simmering pot occasionally boiled over. The issue of May 24, especially, contained expressions decidedly partial to the Populists. Shortly afterward, the executive committee of the North Carolina Alliance indicated its disapproval. Upon hearing of this, Polk, with characteristic decision, tendered at once the *Progressive Farmer's* resignation as the organ of the State Alliance. In taking the startling action he tried to make clear that his paper would continue to be loyal to the Alliance and its principles. It could not and would not, however, be circumscribed in its advocacy of the People's Party—the only present hope for relief and reform. The two dominant parties had openly violated their pledges and repeatedly betrayed the interests of the people; independent political action, based upon Alliance education, remained the last resort. "Fully nine-tenths of the Alliance people of our State," Polk said, "are solemnly impressed with these same convictions. . . ." Therefore the *Progressive Farmer* would go with them and stand by them.[11]

Marion Butler and other members of the executive committee took the view that the Alliance should be preserved as a non-partisan organization; that the state organ should reflect this policy; and that the organ should be under the direction of the state administration. In answer to Polk's letter of resigna-

[9] *News and Observer*, June 5, 1892.
[10] Polk to Denmark, Dec. 16, 1891, March 26, April 6, 12, 1892.
[11] Polk to Sydenham B. Alexander, May 31, 1892, and MS. editorial, undated.

tion, Syd Alexander, the chairman, stated that the committee had made its complaint without naming any party, and that Polk had probably tendered the resignation through a misunderstanding.[12] Polk, however, believed he had reached the parting of the way, and he had made his choice.

The resignation of the *Progressive Farmer* caused a sensation in North Carolina. "Everybody is talking about it," Ramsey wrote Polk. "The politicians say it will ruin the paper and the Alliance. But, as they look so blue, it is safe to say that they are more uneasy about 'the party' than anything else."[13] In an editorial entitled *"The Fall of Polk,"* the *News and Observer* asseverated: "Col. Polk will no longer be in the swim.... From now on his career will be downward."[14] Yet Alliance men in general seemed to favor the resignation, although a division of opinion on the matter was inevitable. W. H. Worth, state business agent, and W. S. Barnes, state secretary, both felt sure that the next convention of the State Alliance would endorse the Colonel's stand and readopt the *Progressive Farmer*.[15]

Late May and early June brought untold anguish to Polk. The political situation in his home state deeply troubled him. The Alliance caucus of May 17 revealed all too well the cleavage between the Democratic and Populist wings of the order. The Democratic state convention the following day not only nominated for governor an outstanding Alliance man in the person of Elias Carr but proved that the Bourbon Democrats would yield completely to the Alliance Democrats in order to check the Populists. Marion Butler's plan for Democratic-Populist fusion in state politics, which because of the Republican-Negro menace could be

[12] Alexander to Polk, June 2, 1892; Clinton *Caucasian*, June 9, 1892.
[13] Ramsey to Polk, June 4, 1892.
[14] *News and Observer*, June 5, 1892.
[15] Denmark to Polk, June 4, 1892. At its annual meeting, after Polk's death, the state body did "endorse *The Progressive Farmer* as the organ of the State Alliance." Still believing that Polk had tendered his paper's resignation through a misunderstanding, the executive committee had never officially accepted it.

counted on to receive much support, clashed with the Polk policy of independent political action on all fronts. Then came the resignation of the *Progressive Farmer*—a most trying decision for Polk to make.

As June opened, Ramsey and Denmark received from Polk four pages of material for the next issue of the paper. He had written one page but had dictated the rest. In a covering note J. H. Turner of Georgia, national secretary of the Alliance, mentioned that "Col. Polk is quite unwell. . . ." The next mail brought a letter from Dr. J. M. Hays, Polk's physician, stating that he had forbidden the Colonel any unusual physical or mental exertion for a few days. Denmark then wired for particulars, and Turner replied: "One of Colonel's old spells. No danger. He is better. Will keep you informed."[16] On Tuesday, June 7, Denmark received the following note that Polk had dictated to Macune:

> I fear you are unnecessarily alarmed from the dispatch you sent Mr. Turner. . . . The attack was about like the one which I had at Ocala . . . the difference being that this is more persistent. . . . Be assured that I will . . . inform you if my case should grow worse or become serious. . . . Of course I have felt that this is the most important week in the work on my paper that has ever occurred in its history. No one can realize how deeply I regret that I have been unable to give it my attention. . . .[17]

Polk's malady was hemorrhage of the bladder. Caused by a tumor, it had afflicted him at intervals for about four years. His incessant traveling, vigorous speaking, and long hours of writing, conferring, and presiding unfailingly aggravated the condition. Any prolonged strain or excitement usually brought on an attack. Yet Polk, a zealot enlisted in a cause, would not spare himself, even though he fully realized his danger. His severest previous attack had immediately followed the Ocala convention. The present one had begun on May 27.

[16] Telegram, Turner to Denmark, June 4, 1892.
[17] Polk to Denmark, [June 4, 1892].

When Denmark arrived in Washington on Wednesday, June 8, he found the Colonel "completely exhausted, physically" but "mentally about as clear as ever." Many friends and well-wishers —like Macune, Turner, Tom Watson, and General Julian S. Carr—had paid calls that Polk, a sociable man, thoroughly enjoyed. Later in the day, however, he twice suffered heart failure, though each time he was revived. In fact, he rallied to such an extent that his observers thought he might completely recover. And Mrs. Polk came to him on Thursday. Yet he soon grew noticeably weaker, and his suffering gradually increased. On Friday signs of uraemia appeared, and, in the faint hope that an operation could save him, he was removed from his residence at 717 Twelfth Street to the Garfield Memorial Hospital. He lost consciousness that evening. Sinking slowly, he breathed his last at eleven-fifteen o'clock, Saturday morning, June 11.[18]

The sudden death of Polk—at fifty-five—was a stunning blow. Only members of the family and close associates had known the precariousness of his physical condition. His friends and followers in general had assumed his health to be excellent; they had always marveled at his tireless energy and robust constitution. At the political conventions in Raleigh three weeks before his death, Marion Butler declared, Polk "never looked better . . . he seemed to have the promise of still a score of years or more." It quickly became apparent, none the less, that he died from overwork. Perhaps a reckless enthusiasm led him to undertake more than his body could stand. Or perhaps he was driving to accomplish as much as possible before the inevitable end. After Polk's death a California Populist recalled:

> Within a year it was my privilege to spend a day in his company, traveling on a train. He then appeared to me to be overworked. I said so to him, and suggested that he should take care of himself, as we could ill-afford to lose him. He answered that he had but one life to live; that he was devoting his

[18] Oxford *Public Ledger,* June 17, 1892; *Progressive Farmer,* June 21, 1892.

energies to a cause that was dearer to him than his life, and that if he was called away others would be found capable and earnest enough to take up the work where he left off; and that if he could look back in his dying moments and feel that he had done his duty to his family, his country and his God, he would have no regrets, no matter when the moment came.[19]

Polk died poor. His singular devotion to the farmers' movement during the last six years of his life completely transcended the thoughts of money-making that had engaged him in the early 'eighties. His personal debts, which included a pledge of $500 to the Baptist girls' school, and the debts of the *Progressive Farmer* amounted to approximately $3,000.[20] They could be paid only if the paper continued to operate successfully, and if all sums due the estate were assiduously collected. At the time of Polk's death the Alliance owed him $853.54 in salary. Two years later Denmark was urging the secretary-treasurer to pay the last $235.54, explaining that even when the estate were finally settled there would be little money left.[21] Butler remarked:

> How often do we see men enter public life poor, but suddenly become rich—how, the public seldom knows. Col. Polk dies poor, and there probably has never lived a man who could have prostituted his position for greater financial gain. He was not only a man who could not be bought at any price, but he was a man who spur[n]ed with the supremest contempt and indignation any suggestion of a deal or trade, however slight or seemingly plausible.[22]

Alliance men and Populists felt not only shock but a deep sense of loss at the death of Polk. His successor as president of the Alliance, H. L. Loucks, struck near the truth when he said: "Brother

---

[19] J. J. Morrison, in San Francisco *People's Press,* June 25, 1892.
[20] MS. "Inventory and account of the property of L. L. Polk deceased," undated.
[21] Denmark to D. P. Duncan, copy, July 24, 1894.
[22] *Caucasian,* June 16, 1892.

Polk . . . was the one man whose place can not be filled. He was the one around whom all our hopes centered as they can around no other man."²³ H. E. Taubeneck, chairman of the People's Party executive committee, wrote Ignatius Donnelly: "The death of Col. Polk was a severe blow to our cause and it is very hard to find a man to fill his place as he did."²⁴ Such leaders, all over the country, agreed that the esteem in which the rank and file held Polk, the influence of his crusade against sectionalism, his refusal to nurse grudges or resentments, and his absolute integrity had been factors of incalculable benefit to the People's cause. Even his old enemy the Topeka *Capital* declared that he "did more to give the party a national standing than any other man in it."²⁵

When death had thus eliminated Polk, their first choice, People's Party leaders unofficially offered the Presidential nomination to Judge Walter Q. Gresham of Indiana, a widely known independent Republican who advocated tariff and monetary reform. Gresham, however, declined to be the candidate. Then, after rejecting other possibilities—Ignatius Donnelly, for instance, because of idiosyncrasies that recalled Horace Greeley, and Leland Stanford because of monopolistic taints—the leaders decided that General James B. Weaver would be most logical and most eligible. Weaver, therefore, won the nomination at Omaha, defeating Senator James H. Kyle of South Dakota. For second place on the ticket the convention chose a former Confederate, General James G. Field of Virginia, over Ben Terrell of Texas.

Many observers regarded the nomination of Weaver as a serious tactical error, principally because he was already associated in the public mind with political lost causes. Both Republicans and Democrats, said the Washington *Star,* greeted the news with "something closely approaching a sigh of relief."²⁶ A strong new

---

[23] Emory A. Allen, *The Life and Public Services of James Baird Weaver,* p. 69.
[24] H. E. Taubeneck to Ignatius Donnelly, June 16, 1892, Donnelly Papers.
[25] Topeka, Kansas, *Daily Capital,* June 12, 1892.
[26] Quoted in *Public Opinion,* XIII, 320 (July 9, 1892).

man, such as Polk, had he lived, or Gresham, or even Kyle, would have contributed a greater element of uncertainty to the campaign. In the fall elections, none the less, the Populists received over one million popular votes and twenty-two electoral votes—an ex--cellent showing for the new party. With Democratic help, the People's Party carried Kansas, North Dakota, Colorado, Idaho, and Nevada, and almost won in Nebraska, South Dakota, and Oregon. Though the Populists failed to break the "solid South," in Alabama, Georgia, Mississippi, and North Carolina they polled an impressive vote. Southern Populists, and above all, North Carolina Populists, felt most keenly the loss of leadership that Polk's death occasioned.

Following the nomination of Cleveland by the Democrats and Harrison by the Republicans in June, and of Weaver by the Populists in July, the People's Party of North Carolina held its state convention in August. Unfortunately, the delegates rejected the able and realistic Harry Skinner as their nominee for governor and picked instead Dr. Wyatt P. Exum, a hot-tempered extremist. Then in September the Republicans put up a ticket, headed by D. M. Furches. The November election returned Grover Cleveland to the White House and made Elias Carr governor of North Carolina. Democratic candidates in the state received comfortable pluralities. Significantly, however, the Populist vote of 47,840 and the Republican vote of 94,684 totaled several thousand more than the Democratic vote of 135,519.

In 1894, two years later, the Populists and the Republicans fused, thus forming a strange union that controlled North Carolina until 1900. Because Negroes again appeared in power in many parts of the state, the period became one of great tension, bitterness, and tumult. The Democrats, although they represented a majority of the white people and were still the largest political party, found themselves helpless against the combination. To combat Fusion they revived all the methods—good and bad—used against the

Radicals during Reconstruction. Chastened and rejuvenated by the rise of the Farmers' Alliance and by the misrule of Fusion, the Democrats returned to office at the beginning of the new century more responsive to the needs of the people.

Polk undoubtedly would have opposed Populist-Republican fusion in 1894 as vigorously as he opposed Populist-Democratic fusion in 1892. The national campaign of 1896 he would have recognized as the crucial contest between "the people" and "the plutocrats" that he had predicted in his Wadesboro speech five years before, and he doubtless would have championed Bryan against McKinley. Yet many Democrats, in their ardor to "make Populism odious," unjustly linked Polk with such Fusionists as Marion Butler, who went to the United States Senate as a Populist, and Daniel L. Russell, the Republican governor who followed Elias Carr. Some Populists and Republicans, too, unfairly claimed the blessing of Polk for their marriage of convenience. "Whatever error Col. Polk may have made," Josephus Daniels has rightly said, "those who have wronged him by connecting his name with fusionism must see they are in error."[27] The black clouds of prejudice and passion that rose in the 'nineties drifted over North Carolina for a generation, all but obscuring Polk's record of constructive achievement.

Similar prejudice in the nation at large long distorted the "agrarian crusade." A well-known American historian was only expressing the fashionable view when, in the year of normalcy 1920, he asserted of the Granger, Greenback, Alliance, and Populist movements:

> Every one of them was based on class selfishness and flourished amid poverty and ignorance. The eccentric fandangoes which the leaders of the movements cut in a number of state and national campaigns are things the farmer of this day, one of the wealthiest and solidest figures in our citizenry, would like to

---

[27] Josephus Daniels, in *News and Observer*, July 29, 1926.

forget. Fortunately such fatuities never did possess the minds or beguile the steps of any considerable number of the cultivators of our soil and the gleaners of our harvests. The farmers who sat at Horace Greeley's feet as they read the *Weekly Tribune* had their "isms", but praise be, they did not contribute the men who strode into our politics to be remembered because of their want of socks, their long beards, their speeches about pitchforks, bloody bridles, and crosses of gold.[28]

More enlightened observers knew better. Like English Chartism of the 1840's, American Populism of the 1890's was a powerful mass movement. It proved to be effective educationally as well as politically. At first the two major parties scorned the demands of the People's Party, labeling them "radical" and "fantastic." After the third party's exhibition of strength in 1892, however, both Democrats and Republicans gradually adopted Populist principles, thus making them "respectable." It was not long before practically all of the old Alliance-Populist demands became law. Populism clearly influenced William Jennings Bryan, Theodore Roosevelt, Robert M. La Follette, and Woodrow Wilson—so much so that James A. Woodburn remarked: "It seems to me it was General Weaver who had grown the feathers in which these later political birds plumed themselves."[29] In the fight for industrial democracy since the Civil War, the "agrarian crusade," the Progressive movement, and Franklin D. Roosevelt's New Deal have been successive, connected steps.

Polk's period of prominence on the national scene amounted to only two and a half years. Yet he ably led the Farmers' Alliance and the People's Party during the most vital months of their existence. Assuredly, his untimely death cheated him of greater fame. It may have been a merciful Providence, however, that removed him on June 11, 1892; relentlessly his physical and mental strain would

---

[28] Ellis P. Oberholtzer, review of Solon J. Buck's *The Agrarian Crusade*, in *American Historical Review*, XXVI, 147 (Oct., 1920).

[29] James A. Woodburn, "Western Radicalism in American Politics," *Mississippi Valley Historical Review*, XIII, 155-61 (Sept., 1926).

"I AM STANDING NOW . . ." 297

have increased, and had he lived longer he might have died at an even more tragic time. A few days after Polk's death Tom Watson, of Georgia and the South, wrote:

> Who has toiled harder for the people . . . ? Who was readier to go; to suffer; to spend and be spent; to risk all; to heal wounds he had not made; to harmonize differences and preach brotherly love?
> Who has done more to destroy sectionalism and to join the hands of the Blue and the Gray?
> No man who has ever lived. . . .
> He named the evils of which we complain; he named the remedy for these evils; he made it clear to all men that the South and West could act together; and when that proof was made, every thinker realized that the Future of the Southern people contained a splendid possibility which its Past had not contained.[30]

Forty-five years after Polk's death William Allen White, of Kansas and the West, testified: "I was a young pharisee of a rather strict caste when Colonel Polk came to Kansas but I saw the light on the Damascus Road ten years later and have always been convinced that he was one of the great pioneers who left their bones to whiten on the road to progress, marking the way."[31]

Following the funeral services at the First Baptist Church of Raleigh on Sunday afternoon, the day after his death, the remains of Leonidas LaFayette Polk were laid to rest in Oakwood Cemetery. On a tree-shaded knoll overlooking a little valley and a rivulet, an unusual monument marks his grave. A massive granite base is surmounted by a square pedestal of dark marble. But no shaft rises from the pedestal; the Polk Memorial and Relief Association failed to collect funds enough to complete the monument. In letters already weather-worn and dim, three sides of the pedestal relate the main events of his career. The fourth side bears two sentences, eloquent and prophetic, from his Winfield speech of

[30] *People's Party Paper*, June 17, 1892.
[31] William Allen White to author, June 24, 1937.

July 4, 1890. Polk had said: "I am standing now just behind the curtain, in the full glow of the coming sunset. Behind me are the shadows on the track, before me lies the dark valley and the river, and when I mingle with its dark waters I want to cast one lingering look upon a country whose government is of the people, for the people, and by the people."

The memorial in Oakwood symbolizes both his life and the cause for which he was fighting: each, when he died, seemed sadly unfinished. Monuments more significant than stone, however, recall L. L. Polk in North Carolina. And the reinvigoration of American democracy during the first half of the twentieth century is in great measure a tribute to those who, like Polk, fought hardest when the issue was most in doubt.

BIBLIOGRAPHY

Manuscripts

The L. L. Polk Collection

Most important of the sources of information on Polk is this large, rich, and varied mass of material in the possession of Miss Leonita Denmark, of Raleigh, North Carolina. A private collection, it is uncatalogued, although the contents are conveniently arranged by topic and by chronology. Letters from Polk to his wife, 1862-65, and to his son-in-law, 1891-92, are especially revealing. Letters received by Polk cover fairly well the period 1877-92 and are voluminous for his three years as Commissioner of Agriculture. Business records that illuminate Polk's commercial enterprises of the 'seventies and 'eighties form a great portion of the manuscript material. The Collection also includes printed material. Of prime value are bound volumes containing the almost complete issues of the Polkton *Ansonian* for 1874-75 and 1876-77 and the *Progressive Farmer* from 1886 to the late 'nineties. Issues and clippings of other newspapers, useful particularly for the years 1890-92, are plentiful. The published proceedings of the farmers' organizations with which Polk was connected, books and pamphlets that were a part of his personal library, a number of photographs, and miscellaneous items round out the Collection.

Other Collections

Ashe, Samuel A., North Carolina Department of Archives and History, Raleigh

Butler, Marion, Southern Historical Collection, University of North Carolina Library, Chapel Hill
Henderson, John S., Chapel Hill
Kingsbury, Theodore B., Chapel Hill
North Carolina Grange, Duke University Library, Durham
Smith, Ed. Chambers, Durham

Of these, the Ashe, Butler, and Henderson Papers prove most useful to the Polk student; they throw valuable light on North Carolina politics during the important years 1890-92. Several interesting letters by, to, and about Polk may be found in the "miscellaneous files" at Raleigh and at Durham and in the Ignatius Donnelly Papers, Minnesota Historical Society, St. Paul. Also useful are two published collections:

Grimes, Bryan, *Extracts of Letters . . . to His Wife . . .* (Pulaski Cowper, comp.), Raleigh, Alfred Williams & Co., 1884.

Worth, Jonathan, *Correspondence* (J. G. deRoulhac Hamilton, ed.), 2 vols., Raleigh, Edwards & Broughton, 1909.

Published Works of L. L. Polk

Speeches

Address . . . Delivered at Indianapolis, Ind., Nov. 18, 1891, Washington, *National Economist,* 1891.

Address . . . Delivered before the Inter-State Convention of Farmers . . . Atlanta . . . 1887, Atlanta, Jas. P. Harrison & Co., 1887.

Agricultural Depression: Its Causes—the Remedy: Speech before the Senate Committee on Agriculture and Forestry, April 22, 1890, Raleigh, Edwards & Broughton, 1890.

The Protest of the Farmer: Address . . . to Citizens' Alliance No. 4 of Washington, D. C., at Concordia Hall, April 14, 1891, [Washington, *National Economist,* 1891].

Articles

"The Farmers' Discontent," *North American Review,* CLIII, 5-12 (July, 1891).

"Sectionalism and the Alliance," in Nelson A. Dunning and others, *Farmers' Alliance History and Agricultural Digest* (listed separately below), pp. 249-53.

Department of Agriculture Publications

These are arranged chronologically. Each was printed in Raleigh in the year given.

First Quarterly Report . . . (July 17, 1877).
Monthly Crop Reports, 1877-78.
Third Quarterly Report . . . (Jan. 15, 1878).
Report on the General Condition of the Agricultural Interests of North Carolina . . . (March, 1878).
Fourth Quarterly Report . . . (April 16, 1878).
Second Quarterly Report . . . for the Year 1878.
Report . . . for 1877 and 1878, 1879.
Handbook of North Carolina: Embracing Historical and Physiographical Sketches of the State, with Statistical and Other Information Relating to Its Industries, Resources and Political Conditions, 1879.
Report on the Work of the Department of Agriculture (Jan., 1880).

OFFICIAL PUBLICATIONS

United States

United States Census, 1850-1890.
Wiley, Calvin H., "North Carolina," in [serial number 2476] 49th Congress, 2nd session (1886-87), *House Executive Documents,* XVII, 214-60.

North Carolina

Each of these was published in Raleigh by the state printer.

Bureau of Labor Statistics, *Annual Reports, 1887-1891.* These volumes contain valuable information on social and economic conditions.

Convention of 1865-66, *Journal*.
Department of Agriculture, *Bulletin*, monthly, 1880-1887.
House Journal, 1860-91.
Public Documents, 1860-91.
Public (and *Private*) *Laws*, 1861-91.
Senate Journal, 1860-91.

In the Anson County courthouse at Wadesboro are located a "Record of Inventories, 1849-1856," a "Record of Deeds," indexes to deeds, and similar records that furnish an insight into the economic and social status of Polk and his forbears. Useful also in this connection is the Anson County index in the Land Grant Office (Secretary of State), Raleigh.

Private

Battle, Kemp P., *Reports . . . to the Board of Trustees of the University of North Carolina, January 20th, 1887*, Raleigh, Edwards & Broughton, 1887.
Davidson College, *Catalogue . . . , 1855-58*.
North Carolina Baptist State Convention, *Minutes, 1880-1892*.
North Carolina College of Agriculture and Mechanic Arts (beginning 1917 N. C. State Coll. of Agr. and Engineering), *Record*, 1904-25.
North Carolina Press Association, *Historical Records 1873-1887* (J. B. Sherrill, comp.), 1930.

Three manuscript record-books in the Davidson College Library provide entertaining information on Polk's student days: Faculty Minutes covering the year 1856, "Record of Minutes of the Eumenean Society [1852-1859]," and "Eumenean Society Treasurer's Book" covering 1855-1856. The following official publications, because of their special importance for the study of Polk, are listed separately:

Farmers' and Laborers' Union of America, *Proceedings, 1888-89*.
Inter-State Farmers' Association, *Proceedings, 1887-89*.

BIBLIOGRAPHY 303

National Farmers' Alliance and Co-operative Union of America, *Proceedings, 1887.*
National Farmers' Alliance and Industrial Union, *Proceedings, 1890-91.*
North Carolina Farmers' State Alliance, *Proceedings, 1890-92.*
North Carolina State Grange, Patrons of Husbandry, *Proceedings, 1875-1887.*
Proceedings . . . of Atlantic Council, Patrons of Husbandry. . . . Kinston, N. C., Dec. 18th, 1873 (broadside).

NEWSPAPERS

Aside from Polk's own *Ansonian* and *Progressive Farmer,* the following best portray his life and work. The newspapers cited in the footnotes but not listed below represent in almost all cases issues and clippings in the Polk Collection.

North Carolina

Charlotte *Southern Home,* weekly, 1872-79, University of North Carolina Library, Chapel Hill.
Clinton *Caucasian,* weekly, 1889-92, State Library of North Carolina, Raleigh. Marion Butler's paper.
Polkton *Ansonian,* weekly, 1875-76, Anson County courthouse, Wadesboro. For the year between Polk's two terms as editor.
Raleigh *Biblical Recorder,* weekly, 1879-92, Raleigh. Organ of the North Carolina Baptists.
Raleigh *Evening Visitor,* daily, 1879-81, 1890-92, Raleigh.
Raleigh *Farmer and Mechanic,* weekly, 1877-85, Raleigh. First the organ of the Department of Agriculture, then a general newspaper.
Raleigh *News,* daily, 1878-80, Raleigh. Polk wrote a great deal for this paper during the summer of 1880.
Raleigh *News and Observer,* daily, 1880-92, Raleigh. The voice of the "Bourbons," edited by Samuel A. Ashe; indispensable to the study of Polk.

Raleigh *North Carolina Intelligencer,* weekly, 1890-91, Raleigh. A conservative paper.

Raleigh *Observer,* daily, 1877-80, Raleigh. An excellent newspaper.

Raleigh *Signal,* weekly, 1880-92, Raleigh and Chapel Hill. Republican.

Raleigh *State Agricultural Journal,* weekly, 1874-75, Chapel Hill. Organ of the Grange.

Raleigh *State Chronicle,* weekly, then daily, 1885-92, Chapel Hill. The voice of the "young progressives," edited first by Walter H. Page and then by Josephus Daniels.

Wadesboro *North Carolina Argus,* weekly, 1859-65, Raleigh, 1873-76, Wadesboro. Particularly valuable for Polk's early political career.

Wadesboro *Pee Dee Herald,* weekly, 1875-76, Wadesboro.

The following agricultural monthlies located at Chapel Hill should be listed:

Raleigh *North-Carolina Farmer,* 1876-83.
Raleigh *North-Carolina Planter,* 1858-61.
Tarboro *Reconstructed Farmer,* 1869-72. A periodical of unusual interest.
Wilmington *Carolina Farmer,* 1868-79.

Other States

Files of the following are in the Library of Congress.

Atlanta *Constitution,* daily, Aug., 1887. For the first Inter-State Farmers' convention.

Atlanta *People's Party Paper,* weekly, 1891-92. Tom Watson's.

Cincinnati *Enquirer,* daily, May, 1891. Fair-minded reporting of the famous "National Union Conference."

Des Moines *Iowa State Register,* daily, 1890-91. See "Topeka," next page.

Indianapolis *Journal,* daily, Nov., 1891. Annual Alliance meeting.

St. Louis *Globe-Democrat,* daily, Dec., 1889, Feb., 1892. For two of the most significant of the farmers' conventions.

Topeka *Capital,* weekly edition, 1890-91. An engaging study in vituperation, called forth by three Polk visits to Kansas.

Washington *National Economist,* weekly, 1889-92. The official organ of the Alliance, edited by Charles W. Macune.

Washington and New York, *Public Opinion,* weekly, 1890-92. Collection of editorials from newspapers of various political beliefs.

WRITINGS OF POLK'S CONTEMPORARIES

Allen, Emory A., *The Life and Public Services of James Baird Weaver...,* People's Party Pub. Co., 1892. A campaign tract.

American (beginning 1875 *Appleton's*) *Annual Cyclopaedia and Register of Important Events, 1861-1892,* New York, D. Appleton & Co.

Andrews, Sidney, *The South since the War,* Boston, Ticknor & Fields, 1866.

Campbell, George, *White and Black: the Outcome of a Visit to the United States,* New York, R. Worthington, 1879.

Chamberlain, Henry R., *The Farmers' Alliance: What It Aims to Accomplish,* New York, Minerva Pub. Co., 1891.

Drew, Frank M., "The Present Farmers' Movement," *Political Science Quarterly,* VI, 282-310 (June, 1891).

Dunning, Nelson A., and others, *Farmers' Alliance History and Agricultural Digest,* Washington, Alliance Pub. Co., 1891.

Garvin, William L., and S. O. Daws, *History of the National Farmers' Alliance and Co-operative Union of America,* Jacksboro, Tex., J. N. Rogers & Co., 1887.

Grady, Henry W., "Cotton and Its Kingdom," *Harper's New Monthly Magazine,* LXIII, 719-34 (Oct., 1881).

Hundley, Daniel R., *Social Relations in Our Southern States,* New York, Henry B. Price, 1860.

Kelley, William D., *The Old South and the New*, New York, G. P. Putnam's Sons, 1888.

King, Edward, *The Great South: a Record of Journeys...*, Hartford, American Pub. Co., 1875.

Olmstead, Florence H., *Alliance Nightingale*, Douglass, Kan., 1890. A song book.

Skinner, Harry, "The Hope of the South," *Frank Leslie's Illustrated Newspaper*, LXIX, 290 (Nov. 30, 1889). Germ of the Alliance's sub-treasury plan.

Somers, Robert, *The Southern States since the War, 1870-1*, New York, Macmillan, 1871.

Suggestions for the Establishment of a Polytechnic School in North Carolina, Fayetteville, Edward J. Hale & Son, 1856.

Vincent, Leopold, comp., *Alliance and Labor Songster*, Winfield, Kan., H. & L. Vincent, 1890.

Watauga Club, *The Need of an Industrial School in North Carolina, Together with the Estimates of the Cost of Establishing and Maintaining It: a Memorial to the General Assembly*, Raleigh, *Daily State Chronicle*, 1885.

Wilcox, Ella W., "Reform" (poem), *Arena*, V, 748 (May, 1892).

BIOGRAPHICAL AND AUTOBIOGRAPHICAL MATERIAL

Battle, Kemp P., *History of the University of North Carolina*, 2 vols., Raleigh, Edwards & Broughton, 1907, 1912.

———, *Memories of an Old-Time Tar Heel* (William J. Battle, ed.), Chapel Hill, University of North Carolina Press, 1945.

Connelley, William E., *Ingalls of Kansas: a Character Study*, Topeka, 1909.

Daniels, Josephus, "Leonidas LaFayette Polk," Raleigh *News and Observer*, July 29, 1926. An excellent interpretation of Polk's career.

Dowd, Clement, *Life of Zebulon B. Vance*, Charlotte, *Observer* Printing & Publishing House, 1897.

Hendrick, Burton J., *The Life and Letters of Walter H. Page*, 3 vols., Garden City, N. Y., Doubleday, Page & Co., 1922.

———, *The Training of an American: the Earlier Life and Letters of Walter H. Page, 1855-1913*, Boston, Houghton Mifflin Co., 1928.

Kingsbury, Theodore B., "Samuel A'Court Ashe," *Biographical History of North Carolina from Colonial Times to the Present* (Ashe, ed., 8 vols., Greensboro, Charles L. Van Noppen, 1905-17), I, 66-75. The sketches appearing in this work are useful but generally uncritical and must therefore be used with caution.

Page, Walter H., "Address at the Inauguration of President Winston," *N. C. University Magazine*, XXII (1891-92), 61-71.

———, *The Southerner: a Novel, Being the Autobiography of Nicholas Worth*, New York, Doubleday, Page & Co., 1909.

Peele, William J., "Col. L. L. Polk: a Brief Sketch of His Life and Work," *North Carolina Baptist Almanac for the Year 1893*, pp. 46-49. A sympathetic review.

Poe, Clarence, *Colonel Leonidas Lafayette Polk: His Services in Starting the N. C. State Coll. of Agr. and Eng.*, Raleigh, *Progressive Farmer*, 1926. Sympathetic biographical sketch and estimate.

Polk, William H., *Polk Family and Kinsmen*, Louisville, Bradley, 1912.

Polk, William M., *Leonidas Polk: Bishop and General*, 2 vols. (rev. ed.), New York, Longmans, Green & Co., 1915.

[Robson, Charles], *Representative Men of the South*, Philadelphia, Chas. Robson & Co., 1880. Contains a good account of Polk up to the age of forty, with particular emphasis upon his Civil War career.

Simmons, Furnifold M., *F. M. Simmons, Statesman of the New South: Memoirs and Addresses* (J. Fred Rippy, comp. and ed.), Durham, Duke University Press, 1936.

"Sketch of Harry Skinner," *North Carolina Bar Association, Proceedings, 1915*, pp. 238-41.

Whitaker, Richard H., *Reminiscences, Incidents and Anecdotes,* Raleigh, Edwards & Broughton, 1905.

Wilson, Peter M., *Southern Exposure,* Chapel Hill, University of North Carolina Press, 1927.

Winston, Robert W., *It's a Far Cry,* New York, Henry Holt & Co., 1937.

Special Studies

Andrews, Benjamin F., "The Land Grant of 1862 and the Land-Grant Colleges," United States Bureau of Education, *Bulletin, 1918,* No. 13.

Barr, Elizabeth N., "The Populist Uprising," *Standard History of Kansas and Kansans* (William E. Connelley, ed.), II, 1115-95.

Buck, Paul H., *The Road to Reunion, 1865-1900,* Boston, Little, Brown & Co., 1937.

Buck, Solon J., *The Agrarian Crusade: a Chronicle of the Farmer in Politics,* New Haven, Yale University Press, 1921.

―――――, *The Granger Movement: a Study of Agricultural Organization and Its Political, Economic and Social Manifestations, 1870-1880,* Cambridge, Harvard University Press, 1913.

Dabney, Charles W., *Universal Education in the South,* 2 vols., Chapel Hill, University of North Carolina Press, 1936. Contains a valuable account of the Watauga Club of Raleigh.

Hicks, John D., "The Farmers' Alliance in North Carolina," *North Carolina Historical Review,* II, 162-87 (April, 1925).

―――――, *The Populist Revolt: a History of the Farmers' Alliance and the People's Party,* Minneapolis, University of Minnesota Press, 1931.

Johnston, Robert Z., "The Administration of Rev. Drury Lacy, D.D., Third President of Davidson College," *Davidson College Semi-Centenary Addresses* (Raleigh, E. M. Uzzell, 1888), pp. 121-30.

Kenan, Thomas S., "Forty-Third Regiment," *Histories of the Several Regiments and Battalions from North Carolina in the Great War, 1861-'65* (Walter Clark, ed.), III, 1-18.

Oberholtzer, Ellis P., review of Solon J. Buck's *The Agrarian Crusade,* in *American Historical Review,* XXVI, 147-48 (Oct., 1920).

Peele, William J., "A History of the Agricultural and Mechanical College," *North Carolina Teacher,* VI, No. 1, 12-25 (Sept., 1888).

Shaw, Cornelia R., *Davidson College,* New York, Fleming H. Revell Press, 1923.

Turner, Frederick J., *The Frontier in American History,* New York, Henry Holt, 1921.

Turner, J. Kelly, and John L. Bridgers, *History of Edgecombe County, North Carolina,* Raleigh, Edwards & Broughton, 1920.

Underwood, George C., "Twenty-Sixth Regiment," *Histories of the Several Regiments* ... (Walter Clark, ed.), II, 303-423.

Vann, Richard T., "Historical Sketch of Meredith College," Meredith College *Quarterly Bulletin,* Ser. 4, No. 2, pp. 3-15 (Jan., 1911).

Woodburn, James A., "Western Radicalism in American Politics," *Mississippi Valley Historical Review,* XIII, 143-68 (Sept., 1926).

General Works

Ashe, Samuel A., *History of North Carolina,* 2 vols., Raleigh, Edwards & Broughton, 1925.

Cobb, Irvin S., *North Carolina,* New York, George H. Doran Co., 1924.

Connor, Robert D. W., *North Carolina: Rebuilding an Ancient Commonwealth,* 4 vols., Chicago, American Historical Society, 1929.

Hamilton, J. G. deRoulhac, *North Carolina since 1860* (*History of North Carolina,* III), Chicago, Lewis Pub. Co., 1919.

Tarbell, Ida M., *The Nationalizing of Business,* New York, Macmillan, 1936.

Wilson, Woodrow, *A History of the American People,* 5 vols., New York, Harper & Bros., 1902.

Readers who may wish a more extensive citation of sources

should see the footnotes and bibliography of this author's "Leonidas LaFayette Polk: a Study in Agrarian Leadership" (1947), a bound typescript in the Library of the University of North Carolina at Chapel Hill.

Chapters VI and VII of the present book appeared, in slightly altered form, as a two-part article entitled "Leonidas LaFayette Polk and the North Carolina Department of Agriculture," in *North Carolina Historical Review*, XX, 103-21, 197-218 (April and July, 1943).

INDEX

Advertising, in *Progressive Farmer*, 153-54
"Agrarian crusade," estimated, 262, 295-96
Agrarian discontent. *See* Farmers
Agricultural and Mechanical College. *See* North Carolina College of Agriculture and Mechanic Arts
Agricultural college, campaign for in North Carolina, 170-80
Agricultural Wheel, 206
Agriculture, Polk on decline of, 9 f., 197-98, 264
Aiken, D. Wyatt, Grange organizer, 99
Alabama, poverty in, 197
Albright, James W., 128
Alderman, Edwin A., 252
Alexander, Dr. Annie L., 152
Alexander, Sydenham B., urges Grange to foster education, 101; and the North Carolina Department of Agriculture, 108, 127 ff., 133; advises Polk on editing *Progressive Farmer*, 150 f.; supports industrial school and agricultural college bills, 165, 178; seeks nomination as governor, 229 f.; Polk's relations with, 248, 261; on resignation of *Progressive Farmer*, 289
Alliance. *See* Farmers' Alliance
American Revolution, 26 f., 36
Anderson, David, 143
Anson County, Polk land in, 22 ff.; described, 24 f.; political bent of in 1860, 42 f.; Polk organizes the militia in, 49; House campaign of 1864 in, 64-65; Kilpatrick's raid in, 75; supports new railroad, 76-77; farmers' clubs in, 158; Farmers' Alliance in, 238. *See also* Polkton *and* Wadesboro
"Anson Plough Boys," 50
Ansonian. See Polkton *Ansonian*
Appomattox, 14, 74
Ashby, H. S. P., 217
Ashby, N. B., 263
Ashe, Samuel A., attacks Polk, 232-39; Senator Vance's relations with, 243, 249 ff.; on N. C. politics, 276; mentioned, 281
Ashe, Thomas S., Polk's friendship with, 29, 62-63, 71
Asheville, farmers' meetings at, 117 f., 206
Atkinson, Edward, Boston economist, 137
Atkinson, George F., University professor, 151-52
Atlanta, Exposition of 1881, 137, 141 f.; farmers' conventions in, 202 ff., 212, 232
Atlanta *Constitution,* on Polk, 203
Austin, C., 107n
Aycock, Charles B., on Polk, 247
Ayer, Hal W., 256

Badger, George E., 129
Baltimore, Md., 79, 112
Bannister, Cowan and Company, 91
Baptist Female Seminary, of Raleigh, Polk's daughters attend, 139; characterized, 184-85
Baptist school for girls, campaign for in North Carolina, 185-89

INDEX

Baptist State Convention, of N. C., 183 ff.
Barbee, J. S., 237
Barnes, W. S., 289
Barringer, D. M., 91
Barringer, V. C., 46
Battle, H. W., 185
Battle, Kemp P., work of in establishing N. C. Department of Agriculture, 104 f., 108; asks Polk to speak at Chapel Hill, 117; seeks to oust Polk as Commissioner of Agriculture, 126 ff., 180; opposes industrial school, 167 f.; opposes agricultural college, 173 ff., 179; estimates Polk, 180n, 182; attends banquet for Polk, 213
Battle, Richard H., 143
Beaumont, Ralph, labor leader, 3 ff., 225
Beddingfield, Eugene C., 241, 246
Bellamy, Edward, 263
Benbow, D. W. C., 122, 161
Bennett, Risden Tyler, 63
Benton, W. H., family, 29
Bible, the, in Polk home, 23, 38, 57
Big business, Polk on, 265 f.
Biggs, Asa, 91
"Bill Arp," 153
Bingham School, 141
Birmingham, farmers' meetings in, 211, 287
Blaine, James G., 256
"Bloody shirt." See Sectionalism
Board of Agriculture, origin and composition of, 107 f.; Polk's relations with, 116 ff., 126 ff.; fight to reorganize, 129-33, 176 f.; and the industrial school, 165 ff.; farmers meet with, 175-76, 179
Boone, J. B., 184
Boston, Fair of 1883, 137-38, 145; Polk enters business in, 145, 149
"Bourbons," in North Carolina, 133, 136, 147-49, 175, 229 ff., 238 f., 243-44, 279 ff., 289
Bragg, Thomas, 91
Brain-power, Polk on, 7-8

Bribery of legislatures, 230-31
Brily, James, 52
Broadaway, John, Polk's guardian, 29, 37
Broughton, N. B., 185
Bryan, William Jennings, 295 f.
Buck, Paul, quoted on South, 116
Burgwyn, W. H. S., 202
Burnside, Gen. Ambrose E., 50
Butler, Gen. Benjamin F., 54
Butler, Marion, analyzes Bourbon tactics, 239; on Polk, 259, 291 f.; sketch of, 278; in N. C. campaign of 1892, 278 ff., 289-90; on resignation of *Progressive Farmer*, 288; as a Fusionist, 295
Buxton, R. P., 135 f.

Cade, Baylus, 231
Caldwell, Tod R., 82
Calhoun, John C., 35
Calhoun, Patrick, 257 f.
California, Farmers' Alliance and People's Party in, 270-71
Cameron, John D., 120
Campbell, Sir George, on Polk, 115; describes Raleigh, 140
Cantwell, Edward, 46
"Captain Bogardus and Sons," 141
Carolina Central Railroad, 42, 76-77
Carr, Elias, elected president of North Carolina Farmers' Association, 176; Senator Vance's correspondence with, 241-42, 250 f.; Polk's relations with, 261; nominated for governor, 280 f., 289; elected governor, 294 f.
Carr, Julian S., 187, 280, 291
Casey, Lyman Rufus, 245
Catawba County, resources of, 115
Chapel Hill, agricultural experiment station at, 104 f., 112, 132, 144; Polk speaks at, 117-18; mentioned, 167
Charlotte, N. C., mentioned, 26, 32, 42, 77, 82, 151
Chartism, Populism compared with, 296
Chatham County, agricultural distress

INDEX   313

in, 198
Chautauqua, 3 ff., 6, 8
Cheek, W. H., 127
Chowan Baptist Female Institute, 188
Cincinnati, "National Union Conference" at, 269-70
Clark, Charles C., 48
Clay, Henry, 37, 40, 83
Clemson College, 179
Cleveland, Grover, 232, 276; Southern attitude toward, 282 f., 286; nomination and election of in 1892, 294
Clingman, Thomas L., 90-91
Clinton *Caucasian,* 278
Clover, Benjamin H., with Polk at Winfield, Kansas, 4 ff., 14f.; on hard times, 192-93; vice-president of Farmers' Alliance, 212-13, 285; on attacks upon Polk, 239
Cobb, Irvin S., on North Carolina, 118, 147
Colored Alliance, 207, 273
Congress, and the sub-treasury bill, 18 ff., 219 f., 227, 266; Reconstruction legislation of, 83; farmers' feeling toward, 254 f.
Connor, Robert D. W., quoted, 148
Conscientious objectors, 48-49
Conservatives, during Reconstruction, 83 ff.
Convict labor, Polk on, 155
Co-operatives, Grange, 100; Farmers' Alliance, 201-2, 207 f., 272
Cotton. *See* Diversification of agriculture
Cotton Mills, North Carolina, 82, 137 f.
Cotton planters, protection of, 216, 219
"Country merchant," 193
Cowley County, Kansas, 3 f., 192
Crawford, Samuel J., 224
Crop lien system, 193, 195-96, 198-99
Crumpler, Thomas N., 46

Dabney, Charles W., as State Chemist, 129, 131, 137, 161; and the industrial school, 165; and the agricultural college, 177 f.

Daniels, Josephus, criticizes N. C. Department of Agriculture, 129, 132; on Polk, 146, 182, 210; as editor of Raleigh *State Chronicle,* 166, 281; accompanies Polk to Atlanta, 212; and state printing contract, 234; defends Polk, 238, 295; on Democratic Party, 276; mentioned, 213, 247
Daniels, Mrs. Josephus, 212
Dargan, A. J., 65
Davidson College, picture of in middle 1850's, 31-36, 40; mentioned, 238
Davis, Jefferson, 222
Davis, Stephen W., 48
Democratic Party, in North Carolina, on eve of Civil War, 41 ff.; just after Civil War, 73, 83; challenge to, 86, 149; during early 1880's, 136-37; in campaign of 1890, 229, 248 f.; characterized, 276; in campaign of 1892, 277 ff., 289; during election of 1892 and Fusion period, 294-95; national, farmers' dissatisfaction with, 194; in campaign of 1890, 226 f., 242; and the "money power," 255, 277, 282 f., 286; in campaign of 1892, 293 f. *See also* "Bourbons" *and* Conservatives
Denmark, James W., Polk's correspondence with, 235, 261, 270, 272, 278, 281, 287, 290; mentioned, 154, 291 f.
Denson, C. B., 120
Department of Agriculture. *See* North Carolina Department of Agriculture
Des Moines *Iowa State Register,* on Polk, 228
Diggs, Annie L., 222
Diphtheria. *See* "Polk's Diphtheria Cure"
Diversification of agriculture, 95-98, 154-55, 194
Dixon, Thomas, 165
Dockery, Alfred, 48
Dodd, W. H., 142 f., 145
Dodd, Polk and Company, 142 f., 146
Dodge, Jacob R., 19
Dogs, Polk attacks sheep-killing of, 113-14; tax on suggested, 177

Dollar, high cost of the, 18-19, 264-65
Donnelly, Ignatius, Alliance leader, 222, 263, 269, 274, 285, 293
Dowd, J. W., 123
Dozier, Nellie F., farm girl, 264
Drexel, J., 91
"Duel," Ashe vs. Polk, 237
Duffy, P. F., 232
Dunlap, B. I., 85
Dunning, Nelson A., 263
Durham, Dukes' tobacco industry of, 82; wants Baptist school for girls, 187 f.
Durham *Globe,* on Polk-Vance contest, 248-49

Early, Gen. Jubal A., 55
Eaves, J. B., 178
Edgecombe County, 130; Farmers' Alliance in, 205
Education, in North Carolina, Grange's interest in, 101, 252; Governor Jarvis cites need for, 137; during 1880's, 200; contributions of "farmers' legislature" to, 251 f.
Edwards, John, 29
Edwards and Broughton printing house, 81, 134
Elias, Kope, 178
Ellis, Gov. John W., in crisis of 1860-61, 43 ff.; recommends a Board of Agriculture, 103
Emporia, Kansas, farmers' rally at, 223-24
Enniss, J. H., editor, 130
"Equal taxation," N. C. political issue, 41-42
Erwin, Marcus, 46
Eumenean Literary Society, Davidson College, 34-36
Evans, Jonathan, 108, 127 f., 131
Exum, Dr. Wyatt P., 294

Farley and Company, fraudulent firm, 100
Farmer and Mechanic. See Raleigh *Farmer and Mechanic*

Farmers, characterized, 10; revolution of, 10-11, 190-91, 266, 286; reasons for unrest of, 11-12, 98-99, 149, 190-200, 264-66; Polk on need for organizing, 12, 157, 203; in politics, 15. *See also* Middle-class farmer.
Farmers' Alliance, strength of in 1890, 3, 227; and politics, 14-16, 209, 220, 255, 269, 271, 288; educational and social aspects of, 195, 262-64; North Carolina Negroes condemn, 200; origin and growth of, 201-2, 204-7; principles of, 207-10, 213, 252; defeats jute-bagging trust, 211; demands on Congress, 215, 241, 255-56; and the sub-treasury plan, 217-20, 255, 271; policy toward sectionalism, 220 ff., 228; attitude toward third party, 268-69, 271, 276; decline of, 271-72. *See also* Ocala
Farmers' and Laborers' Union of America, 206
Farmers' clubs, in North Carolina, 156-62
Farmer's home, Polk's tribute to, 6; recommendations for improvement of, 160
Farmers' institutes, in N. C., 161
"Farmers' legislature." *See* North Carolina General Assembly of 1891
Farmers' Mutual Benefit Association, 206, 273
Farmers' Union of Louisiana, 206
Fayetteville, N. C., industrial possibilities of, 139; mentioned, 143, 170, 206
Fayetteville *Carolinian,* on need for agricultural college, 170
Felton, W. H., 202
Fence reform, Polk champions, 114
Ferebee, Dennis D., 48
Fertilizers, commercial, regulation of in N. C., 111-12, 129
Field, James G., 293
First Baptist Church of Raleigh, 183, 188, 297
Fish culture in N. C., 112-13

INDEX

Fishburne, Clement Daniel, 33
Florida, 254
Food of Confederate soldiers, 58 f., 67
Forsyth County, 150; farmers' clubs in, 158
Forty-third Regiment, N. C. volunteers, campaigns of the, 51-56; rations of the, 58, 67
Fourteenth Amendment, 190
Fowle, Daniel G., 62, 229, 280
French, G. Z., 103
French Academy of Medicine, 146
Fries, Henry E., 161, 178
Furches, D. M., 294
Fusion, in North Carolina, 278-79, 294-95

Gaddy, Joel T., 36 f., 65
Gaddy, Mary A. Bennett, 36
Gaddy, Risden Bennett, 31, 36 f., 49, 78
Gale, C. D., 80
Garfield, James A., 135
Gatling, John, becomes part owner of Raleigh *News*, 134; supports industrial school bill, 165
George, Milton, reform editor, 201
Georgia, Grange growth in, 99; Farmers' Alliance in, 212, 224, 256 ff.; mentioned, 103, 171
"Georgia senatorial affair," 256-58, 272
Gettysburg, 52 f.
Gilbert, J. L., 237
Gilded Age, the, 146, 190
Goldsboro, "Southern Rights" convention at, 45; Grange convention at, 104-5
Gompers, Samuel, 269
Gordon, John B., 202, 257 f.
Gould, Jay, 191
Grady, Henry W., and the "New South," 137 f., 142, 147-48; invites Polk to Atlanta, 212 f., 232; mentioned, 202
Graham, W. A., 91
Grand Army of the Republic, 285
Grange (Patrons of Husbandry), urged by Polk to set up N. C. headquarters and museum, 94-95, 102, 114; activities of in N. C., 98-105, 122, 171; mentioned, 201, 207
"Granger laws," 230
Grant, Gen. Ulysses S., Polk's tribute to, 14; mentioned, 54, 56, 72
Greeley, Horace, 37, 293, 296
Greenback movement, 136, 269
Greensboro, farmers' meetings in, 161, 175 f., 205, 244; wants Baptist school for girls, 187 f.; mentioned, 94, 122, 185
Greensboro *Patriot*, 244
Gregory, Nat. A., 120
Gresham, Walter Q., 293 f.
Grimes, Gen. Bryan, arrests Polk, 66 f., 70
Guide to Capitalists and Emigrants, 90 f.
Guilford County, 99, 161
Gwaltney, W. R., 185

Hale, Peter M., editor, 134
Hall, Capt. Robert T., 66-67
Hamilton, Alexander, 190
Hamilton, J. G. deRoulhac, quoted, 125
Hampton, Gen. Wade, 75
Hancock, Winfield Scott, 135, 138
Handbook of North Carolina, by Polk, summarized, 118-20; mentioned, 123
Hargrave, J. R., 69
Harrison, Benjamin, 232, 282, 294
Hatch Bill of 1887, 177-78
Haw River, cotton mill at, 82
Hawley, F. O., 80
Hayes, Rutherford B., 84, 135
Hays, Dr. J. M., Polk's physician, 290
"Hayseed Socialists," 18, 220, 227
Henderson, John S., and Farmers' Alliance and People's Party, 240, 277-78
Hendrick, Burton J., criticized, 167n, 180
Hicks, John D., quoted, 213
Hicks, W. J., 142
High Point Female College, 188
Hill, Daniel Harvey, 33 f., 51, 63

Hoke, R. F., 104
Holden, William Woods, mentioned, 46, 62, 74, 91; praises Polk and Vance, 122
Holladay, Alexander Q., 213
Holman, Mr., of Boston, 145 f.
Holt, Thomas M., entertains members of the press, 82; and the N. C. Department of Agriculture, 103, 106 ff., 127, 130 f.; buys Raleigh *News*, 134; becomes lieutenant-governor and governor, 229-30; in campaign of 1892, 280-81; mentioned, 161, 213
Hudson, J. K., Kansas editor, 224, 226
Hufham, J. D., 185
Hunter, Gen. David, 54 f.
Hyde County, 51

Illiteracy in North Carolina, 200, 226
Immigration, campaign for in N. C., 90-92, 115-16; Polk's ideas on, 92-95, 114-15
Implements and machinery, agricultural, 142-43
Indiana, 208
Indianapolis, Farmers' Alliance convention at, 270 f., 284
Industrial school, campaign for in N. C., 164-68
Industrialism in N. C. See Cotton mills
Ingalls, John J., Farmers' Alliance opposes, 222-23, 228; attacks Polk, 224-25, 233 f.
Inter-State Farmers' Association, 202-4, 206, 211
Iowa, Farmers' Alliance in, 260, 270

Jackson, Andrew, 190
Jackson, Gen. Thomas J. ("Stonewall"), 54, 61
Jacksonville, Fla., 254
James I of England, 24
Jarvis, Thomas J., praises fertilizer law, 112; and the N. C. Department of Agriculture, 125 ff.; as governor, 135 ff.; warns Democrats against reaction, 149; addresses farmers' convention, 176; on the Farmers' Alliance, 239; mentioned, 145
Jefferson, Thomas, 148, 190
Jernigan, Thomas R., 281
Johnson, Andrew, 74
Jones, Evan, 212
Jones, Col. J. T., 63
Jute-bagging trust, 211

Kansas, farmers' revolt of 1890 in, 3, 20, 222 ff., 226, 228; plight of agriculture in, 9 f.; mentioned, 201, 258
Kelley, Oliver Hudson, Grange founder, 98, 100
Kelley, William D., on Southern poverty, 197
Kenan, Thomas S., leads 43rd N. C. Regiment, 51; defends Polk, 69; mentioned, 105
Kerr, Edwin W., "railroad senator," 278
Kerr, W. C., 91; and the N. C. Department of Agriculture, 104 ff., 119 ff.
Kilpatrick, Gen. Hugh Judson, makes cavalry raid on Anson County, 16, 75
King, Edward, describes Raleigh, 140
Kinston, N. C., in Civil War, 51, 55, 57 ft, 61, 65
Kitchin, W. H., on Cleveland, 283
Knights of Labor, co-operates with Farmers' Alliance, 207; favors third party, 268; mentioned, 157, 176, 266, 273
Kolb, Reuben F., 202
Kyle, James H., 293 f.

Labor, Polk's feeling toward, 266. See also Knights of Labor
Lacy, Drury, 33 f.
Lacy, Drury, Jr., 69
Lacy, W. S., 238
Lafayette, Gen., 27
La Follette, Robert M., 296
Land question, Farmers' Alliance on the, 215

INDEX

Land scrip fund, in N. C., 168 ff.
Lane, Col. J. R., 63
Lawyers, farmers' attitude toward, 209
Leak, J. A., 85
Lease, Mrs. Mary E., as a Farmers' Alliance leader, 222, 224, 235, 274; on woman suffrage and prohibition, 275
Leazer, Augustus, supports industrial school and agricultural college bills, 165, 178; in politics, 229 f., 240
Ledoux, Dr. Albert R., State Chemist, 112, 117, 120 ff., 129
LeDuc, William G., 115
Lee, Gen. Robert E., 14, 52 ff., 60, 72
Lee, Stephen D., 172
Leland, John Adams, 33
Lewis, Col. W. G., arrests Polk, 69
"Liberal Democratic" movement in N. C., 136
Liles, Edward R., with Polk in legislature, 43, 46; Polk's political rivalry with, 65, 85; commends Polk's activities, 80, 102; supports Polk for Commissioner of Agriculture, 107; mentioned, 62
Lincoln, Abraham, 43 ff. *passim*, 262
Little, George, 91
Little, Robert A., 31
Littleton, N. C., "Pioneer Agricultural Club" of, 156, 160
Liverpool Cotton Exchange, 216
Livingston, Leonidas F., with Polk in Kansas, 224; and the Georgia senatorial affair, 257 f.; Indianapolis convention drops, 271; mentioned, 202, 217, 269
Long, John S., 120
Los Angeles, Polk speaks in, 270 f.
Loucks, H. L., on Polk, 285, 292-93
Lovill, E. F., 168

McCracken, Isaac, 212, 260
McGehee, Montford, and the N. C. Department of Agriculture, 105 f., 129 ff., 138
McIver, Charles D., 252

McKay, D. McN., letter of to Polk, 149-50
McKinley, William, 295
McManaway, A. G., 185
McRee, J. I., 232 f.
Macune, Charles W., as leader of Farmers' Alliance, 201 ff., 212 f., 268 f., 274; and sub-treasury plan, 217 ff., 242; criticizes Senator Vance, 243; on the Alliance demands, 255-56; and the Georgia senatorial affair, 257 f.; Polk's association with, 259, 290 f.
Madison, James, 27
Manufacturing in N. C. *See* Cotton mills
Marsh, R. H., 185
Marsten, Francis, unusual prayer of, 231
Maryland, Confederates invade, 55, 60
Mason, R. S., 91
Massachusetts Institute of Technology, 164
Mecklenburg County, 24 ff.; fence reform in, 114
Merchant, Polk on the, 266-67
Meredith, Thomas, proposes "female seminary," 185
Meredith College. *See* Baptist school for girls
Mexican War, 33
Middle class, Polk praises the, 20, 265
Middle-class farmer, characterized, 23
Miles, W. R., 202
Militia bill, Polk sponsors, 48-49
Millionaires, 9
Mills, Dr. Columbus, 99, 104
Mississippi, Agricultural and Mechanical College of, 172; poverty in, 197; mentioned, 100
"Money problem," in U. S., 191-92, 227, 264 ff.
Morehead City, N. C. Farmers' Alliance convention at, 206, 235-36, 239
Morgan, W. Scott, 217, 221, 263
Morrill, Justin S., 19
Morrill Land-Grant Act of 1862, 168 ff.

Mountain Creek Farmers' Club, 160-61
"Mummy letters," of Walter H. Page, 166-67
Museum, agricultural, Polk advocates, 94-95; establishes, 114 ff.

Nash County, 263
National Economist. See Washington, D. C., *National Economist*
National Farmers' Alliance and Cooperative Union of America, 206 National Farmers' Alliance and Industrial Union. See Farmers' Alliance
Nationalists, 269
Negroes, Polk's views on, 83-84, 92 ff., 155, 199, 253; problems of following emancipation, 89-90, 114; "exodus" of from North Carolina, 199-200; during Fusion period in N. C., 294. See also Colored Alliance
New Bern, N. C., 50, 238, 240
New Deal, 207, 296
New Freedom, 207
New Hampshire, farm distress in, 17
Newman, J. S., 202
Newspapers. See individual titles
New York City, Polk enters business in, 146, 149
New York *Press,* on Farmers' Alliance, 262
Normal and Industrial School for girls, 251 f.
North, the, reluctance of to invest in the South, 116; South's economic dependence upon, 139, 194. See also Sectionalism
North Carolina, rise of scientific agriculture in, 31, 37; politics on eve of Civil War, 40 ff. *passim;* Civil War campaigns in, 50 ff.; restored to the Union, 73-74; economic and social conditions during Reconstruction period, 82-83, 86-90; gubernatorial campaign of 1876, 86; immigration campaign, 90-95, 114-16, 137; need for diversified farming in, 95 ff., 154-55; Grange's career in, 98-101, 157; Polk on the basic needs of, 109-10, 129; beginnings of industrialism in, 138; Civil War heritage and Bourbonism in, 147-49, 163, 251; farmers' clubs in, 156-62, 204, 229; agricultural and social conditions during 1880's, 195-200; Farmers' Alliance in, 204-6, 208, 223, 263, 271, 280 f.; campaign of 1892 in, 276-81; election of 1892 and Fusion period in, 294
North Carolina Board of Immigration, Statistics, and Agriculture, urges immigration, 91, 93; slights agriculture, 103
North Carolina Bureau of Labor Statistics, 196
North Carolina College of Agriculture and Mechanic Arts, 178 ff., 229, 251 f.
North Carolina Constitution of 1835, 41
North Carolina Constitutional Convention of 1875, 103-4
North Carolina Convention of 1861, 45-46
North Carolina Convention of 1865-66, 73-74
North Carolina Department of Agriculture, establishment of, 103-8; program of, 110-15, 120, 132; opposition to, 122 ff., 132-33, 177. See also Board of Agriculture
North Carolina Farmers' Association, 176 f., 205-6, 229
North Carolina farmers' conventions of 1887, 175-77
North Carolina Farmers' State Alliance, 205 f.
North Carolina General Assembly, of 1860-61, 43 ff.; of 1864-65, 71-72; of 1876-77, 104 ff.; of 1879, 125 f.; of 1881, 130; of 1883, 130 f.; of 1885, 165; of 1887, 177 f.; of 1889, 230 f.; of 1891, 188, 248 ff.
North Carolina Land Company, 90-91
North Carolina Press Association, 81-82

INDEX 319

North Carolina State Agricultural Society, 31, 82, 140; sponsors State Fair, 141
North Carolina State Fair, 31, 115, 141; of 1881, 141 ff.
North Ireland, 24
Northen, W. J., 202
"Northern Alliance," sketch of, 201, 206 ff., 219, 268, 273
"Northwestern Alliance," 206
Norwood, Thomas M., 257 f.

Oak Ridge Alliance, Polk and, 205, 212 ff.
Oakwood Cemetery, Raleigh, 297 f.
Ocala, Fla., Farmers' Alliance convention at, 254-59, 268
Ohio legislature, prayer for, 231
"Old Fogy," pseudonym of Rittenhouse, 256
Omaha, People's Party convention at, 275, 279 ff., 293
One-crop system. See Diversification of agriculture
Overby, R. R., 185
Overproduction theory, farmers repudiate, 19, 191
Oxford, N. C., 187 f.

Page, Mrs. C. M., 52
Page, Walter H., describes Raleigh, 140; and the industrial school, 163 ff.; estimated, 180-81; favors Polk for governor in 1884, 247; mentioned, 121
Paris Exposition of 1878, 115
Parker, D. Reid, 202
Passes, free, on railroads, 85, 192, 230-31
Patrons of Industry, 273
Peace Institute, Raleigh, 82
"Pee Dee Wildcats," 50
Peele, William J., urges industrial school, 163 ff.; on Polk, 182; on Democratic Party and Democratic principles, 276; mentioned, 213

Peffer, William A., Alliance leader, 222, 228, 235, 263, 285
Pell, W. E., 90
Pennsylvania, Polks in, 25 f.; Confederates invade, 52, 60
People's Party, in Kansas, 3, 222, 224, 226, 233, 268 f., 271; national, birth of, 270, 273 ff.; attitude of toward major parties, 282; Polk predicts success for, 284, 287; in election of 1892, 294; lasting impress of, 296; in North Carolina, 281, 289, 294-95
Petersburg, Va., 52 ff., 144
Pettigrew, Gen. J. Johnston, 51
Philanthropic Literary Society, Davidson College, 34 ff.
Pickler, John A., 219, 244
Picot, Professor, 101
Piney Grove, Sabbath School, 38; Church, 49
Plymouth, N. C., in Civil War, 54, 60-61
Poe, Clarence, 181
Polk, Andrew (father of L. L. Polk), sketch of, 7, 22 ff., 27 ff.
Polk, Colin Caraway, 24, 28
Polk, James (half-brother of L. L. Polk), 24, 30
Polk, Juanita (daughter of L. L. Polk), 141-42
Polk, L. L., and Company, 142-43, 146
Polk, Leonidas, bishop and general, 27-28
Polk, Leonidas LaFayette, described, 4-5, 21, 59-60; oratorical abilities of, 5 f., 13, 21, 143, 210, 264, 270; speech of at Winfield, Kansas, 5-21, 22, 75, 297-98; labors on the farm, 7, 75-76; travels of, 8, 223, 270 f.; on sectionalism, 12-14, 20-21, 221, 223, 228; confesses partisanship, 17; predicts a "people's party" that will oppose "the plutocrats," 18, 267, 295; birth and boyhood of, 28-31; characterized, as a youth, 30; as a student at Davidson College, 34 ff.; marriage of, 36-37, 56-57; reading and religious

thinking of, 37-39; enters politics, 40 ff.; in Legislature of 1860-61, 46-49; raises troops, 49 f.; with 26th N. C. Regiment, 50-51, 144; with 43rd N. C. Regiment, 51-56; war letters of to wife characterized, 56; attitude of toward liquor, 57 f., 78, 184; shows war-time leadership qualities, 63-64; re-elected to legislature as "army candidate," 64-65; court-martialed, 66-70, 236-37; fellow officers characterize, 71; in Legislature of 1864-65, 71-72; in Constitutional Convention of 1865-66, 74; builds town of Polkton, 77-80; as Polkton merchant, 78-79; as editor of Polkton *Ansonian*, 77, 80 ff., 96 f., 102, 151, 154, 260-61; political views and activities of during Reconstruction, 83-86; attitude of toward the Negro, 83-84, 92 ff., 155, 199, 253; ideas of on immigration to N. C., 92-95, 114-15, 155; urges diversification of agriculture in N. C. and South, 95-98, 154-55, 194; work of in Grange, 101 ff.; role of in creating the N. C. Department of Agriculture, 104 ff.; characterized, as Commissioner of Agriculture, 121, 124-25, 128; as corresponding editor of Raleigh *News* and *News and Observer*, 128, 134 ff., 140, 151, 154, 232; attempts to reorganize Board of Agriculture, 129 ff.; as a "regular Democrat," 136-37; favors small, diversified industries, 138-39; moves family from Polkton to Raleigh, 139-40; as secretary of State Fair of 1881, 141; as Raleigh merchant, 142-43, 146; develops "Polk's Diphtheria Cure," 144-46, 149; as editor of *Progressive Farmer*, 149-56, 261, 287-89; organizes farmers' clubs in N. C., 156 ff., 175, 204, 229; attitude of toward Watauga Club's industrial school idea, 166, 171; crusades for agricultural college, 171 ff.; church activities and attitudes of, 183-84; role of in establishing Baptist school for girls, 185-88, 292; as president of Farmers' Alliance, 188, 248, 259-60, 264, 270-71, 286 f.; and the Inter-State Farmers' Association, 202 ff., 211; rise of in Farmers' Alliance, 204-5, 210-14; and the sub-treasury plan, 217 ff.; tours Kansas, 223-26, 233; and N. C. politics, 1888-89, 229 ff., 239-40; Samuel A. Ashe attacks, 232-39; clashes with Senator Vance over sub-treasury bill, 240 ff., 244-51; supports teacher-training and public education, 252-53; at Ocala convention, 254 ff., 258, 284, 286, 290; and the Georgia senatorial affair, 257; financial status of, 260-61, 292; attitude of toward third party, 268 ff., 271, 276-77; and the St. Louis "Industrial Conference," 272-75, 284 ff.; in the N. C. campaign of 1892, 277 ff.; and fusion, 278-79, 295; platform of, 283-84; as probable Presidential nominee, 281, 284-87; last illness and death of, 289-92, 297; estimated, 292 ff.

Polk, Lula (daughter of L. L. Polk), 60

Polk, Marshall (half-brother of L. L. Polk), 24, 30

Polk, Sarah Pamela Gaddy (wife of L. L. Polk), marriage of, 36-37, 56-57; "back home" during the war, 56 ff., 68 f.; makes post-war adjustment, 75 f.; attends Ocala convention, 254; during Polk's fatal illness, 291

Polk, Serena Autry (mother of L. L. Polk), 28 ff.

Polk, Thomas (grandfather of L. L. Polk), 24, 26

Polk, Col. Thomas, sketch of, 26

Polk, Thomas Jefferson (half-brother of L. L. Polk), 24, 29-30

Polk, William (great-great grandfather of L. L. Polk), 25 f.

Polk, Col. William, sketch of, 26-27

INDEX 321

Polk and Gaddy, country store, 78
Polk family, history of, 24-27
"Polk Hall," 181
Polk Memorial and Relief Association, 297
"Polk's Diphtheria Cure," 144-46
Polkton, N. C., sketch of, 77-80
Polkton *Ansonian,* Polk's editorship of, 77, 80-81, 151; Polk's articles on immigration in, 92-95
Pollok, Robert Bruce, 25
Pond Mill Grange, Polk joins, 101-2
Pool, John, 43
Populism, Populists. *See* People's Party
Potecasi, N. C., grange high school, 101
Pou, James H., 178
Powderly, Terence, 269
Presbyterians, and Davidson College, 31-32
Prices, paid by Confederate soldiers, 58-59
Primary elections and conventions, 239-40
Pritchard, T. H., 185
Progressive Farmer, analyzed, 149-56; circulation and influence, 210, 287-88; editors of, 231-32; clashes with Raleigh *News and Observer,* 234 ff.; and Senator Vance, 243 ff.; financial condition of, 260-61, 292; as organ of State Alliance, 263 f., 288 ff.; on decline of Alliance, 271-72; in N. C. campaign of 1892, 280; mentioned, 171, 173, 177 f., 181 f., 197, 214, 253, 256
Progressive movement, 207, 296
Prohibition, in North Carolina, 38, 136, 184
Prohibitionists, at St. Louis, 273, 275
Pullen, R. Stanhope, 177
Pure food law, Farmers' Alliance favors, 255, 259

Radicals, during Reconstruction, 83 ff., 295

Railroad commission, struggle for in N. C., 230 ff., 251-52
Railroads, and Western farmers, 192, 201; and N. C. farmers, 197, 230 ff.
Raleigh, N. C., press convention of 1874 in, 81-82; farmers' meetings in, 103, 157, 161, 175 f., 204 ff.; described about 1880, 140; commercial activities during 1880's, 142 ff., 150, 154; and industrial school campaign, 164 ff.; and Baptist school for girls, 185, 187 ff.; mentioned, 47, 59, 68, 177, 180 f., 210, 231 f.
Raleigh *Biblical Recorder,* on Polk, 188
Raleigh *Farmer and Mechanic,* sketch of, 120 ff.; on Polk's business failures, 143, 146; influence of on *Progressive Farmer,* 151
Raleigh *News,* sketch of, 134 f., 140; mentioned, 128, 151, 183
Raleigh *News and Observer,* 132, 140; on Polk, 182, 259; clashes with Polk and *Progressive Farmer,* 231 ff., 289; supports Thomas M. Holt for governor, 281; on *Progressive Farmer's* influence, 287-88
Raleigh *Observer,* quoted, 86, 106 f.; characterized, 134; mentioned, 140
Raleigh *State Chronicle,* sketch of, 124, 132, 166; favors Baptist school for girls, 187-88; characterized, 234, 246; favors Polk for governor in 1884, 247; clashes with Polk and *Progressive Farmer,* 280-81
Ramsey, J. L., as editor of *Progressive Farmer,* 231 f., 235, 261, 288 ff.; arraigns Senator Vance, 243 f.; in N. C. campaign of 1892, 280
Ransom, Matthew Whitaker, 145, 249 f.
Rapidan River, in Civil War, 53, 60
Reade, Edwin G., quoted, 73
Recipes, in *Progressive Farmer,* 152
Reform Press Association, 262-63
Republican Party, in North Carolina,

during early 1880's, 136, 148; in campaign of 1892, 279; national, in campaign of 1890, 224 ff., 239, 242; and the "money power," 255, 277, 282 f., 286; in campaign of 1892, 293 f.; mentioned, 256, 262. *See also* Radicals
Richardson, Charlie, boy orator, 224
Richmond and Danville Railroad, 229
Rittenhouse, D. H., exposure of, 256
Roads, rural, Polk campaigns for, 155
Roark, Tar Heel horse-swapper, 16-17
Roberts, W. P., 106
Robinson, John, 133, 161
Robinson, Sallie, 119
Robinson, Thomas J., 117
Rochdale plan, 100
Rockingham, N. C., farmers' meetings in, 161, 205
Rockwell, Elijah Frink, 33
Rodman, William B., 90
Roosevelt, Franklin D., 296
Roosevelt, Theodore, 296
Ruffin, Edmund, Polk compared with, 118
Russell, Daniel L., 295

St. Louis, Farmers' Alliance convention of 1889, 14, 206 ff., 212-13, 215, 217 f., 221, 244, 254, 274; "Industrial Conference" of 1892, 272-75
St. Mary's School, Raleigh, 82
Salem Academy, girls' school, 37
Salisbury prison, 225
Sampson County, 278
Sanderlin, George W., 280
Saunders, William L., editor, 134
Scales, Alfred M., opposes industrial school, 168; and the farmers, 175 f.
Scarborough, John, 107n
"Scotch-Irish" migration, 24-25
"Second American Revolution," 190
Sectionalism, Polk on, 12-14, 20-21, 221, 223, 228; Farmers' Alliance policy toward, 220 ff., 228; Polk's campaign against, 270-71, 285 f., 293, 297

Settle, Thomas, 86
Sevier, John, 164
Seymour, Horatio, 91
Sheep husbandry, in North Carolina, 113-14
Sheridan, Gen. Philip H., 55
Sherman, Gen. William T., 75
Shotwell, Randolph Abbott, as editor of Raleigh *Farmer and Mechanic,* 120, 123-24, 128, 130
Shreveport, Farmers' Alliance meeting at, 206, 211, 215
Silver, free, 191, 217
Simmons, Furnifold M., and Farmers' Alliance and People's Party, 240, 277-78
Simpson, F. L., 48
Simpson, Jerry, Alliance leader, 222, 269
Single-Taxers, 269
Sixth Army Corps, U. S., 55
Skinner, Harry, and sub-treasury plan, 215-17; rejected as gubernatorial nominee, 294
Smith, Charles Henry ("Bill Arp"), humorist, 153
Somerset County, Maryland, 25
South, the, impact of Civil War on, 50, 57; initial reaction of to military defeat, 74-75; small country stores in, 78-79; under Reconstruction, 83 f., 87 ff.; need for diversified farming in, 96-98, 154-55, 194; attitude of young men in during 1880's, 163; plight of the farmer in, 193-95, 202-3; and sub-treasury plan, 216 ff.; Farmers' Alliance in, 226 f.; and the third-party movement, 269, 276; Polk's political strength in, 284 ff.; Populist showing of in 1892, 294. *See also* North Carolina, Sectionalism
South Carolina, Grange growth in, 99; similarity to North Carolina, 178-79; poverty in, 197; mentioned, 25-26, 44, 211
"Southern Alliance." *See* Farmers' Alliance

Southern Relief, 76
Speaker of the House, contest for in 1891-92, 283-84
Spencer, Mrs. Cornelia Phillips, writes Polk, 115; writes for *Farmer and Mechanic,* 120
Stanford, Leland, 293
Stanly County, Polk's "grangeing" in, 102
Stedman, Charles M., 229
Stores, country, in the South, 78-79
Street, H. H., 48
Streeter, Alson J., urges third party, 203-4
Strowd, W. F., 103
Stuarts, the, English rulers, 24
Sub-treasury bill, attitude of Congress toward, 18 ff., 266; attitude of Senator Vance toward, 219, 241 ff., 249 ff.
Sub-treasury plan, 215-20
Suggestions for the Establishment of a Polytechnic School in North Carolina, 170
Swain, David L., 167
Swaine, Fred, 275
Swift Creek Farmers' Club, 175

Tarboro *Reconstructed Farmer,* on Negro labor, 89-90; mentioned, 103
Tariff, as a sham issue, 17, 266, 282
Tate, Miss, Greensboro prima donna, 82
Taubeneck, H. E., on Polk's death, 293
Terminal Company, of Georgia, 258
Terrell, Ben, Alliance leader, 232, 273 f., 293
Texas, Farmers' Alliance in, 201-2, 204
Thigpen, James R., 103, 108, 127
Third party, movement toward, 204, 268-69; fear of in South, 207, 226, 233, 235, 272; sentiment in Farmers' Alliance, 255, 262, 268-69
Thorne, John D., 279
Threadgill, Sheriff, of Anson County, 64

Tilden, Samuel J., 84, 135
Tillman, Benjamin R., Polk's contact with, 178-79
Tillman movement in South Carolina, 252
Topeka *Capital,* attacks Polk, 224-26, 233 f., 238; pays posthumous tribute to Polk, 293
Tracy, Harry, Alliance lecturer, 263
Trinity College, "The Farmers' Circle" of, 158
Troy, W. C., 105 ff.
Turner, Frederick J., 191
Turner, J. H., 213, 290 f.
Twenty-sixth Regiment, N. C. volunteers, 50-51
Tyrrell County, 51

Union Labor Party, 222
United States, material progress of, 6 ff.; cotton production of, 216
United States Senate Committee on Agriculture and Forestry, hearing before, 219-20, 241 f.
University of North Carolina, and the land scrip fund, 168 ff.; mentioned, 26 f., 278. *See also* Battle, Kemp P.
University of the South, Sewanee, 27

Vance, Robert B., 144
Vance, Zebulon B., sketch of, 50-51; Polk's war-time feeling toward, 62 f., 65, 68; Polk supports for governorship in 1876, 85-86; supports Department of Agriculture and Polk, 104 f., 108, 118, 125, 130; W. W. Holden praises administration of, 122; struggles with Farmers' Alliance and Polk over sub-treasury bill, 240-51, 257; mentioned, 91, 128, 144 ff., 150
Vandervoort, Paul, 285
Vann, R. T., 185
Vicksburg, 53, 62
Virginia, religious restrictions in, 25; secession of, 45; Civil War campaigns in, 51 ff.; diversified agriculture of,

57, 95-96; fish and game laws, 113; mentioned, 171, 211
Virginia Theological Seminary, 27

Wadesboro, N. C., the "speaking" at, 30; "Dixie Floral Fair" at, 183; Polk speaks at, 267; mentioned, 42, 77
Wadesboro *North Carolina Argus,* announces Polk's first candidacy, 43; Polk's communications to, 47, 49, 58, 65, 68; describes Kilpatrick's raid, 75
Waite, Davis H., 285
Wake County, Farmers' Alliance in, 205, 238
Wake Forest College, 185 ff.
Walkup, S. H., 46
"Wall Street," 18 f., 212, 237, 277, 283
War of 1812, 27, 36
"War of Sugar Creek," 26
Warren, E. B., 202, 205
Washington, D. C., grandeur of, 6; poverty in, 19; Confederate threat to, 55; as headquarters of Farmers' Alliance, 213, 259; Polk's last illness and death in, 291
Washington, D. C., *National Economist,* quoted, on prices, 195; on sub-treasury plan, 218; on Polk, 228; on third-party sentiment, 268; mentioned, 243, 257, 259
Washington, George, 17, 26, 37
Watauga Association, 164
Watauga Club, of Raleigh, and campaign for industrial school, 163-67, 178, 180 f.
Watson, Tom, and Polk, 285, 291, 297
Weaver, James B., as Farmers' Alliance leader, 222, 260, 269, 274; as People's Party candidate for President, 285, 293 ff.
Weldon, N. C., Fair, 141, 143
West, the, Polk's first impressions of, 8; plight of the farmer in, 192-93; and the sub-treasury plan, 216 ff.; campaign of 1890 in, 222 f., 226 f.; Polk's political strength in, 285 f.
West Point, 27, 33
Wheeler, Gen. Joseph, 75
Wheeless, Zenobia, farmer's wife, 263-64
Whig Party, in North Carolina, on eve of Civil War, 40 ff.; just after Civil War, 73, 83; national, mentioned, 190
"Whiskey ring," 283
White, William Allen, on Polk, 297
Wilcox, Ella Wheeler, poem of, 275
Wiley, P. A., 142
Willard, Frances E., 275
Williams, Willis R., 165, 178
Wilmington, N. C., 42, 76 f., 79, 140
Wilmington and Weldon Railroad, 54, 196
Wilmington *Carolina Farmer,* advocates farmers' clubs, 156-57; cautions State University, 169-70
Wilmington, Charlotte, and Rutherford Railroad, 42, 76-77
Wilson, Charles, 117
Wilson, Peter M., as secretary of the Board of Agriculture, 117, 121, 128, 161; on Polk as Commissioner of Agriculture, 118, 121; on Boston Fair of 1883, 138; on Polk's chances for Presidential nomination, 285-86
Wilson, S. Otho, 175-76
Wilson, Woodrow, 36, 164, 191, 296
Winchester, Va., battle at, 66 f., 70
Winfield, Kansas, July 4 celebration, 3-4; Polk's speech at, 5-21, 22, 75, 297-98
Winfield, Kansas, *American Nonconformist,* 282
Winslow, Arthur, 164-65
Winston, N. C., in middle 1880's, 150; mentioned, 82, 153 f., 210
Winston, Robert W., 165
Winthrop College, 252
Woman suffragists, at St. Louis, 273, 275
Women, role of in South during Civil

War, 57; adjustment problems of after the war, 74 f.; *Progressive Farmer* material for, 152-53; in farmers' clubs, 160; education of, 184-89, 252-53; in Farmers' Alliance, 263-64
Woodard, J. S., 170-71
Woodburn, James A., quoted, 296
Woodfin, Henry G., 48

Worth, John M., 123
Worth, Jonathan, 47, 74, 91
Worth, W. H., 270n, 289

Yarborough House, Raleigh, 47-48, 105, 213

"Zeke Bilkins," 153

www.ingramcontent.com/pod-product-compliance
Lightning Source LLC
Chambersburg PA
CBHW021353290426
44108CB00010B/219